The **ƒORESIGHT** **PRINCIPLE**

The *f*ORESIGHT *P*RINCIPLE

Cultural Recovery in the 21st Century

RICHARD A. SLAUGHTER

Foreword by Hazel Henderson

Praeger Studies on the 21st Century

PRAEGER

Westport, Connecticut

Published in the United States and Canada by Praeger Publishers,
88 Post Road West, Westport, CT 06881
An imprint of Greenwood Publishing Group, Inc.

Printed in the United States of America

The paper used in this book complies with the
Permanent Paper Standard issued by the National
Information Standards Organization (Z39.48–1984).

10 9 8 7 6 5 4 3 2 1

English language edition, except the United States and Canada,
published by Adamantine Press Limited, 3 Henrietta Street, Covent
Garden, London WC2E 8LU, England.

First published in 1995

Library of Congress Cataloging-in-Publication Data

Slaughter, Richard.
    The foresight principle : cultural recovery in the 21st century /
Richard A. Slaughter.
       p. cm.—(Praeger studies on the 21st century, ISSN 1070–1850)
    Includes bibliographical references and index.
      ISBN 0–275–95292–4 (alk. paper).—ISBN 0–275–95293–2 (pbk. :
alk. paper)
    1. Social change. 2. Culture. 3. Civilization, Modern—20th
century. I. Title.
HM101.S613   1995
303.49'09'05—dc20   94–49380

Library of Congress Catalog Card Number: 94–49380

ISBN: 0–275–95292–4 Cloth
      0–275–95293–2 Paperback

This book is dedicated to Rohan, Lorien, Nadine and their descendants.

They will know better than I which path our global megaculture actually took and whether our efforts to consider the 21st century made any difference.

Contents

Foreword

It is a pleasure to welcome *The Foresight Principle* and its lucid, comprehensive map of the growing futures research movement. Richard Slaughter is a futurist *par excellence* as well as a valued colleague. This book fills a deep need in today's cultural transitions and confusions – expanding the contexts for further human development. Change is occurring at many levels: personal, community, corporate, national, and in ecological and global restructuring processes.

Richard Slaughter is a superb teacher. He has provided a broad, coherent framework for thinking about all those dimensions of our current transition from the dominant culture of the past three hundred years based on instrumental rationality, reductionist science, and the efforts to create an earthly paradise of material abundance. Slaughter recognizes the achievements of this era and its ideology of industrialism and summarises the new problems its limited world view, short-term philosophy and epistemology have created – from ecological destruction to social pathologies and personal angst. Yet Slaughter uses all this as prologue to a careful assessment of our human potentials and possibilities for social innovation to transcend our current dilemmas. I subscribe to precisely this kind of disciplined and honestly normative futures research.

Too often in meetings of professional futurists there is a gulf of misunderstanding between so-called value free, objective technological and social forecasters and those whose research is clearly based on normative scenarios and ranges of alternative policies for creating *preferred* futures. A similar gulf often separates futurists who are not only researchers, writers, and thinkers but also activists and social innovators. Slaughter masterfully shows the continuum linking all these groups and honours their respective contributions to creating the extended foresight that we humans must now develop.

This book will serve to excite interest in the whole field of futures research and its still budding potential for the next stages of human development. Slaughter's style is clear and direct, without sacrificing subtlety and deep reflection. *The Foresight Principle* serves as both a college text and an exciting introduction to the field for concerned citizens and general readers. Even thoughtful high school students will find it engrossing. Many young people who are in despair and alienation will find a road map here to offer new meaning to their lives beyond the narrow options of today's job market.

I can imagine how many teachers will use this book as a basis for new courses in futures studies and to encourage learning of the new skills of social innovation. As an educator, Slaughter has pioneered such courses and fostered foresight in universities and social institutions in many countries beyond his present home in Australia. I hope this book will be read by all those politicians, administrators, and business people who care deeply for their children and grandchildren. My own experience confirms how widespread such concerns are. I found them in government, during my service as a member of the original Advisory Council of the US Office of Technology Assessment; as an environmental and civic activist; and as an early participant in the burgeoning movement of socially concerned investors and companies.

Most of the millions of people concerned with the future of the planet and the human family become activists – no matter what their walks of life or professional careers. In some way, today's human and ecological crises are activating the most aware humans and awakening consciences world wide. In many cases, the young are leading the way because they have the most at stake. In 1992, the United Nations Earth Summit in Rio produced an outpouring of such concern. Its Global Forum linked activists and citizen groups who share longer time horizons and concern for future generations. While government representatives argued from pre-set positions in the official meetings, thousands of representatives of civic organizations cooperated on mutual agendas. They drafted their own treaties to push their respective governments, and shared manifestos and declarations of new principles for human behaviour and responsibilities toward each other, other species, and the planetary ecosystem.

Nothing less than the outline of an 'Earth Ethics' emerged out of the Earth Summit to provide a backdrop of higher human awareness and moral striving for the agreements signed by the 178 countries present and summarised in *Agenda 21*. It was a personal privilege to participate in this great global gathering and an honor to provide a chapter for the forthcoming United Nations volume, *Ethical Implications of Agenda 21*, on how the global economy and financial system can evolve to meet the challenges of restructuring industrial societies for sustainable development. It is now clear that all societies since World War II have confused *means* (i.e. GNP-measured economic growth) with *ends* (i.e. the goals of truly human, sustainable development on a small, ecologically compromised planet).

One never *expects* social innovation to emerge from existing institutions or world views. Today, the planet is dominated by two sets of large institutions: nation states and global corporations. Neither can be expected to lead in the great transformation to sustainable forms of human development. National governments are losing sovereignty due to six great forces of globalisation, as I have elaborated in *Paradigms in Progress*, the globalisation of industrialism and technology, of finance and information, work and migration, human effects on the biosphere, and the globalisation of the arms race and human cultures. Governments can no longer guarantee security, development, environmental protection, or even coherent macro-economic management to provide jobs to their citizens in face of these global forces.

Today, governments must cooperate, by pooling their sovereignty via many international agreements and treaties, such as those in *Agenda 21* and many existing UN protocols which already protect workers, consumers, and human rights in all countries. At the same time, global corporations are pursuing policies and trade agreements which are still predicated on global competitiveness – tantamount to economic warfare, using the same old rules and GNP scorecards of 'progress' and 'wealth'. A 'third sector' is now visible in the world: a growing global civil society in many countries, composed of citizens and voluntary organisations which are still referred to inappropriately as non-governmental organizations (NGOs). As I have described elsewhere, this diverse network of millions of aware, active, grass-roots futurists, and Earth-keepers are rapidly linking beyond their computer conferences on INTERNET, PEACE NET, ECONET, TOGETHERNET, and many others. An Earth Council was launched in November 1993, based in San Jose, Costa Rica – a prototype 'world people's parliament for a sustainable future'. Based on pre-industrial, deep ecological wisdom from all the world's indigenous cultures, these global civil networks incorporate the best of modern science, ecological wisdom, and green technologies and strategies for restoring the earth.

This emerging global civil society will be served by its own Global Television for Sustainable Development network, covering all continents, to amplify grass roots successes in creating more sustainable models for replication, for appropriate replication elsewhere. As this global civil society emerges and its social innovations are amplified on television, a quantum leap in human learning and empathy is possible. As the global civil society is empowered it can lift some of the burdens from governments in many countries and provide alternatives to passive global consumerism and advertising-driven corporate marketing.

Happily, social innovations, 'greener' technologies, and new rules and agreements are breaking through in most countries. In addition, new quality-of-life scorecards, with data clearly presented from many disciplines (rather than over aggregated in money terms as in GNP) and monitoring all the multiple dimensions of true wealth and human progress, are proliferating, from the United Nation's development programme's *Human Development Development Index* (HDI) to my own *Country Futures Indicators* (CFI).* All 178 countries which signed the *Agenda 21* agreements pledged to overhaul their GNP national accounting systems to include valuing environmental costs and benefits as well as all the productive hours worked which are unpaid and ignored in GNP. As I have pointed out, for decades this 'love economy' of cooperative work such as volunteering, growing food, do-it-yourself housing and repairs, parenting children, caring for elders and the sick, maintaining healthy households, etc. accounts for some fifty per cent of all productive work even in industrial countries, and much more in the 'Two Thirds World' as Elise Boulding, author of Towards a Global Civic Culture, calls the developing countries. Today, we must acknowledge that *all* countries are developing in different ways, hopefully toward a more sustainable future, and many in the North will need to learn from those in the South.

Richard Slaughter identifies many of these trends and social innovations. It is clear that we cannot allow trade negotiators and economic advisors with out-dated economic text books to continue 'levelling the global playing field' from their narrow perspectives, which results only in levelling rain forests and homogenising all the world's cultures. We are learning that cultural diversity needs to be savoured and is as important as biological diversity. In the emerging ecological perspective, diversity, both cultural and biological, is seen as a resource just like coal and oil, except more valuable. Obsolete economic worldviews and methods are reproducing some of the worst features of 19th century capitalism in eastern Europe and Russia as well as in Latin America and Asia. This 'rear view mirror' economics still underlies trade agreements such as the North American Free Trade Agreement (NAFTA) and the Uruguay General Agreement on Trade and Tariffs (GATT).

What is needed today is an overhaul of all the Bretton Woods institutions: the GATT, the International Monetary Fund, and the World Bank which were all set up as part of the United Nations in 1945 and reflect a now vanished world. Today we must level the global playing field *upward* by raising its ethical floor. The girder work underlying this higher floor is composed of the many global agreements already mentioned to protect people everywhere and all the earth's ecosystems. Such an ethical floor should include a 'bandwidth' within which today's wage differentials can be narrowed (in the same way that currency fluctuations are contained today). This can slow the mad rush of corporations and global investors seeking out cheaper labor and unprotected environments.

The transition will be slow and painful from today's helter skelter competition. Meanwhile, we will learn that in a global commons such competitive games end in lose-lose tragedies for all players and the

(* *County Futures Indicators* (CFI) © and trademarked, Hazel Henderson, 1991.)

ecosystems. Economists are learning what systems theorists, ecologists, and futurists already know: what goes around, comes around. When niches in markets fill up, as they have in today's crowded, polluted cities and societies, these markets transform into 'commons' (i.e., closed systems which all players must use cooperatively). Markets are usually open systems and can still support win-lose, competitive games. Today, the seamless global economy *itself* has transformed from the open competitive 'global playing field' of the economic text books into a commons with all the same characteristics of other 'natural' commons: such as the Earth's oceans, air, and electromagnetic spectrum.

All commons require cooperative win-win rules because their resources flow indivisibly and can only be used collectively. Economists need to learn how to identify when a market is filling up and turning into a commons and help devise the best ways of changing the rules from competitive win-lose to cooperative win-win. Most economists still use text book references to open systems, not as commons but as 'common property resources', implying that they must be *owned* by someone. This distortion creates many inappropriate policy approaches and collides directly with the emerging understanding that humans do not own or control the planet but are part of the web of life and must operate within the limits of ecosystem niches. Indeed, we are learning that markets are good servants but bad masters and that the 'invisible hand' is not derived from God but is our own.

All countries today have 'mixed economies' (i.e., various mixtures of markets and regulations), while economists have no theories about these mixes. Indeed, it is more fruitful to look at economies as *sets of rules* derived from the various cultural DNA codes of all societies (their different values, goals, and traditions), as I have elaborated elsewhere. Thus, economists will need the assistance of many other disciplines – from anthropologists to zoologists – and all studies of the human development process will need to be systemic and interdisciplinary. Futurists will play key roles as well, in developing and institutionalising foresight. This book will be an indispensable tool in fostering the multi-cultural dialogues and understanding to move us all along.

Hazel Henderson
December 1993

Preface

The 1990s are important for two key reasons. The first is that something old is coming apart at the seams, while something new is attempting to be born. The 'something old' is the industrial system which has reigned supreme on this planet for over two hundred years, changed it almost beyond recognition and brought it to the edge of catastrophe (so far as humans are concerned). The 'something new' is a renewed culture and worldview which is struggling to emerge from the ruins of the old. The latter does not yet have a name. It is certainly not 'post-industrial', nor 'the information age' and still less 'the age of leisure'.

How can we know that something new is, in fact, being born? Well, we cannot know for certain. There are no future facts. But the evidence is there for anyone to consider. What has most forcefully impressed me during almost twenty years' work in futures is a developing 'congruence of insight'. It is an insight about what has gone wrong, what implications this has for the present and what the outlines of a viable future may look like. The insight emerges from many sources: the words of native peoples all over the world, the fears of young people, the views of social critics and the mature reflections of futurists and others.

I do not believe that the future can be predicted, other than in trivial ways. There are no 'iron laws' that govern the process of human and cultural development. There are rules of thumb, fruitful directions, a host of urgent practical measures – but no blueprint. We cannot engineer the human future so much as reclaim it from the abstracted imperatives of power, profit and planetary degradation that have dominated the 20th century, and then re-direct it in a different mode and a different direction.

The central claim of this book is that, while the future is, in a strictly rational, logical sense, unknowable, that does not leave us helpless. Far from it. Unlike the physical body, the human brain/mind system is not locked into a narrow 'creature present'. It is so beautifully constructed that we are able to roam at will through times past, present and future. What we cannot see directly or deduce, we can model, construct or imagine. The view ahead is certainly not clear in all respects, but neither is it as dark or problematic as many imagine. Once we leave aside the absurd conceit of predicting social futures, we open to a broad array of approaches, techniques, methods and practical arrangements which together provide us with a broad-brush overview of our context in time: past, present and near-term future.

This brings me to my second reason for believing the 1990s to be particularly crucial. There is, of course, always a tendency to believe that one lives 'at the hinge of history' because that is where one is, and hence what one sees with greatest clarity. But viewpoint is deceptive. We always exaggerate the 'mental map' of our time and place. However, the significance of the 1990s is not just a matter of individual biographies or perceptions. Something else has been going on during this time which is a consequence not so much of individual behaviour as of collective impact.

In Victoria, Australia, there is still a small, brilliant bird – the Helmeted Honeyeater. It used to be common in scrubland and forest in this region. Now there are merely a few dozen individuals left. Twenty years ago I lived in Bermuda and there saw the same story – 20-odd pairs of Pterodroma Cahow, the Bermuda Petrel, living where once there had been millions. Despite all the many news reports, TV documentaries and activities of countless conservation and wildlife groups, I don't believe that people really understand just how far the human race has gone in unravelling the threads of life on this planet.

It is my belief that 'the man or woman in the street' cares about their family, their standard of living, their job and the kind of car they drive, or would like to drive. But, on the whole, they tend not to care about distant abstractions such as tropical forests, spreading deserts, vanishing species or even – though it promises to affect them directly – the thinning ozone layer. Somehow during our evolution we adopted the habit of focusing on 'me and my group', 'here' and 'now'.

It is this habitual mode of perception, more than any external threat, that is driving our species to the edge.

So the second reason why the 90s are critical is not that we happen to be here at this time. It is due to the fact that by now we have more than ample evidence that the collective impacts and wider implications of industrialized cultures are far more hazardous than is commonly believed. In short, we are confronted with a terrifying choice: either find a different set of principles and practices upon which to erect a notion of 'the good life' or watch the whole thing decay into the biggest mess this world has ever seen.

A bit strong? I don't believe so. A more sanguine view is that 'necessity is the mother of invention'; that, in other words, human ingenuity (largely as expressed through technical virtuosity) will save the day. In the 1990s I consider that such a view has been decisively undermined. We now know with certainty that technical fixes are limited in their ability to solve systemic problems. We have such a problem: there are too many people living in ways that are too destructive of the global commons. Hence, the global system – the air, the water, the soils, the forests, animals and birds – is sending us the message outlined above.

How should we respond? Well, outright denial is pretty effective, and we've had a lot of practice at it. If we choose this path whole industries will help us to block out reality. A cocky self-confidence is another. There's good reason for it – look at what we have collectively achieved; it's not all bad by a long chalk. Or we can pin our hopes on science and technology. They can always find a better way, right? Wrong. They can help. But they only address a part of reality. They are silent on questions of value, purpose and meaning – the very questions now at stake.

However the human race chooses to deal with this difficult time (and I am in no doubt that there are plenty of possibilities) the answer will, I feel, be bound to involve foresight. That is why I have written this book. That is also why I have explicitly linked it with the theme of 'cultural recovery in the 21st Century'. So perhaps I should here try to clarify what I mean by foresight, and why I believe it to be so crucial for our future.

Webster's dictionary defines foresight as, first, 'an act or the power of foreseeing, presience'; second, 'an act of looking forward, a view forward'; and third, 'action in reference to the future, prudence'. It is significant that each segment of this three-part definition stresses action in regard to the future. This captures the key quality of all successful futures work: it enhances our ability to understand and then to act with awareness. But foresight is not a once-only act, it is constantly repeated in different contexts and in different ways. So a working definition would be as follows: foresight is a deliberate process of expanding awareness and understanding through futures scanning and the clarification of emerging situations. In these terms, it is evident that foresight expands the boundaries of perception forward in at least four ways. First, by assessing possible consequences of actions, decisions etc. Second, by anticipating problems before they occur. Third, by considering the present implications of possible future events. Fourth, by envisioning desired aspects of future societies. This book explores some of the many implications of each.

The key point is this. For a very long time our species has learned painfully through experience. It has dragged itself out of the primeval darkness and constructed an impressive sequence of civilisations. From our present vantage point at the edge of the most powerful civilisation ever, we can look back and see what experience has taught us: how to domesticate cattle, plant crops, make tools, use fire, construct buildings, write and so on. All on the basis of accumulated experience. It has worked so well that we find it hard to realise that we have passed beyond the time when experience serves us well. For that same body of accumulated experience is now sending us spurious messages. It is saying: 'cut that forest', or 'build that power plant' or 'drain that marsh'. But experience is not telling us much about the consequences. Part of the issue is that the age we live in, while sharing much with the past, is genuinely and structurally different.

The Achilles heel of experience, for us, is that it is not persuasive enough to make us institute system-wide adaptive change. If we were limited to experience, we would have to experience catastrophe before we could prevent it. Clearly this is an absurdity. Something is missing. We require a different principle, one that has not yet been properly deployed at the social level, i.e. the foresight principle. Without it, late industrial cultures may very likely collapse in chaos. With it, and a measure of wisdom, these same cultures can move on to new stages of civilised life.

Acknowledgments

I would like to thank Jeremy Geelan for his encouragement during the early stages when this book was merely an idea. I would also like to thank those who have read the manuscript and made comments or helpful suggestions: Profs. Wendell Bell, James Dator, Howard Didsbury and Lester Milbrath. Responsibility for errors, omissions etc. is, of course, entirely my own. A special 'thank you' is due to Hazel Henderson – not only for her generous Foreword, but also for the inspiration her work has provided over the years.

R.A.S.

Introduction

Foresight is not the ability to predict the future (though in some circumstances predictions can be useful). It is a human attribute that allows us to weigh up pros and cons, to evaluate different courses of action and to invest possible futures on every level with enough reality and meaning to use them as decision-making aids. As will be seen below, humans use foresight every day of their lives. They build and buy houses, they have children, save for their old age and take holidays. All involve foresight. The simplest possible definition is: opening to the future with every means at our disposal, developing views of future options, and then choosing between them.

In the early 1990s the whole human species faces a number of choices that will determine not only the character of its future, but even if there will be one. For as the products of instrumental reason have proceeded from the labs to the factories, and from the factories to our living rooms, and as the confidence accompanying this process has caused us to think that we are secure and unthreatened, so, at a deeper level, the collective unconscious knows differently. It knows that now, more than ever, everything is at stake. As the technologies of distraction have become more insidious and compelling, so our proud and powerful culture has steadily moved toward the abyss.

In this sense foresight can be painful. We need to be able to confront the consequences of our collective blindness and not only acknowledge the abyss, but look directly into it. Only in so doing will we understand the need for foresight at the social level. In our dangerous postmodern world, where certainty is so elusive, we need to consider those dystopian futures where the human experiment fails. Such insights are needed to prompt us into action. Fortunately they are not very hard to find. While foresight can indeed cost money, we don't need to invest vast sums in researching the dynamics of late industrial cultures. Enough knowledge about the ways they may overshoot certain important limits via unregarded exponential growth has been garnered over recent years to provide a very clear picture about where we are and what this means.

So foresight can clearly act as a kind of early warning system saying, in effect, 'this is where we do not want to go'. That is a useful message.

What map would be useful without marking clearly areas of difficulty or danger? But there are other, and more creative, uses of foresight. One of them is to begin the process of deciding just exactly what it is we really want, and then putting in place the means to achieve it.

So this book is not just about warnings from the future, threats, things we must do – or else. It is also about the ways we can define essential aspects of futures worth living in – and then move towards them. Part Three is therefore devoted to the theme of cultural recovery in the 21st century.

Most people would probably be very surprised at the amount of 'leverage', 'steering capacity', autonomy and decision-making power that still resides fully in our hands. But times change, the wheel is turning and we would do well not to assume that time is on our side.

The 1990s are genuinely a time of crisis and of opportunity. This has nothing whatever to do with the approach of the year 2000 and the new millennium, important as this is in other, more symbolic, ways. The same crisis and opportunity would be upon us if we called it the year 200 or the year 6000. However, one thing is certain. We will not get to the year 6000, or even 3000 if we cannot re-think, re-image and re-value our place on this small planet in the coming decades.

Foresight stands at the juncture between terror and promise. It permits us to move beyond the conditions and constraints of who we are, where we are and what we may, or may not, have inherited from the past. It says to us something like the following:

'Here, look, these are what the stakes appear to be.'

'What are you going to do about it?'

Establishing the context: looking beyond the industrial worldview

CHAPTER 1

Looking Back

This chapter begins with a brief look at the origins of the western industrial worldview and its development through the scientific and industrial revolutions. The world so created is an impressive one in many respects, so due attention is given to the achievements of this outlook in the present century. I then turn to our current predicament by considering some of the costs of this worldview. This allows a diagnosis to be proposed. That is, an account of what has gone wrong as this century comes to a close.

In order to say anything sensible about the future, one must first look back to the past and ask some key questions. Where did we come from? What are the main themes? What structures, processes and ideas have constructed our present? The thrust of this book is positive. It looks beyond the global problematique to some of the social and cultural innovations that can help our badly-compromised culture back to a condition of health and informed optimism. Yet it is necessary to begin with a diagnosis; otherwise the point of strategies for change will be lost. Hence, looking back is a kind of ground-clearing exercise to help us locate ourselves in the wider process. By understanding a little of the world we have emerged from we can more clearly see the world we live in and those that potentially emerge from it.

The origins of the Western industrial worldview

The medieval world picture was very different from what we now take for granted. To begin with, the earth was regarded as the centre of the universe. A series of crystalline spheres was believed to surround it, beyond which was God, the creator. All of existence was teleological, i.e. had intrinsic purpose. Man was the centre of this world and was its lord and master.

In this view, knowledge was based on the authority of tradition which, in practice, meant religion. So to find out about things it was necessary to consult texts, or those who knew what the texts (dating back to Plato and Aristotle) said. In other words, this was the age of scholasticism. Understanding was reached not so much by experience and experiment (because the former was heavily 'filtered' and the latter had not yet been invented) as by citing authorities.

Time was understood as being either cyclical or static. Nature was alive, vital and had great symbolic significance. In **Morris Berman**'s terms, it was 'enchanted'. It possessed intrinsic meaning which could be experienced concretely. One could observe nature and make deductions from general principles.

It was a world in which, despite recurrent privation and material lack, people were fundamentally at home, situated at the heart of things, with all the consolations of a powerful religious interpretative order. However, it is important not to romanticise the medieval outlook. The point is that people were organically interwoven with each other and their environment and that 'the big questions', to the extent they were consciously formulated, had clear and comprehensible answers. In terms of epistemology and social practice there was a sense of being grounded in a durable reality.

Yet by the end of the 16th century a different view of reality was developing through the work of a number of great thinkers, but particularly through Francis Bacon and René Descartes. Bacon is credited with having invented the scientific experiment – that is, the notion of isolating a part of nature and subjecting it to some form of duress, in order to gain new knowledge. It was he who placed a new value on technology, seeing it as a source of value and meaning.

Descartes, on the other hand, was the radical sceptic who doubted all but his power to reason. His response to scholasticism was to question everything. This could be termed 'healthy' up to a point, but it also raised the issue of radical uncertainty, which remains with us to this day. According to Descartes, human thinking was essentially mechanical, or mathematical. The essence of his method was 'atomism', the view that a thing was nothing more than the sum of its parts. Here, then, are some of the foundations of the mechanical worldview that was later to arise.

Descartes assumed that mind and body were separate, like subject and object. He thus invented dualism, a fundamental split in western consciousness that still haunts us today. The combination of Bacon's method with Descartes' philosophy helped to lay the foundations for a mechanical philosophy, a view of the world as a machine-like entity that could be interrogated in order to discover empirical truths. While on the one hand, this liberated human thought from the claustrophobic confines of religious authority, it also broke the brittle boundaries of that earlier system and opened up the possibility of a new world order based on control and predictability.

Those who followed in this path were bound to encounter difficulties. Hence the story of Galileo whose work on the phases of the moon and other celestial phenomena put him on a collision course with religious authorities. But Galileo's other achievements (notably a series of elegant experiments with pendulums, balls, weights, pulleys and frictionless planes) united rationalism and empiricism in a new way. Now it was possible to invent ways to tease out nature's truths – an act which could only be achieved by a radical distancing of subject and object. Here manipulation became the very essence of truth.

Isaac Newton took up the new tools and applied them. In so doing he completed what amounts to a revolution in the way people looked at the world. For Newton, the Universe could be described as a set of discrete forces acting upon each other. In this view, the solar system, with its Sun at the centre, came to be seen as a vast machine. A machine which, once it was understood, could be turned to human use. Hence there developed a philosophy of nature based on reason, manipulation and control. This is not to say that Newton's account was entirely consistent. For example, his view of gravitation was widely criticised by contemporaries. Yet it is also true to say that, in his lifetime, Newton was considered almost a god because he had revealed some of the primary mechanical forces of the Universe, forces that could now be turned to human use. However, in the process a vitally important question was overlooked. In all the jubilation about new sources of technical power, the all-important question of 'why?' was overtaken by the more immediate issue of 'how?'. Thus was established the split between facts (what is) and values (what ought to be) that has plagued western culture ever since.

Yet those who went on to fuel the industrial revolution were unaware of the loss. All they could see were new machines and new opportunities. In this way a fundamentally alienated consciousness was imposed upon the new system. From the beginning, industrialism was flawed. Yet, for a time – two centuries or more – it worked so well that the flaws were largely disguised and overlooked.

The revolution was built on technical and scientific discoveries: the steam engine, electric power and lighting, mechanisation, new materials, the telegraph, radio, manned flight, the internal combustion engine and mass production. The pre-industrial rural economy was largely wiped out. In England at least, the enclosures drove people from the land. As the 'dark satanic mills' and factories began to spread, so more and more people were needed to work in them, often for very long hours. The reality-principles that had lasted for centuries now no longer seemed adequate. Automatic respect for authority had gone. So, too had the organic union between people and their environment. Even the basic categories of time underwent radical change. Time was now beginning to be money, and, unlike produce, money could be accumulated without limit, regardless of other constraints.

Whereas pre-industrial time had been static or cyclic, moving rhythmically with seasonal variations, now it was urgent, precise, controlled. Along with the ability to create time-tables and make appointments, there also came the anxieties and pressures of mechanical clock time:

being late, running out of time, needing to hurry. Here, as always, we see the aspect of technology as a two-edged sword, always taking something away, even as it bestows new gifts.

The Victorian era was, in many ways, the peak of industrial society. With its technological head-start, British industrial capitalism spread across the globe to create an empire 'upon which the sun never set'. It was a system copied and emulated by other European colonial powers. The ethos of the era was most clearly demonstrated at the Great Exhibition in London in 1851. Here, a series of magnificently-appointed displays showed off the pride of British technical power and skill. Great engines, magnificent sculptures, fountains, and the rest. They all spoke with one voice: pride in the past, confidence in the present, optimism for the future.

But it was not to last. With the coming of the Great War, it became clear that the rational organisation of men and machines, backed by the power of contending states and driven by competing ideologies had led to a literal dead-end. The dreams of utopia, of an earth made new by reason and technical power, died in the mud of Flanders and have since been lost to us for most of the century. Whereas the Victorians had genuinely believed in a new era of peace and prosperity for all of humankind, other forces had been at work to subvert this aspiration.

An uneasy atmosphere prevailed between the First and Second World Wars. Alignments were conceived, agreements were tried. But a different dynamic had been established. Under the pressure of war, and impending war, new resources were poured into the business of making new weapons and weapon systems. Throughout the Second World War science and technology were deployed at every turn to gain competitive advantage. And then, at the close of the war, a new kind of force entered the world.

When the first atomic bomb was dropped in 1945 it sealed forever (or so it seemed) the idea of the future as a desirable place, or state. Instead, it seemed to some to be 'a disaster that had already happened'. The psychic, and hence cultural, fallout from this event has reverberated around the world ever since, generating (among other things) a downbeat Dystopian literature which explores different aspects of future worlds gone sour. This is the territory of *Brave New World*, *Nineteen Eighty-Four* and very many others, be they in print, on celluloid or on TV screens. I will have cause to review them again below. Here let me simply note that there is a direct line, a clear and unambiguous sequence, from the early insights of leading scientists to the world we inhabit today poised on the edge of catastrophe. This leads to a fascinating question: how different might it all have been if foresight had been employed at every stage? One thing is certain: our world would be very different to the way it looks today.

So what early indications can we glean from this look back to the origins of the industrial worldview? A number of things stand out clearly. First, industrial culture was bought at a certain price. In parting company from the medieval period and embarking on a brash new one, it discounted a large part of what most cultures on the planet have considered valuable – what Berman calls 'a whole landscape of inner reality'. Second, the drive for industrial progress instituted a technical/rational dynamic over a human or cultural one, such that it has seemed in the intervening years that science and technology are the dominant forces of industrial culture. Third, that in the heady rush to create, invent, discover and apply, almost no one was paying attention to the wider picture, to the sum of all these new devices and their effects. This is why H.G. Wells continually complained about the lack of foresight in his time. Finally, it follows that over the two centuries of industrialism almost no attention was paid by those who created and sanctioned change to the kinds of futures implicit in the process.

Before discussing the question of costs in more detail, it is important to give this system its due and consider some of its achievements.

Achievements of industrial culture

Those of us who live in cities (i.e. the majority) do not find it easy to appreciate just how far we have come in the last two centuries. Like fish in water, we seldom pause to think about where we have come from or where we may be going. But the backward glance is important. It provides a sense of perspective, a starting point for access to 'the big picture'.

Two or three centuries ago our ancestors would probably have lived in small rural communities or towns. They would not have had electric light, power or any of the machines we now take for granted; no toothbrushes, telephones or antiseptics. They would have risen earlier, with the sun, worked hard, long hours, and gone to bed early. Their lives would have been dominated by seasonal rhythms. Since food would have been a first priority, a great deal of effort would have been devoted to growing, storing and preparing it. There were, of course, no refrigerators, no convenience foods, no long-life milk. Families would have been much larger. But many more women died in childbirth and many more children died young.

Transport would have been largely by foot, horse (and maybe carriage) and boat. Communication between one place and another would have been slow and uncertain, particularly in winter. Access to medical care would have been rudimentary, though an extensive tradition of folk medicine would have been available to many. Given the isolation, the dependence upon the seasons, life would have been intensely local. People would have been born, grown up, married, had families and died in the same village or valley. This 'organic community' would have been severely stratified according to family, wealth and title, and the ownership of land. Yet there would also have been many local rituals and festivals, many connected with the church, which would have given life much of its variety. Indeed, religion played a much greater role in people's lives than it does now. The harvest festival provided a symbolic way of giving thanks for the bounty of the year, while the winter solstice gave assurance that hardship would end and life would return.

To gain a real sense of the past, as indeed of the future, one needs to turn to art, imagination and literature. In numerous stories or novels we find the lived quality of earlier days reconstructed for us. In whatever culture we find ourselves, there are accounts of earlier days. These provide important starting points for our journey into the future. Yet, given the nature of the industrialising process, and the upheavals it engendered, let alone the forced moves from one country to another, it is likely that most of us will have lost touch with our roots, our origins, the specific places and people we are from. This loss of contact with the past is one of the distinguishing features of our time. Hence the effort in uncovering roots, elaborating the family tree, writing, or re-writing, our own histories.

Given all this – our distance from the past, our immersion in the present, our ready acceptance of what is in fact historically unprecedented – it does take an effort of imagination to see the present clearly. Moreover, we tend to be preoccupied with problems and tend to overlook the very real achievements of this culture. So, before proceeding to the costs, let us pause a moment to reflect on these achievements.

Imagine a dusty plain. Brown soil, clumps of bushes, a light scattering of trees, dark, low hills. Not a soul in sight. Just some browsing animals in the middle distance and a flock of bright, noisy birds flying overhead. This is the site of a future Canberra, the capital of Australia. Now see it as your aircraft approaches from the south, circles, gives you a bird's-eye view of a breathtaking cityscape. Lake Burley Griffin, the strong axis of the city from the war memorial to the vast new parliament house set atop a hill. See the way the roads, the curved avenues of houses cluster around this grand design. See the skill and care of master architects who sculpted this new reality out of the dusty plain.

Moments like this can give one a profound sense of pride, wonder, at the human project. This is an achievement! Look at any great city from the air – it may be Bombay, Vancouver, even Los Angeles – and, if the conditions are right, one can feel this sense of participation, of being part of a powerful and accomplished culture.

A complementary insight emerges from contemplating the earth in its barren aspect. On many trips between Melbourne and London I have often woken up over the deserts of Afghanistan or Turkey. Looking down from the sky there seems to be nothing but a vast emptiness. Mile after mile of sand, rock, bare and broken hills. Henry David Thoreau was among the first to clearly understand how vital it is that areas of wilderness are maintained upon the earth. They remain important, in part because they are a benchmark, reminding us of the realm of raw nature which we have transcended so decisively.

We have won more than a foothold on this planet. Our species has transformed it utterly. It has levelled mountains and raised new ones, emptied lakes and created others, removed whole ecosystems and replaced them with farms, roads, buildings and parks. There is no point in romanticising nature. If left alone with it, most of us would die. So we have made ourselves secure by re-shaping our environment to suit our needs. And there are a lot of us; now over five billion. So the transformation is extensive.

The industrial revolution completely changed the landscape through mechanisation and land-clearance. In wealthy countries, small farms were replaced by larger ones. The tractor did away with the horse and fields grew bigger. The grain from the new fields fed the animals, and meat and grain was sent over increasing distances to the developing cities. This is another great achievement. The logistics of food supply to a large city are complex and difficult. Within the cities, health became a problem. It was necessary to invent sewage systems to carry away the waste and to organise water supplies for this and other uses. In the city of man everything had to be re-invented.

The late 20th century infrastructure is a scientific and engineering miracle. We are so used to it that we take it for granted. Yet, if one looks in the right places, there are still people who take a pride in this kind of technological virtuosity. Though it has become unfashionable to say so, the curve of a road can be beautiful; the span of a bridge can inspire; the vault of a building fill one with wonder.

These miracles are obvious and commonplace. There are so many of them! Yet within the new infrastructure are many more. There are machines of every kind. Machines that calculate vast numbers in moments; peer into the depths of matter and the limits of space/time; fling messages across continents and seas; and so on. They support a bewildering variety of human enterprises: medicine, sport, entertainment, defence, governance, politics. So, in one sense, the achievements of this culture are not to be measured or found in the outer world of its physical structures, so much as in the inner worlds of its people – people who can now live lives of greater variety and interest than ever before.

It is salutary to think that the 'ordinary' man or woman of the late 20th century, living in a developed western country, has access to more luxury, more significance, more goods and services of every kind than the kings and queens of the past could ever have dreamed of. This too is an achievement.

But the achievements, real as they are, have indeed been bought at great cost. So having given the 'city of man' its due, I turn now to the darker side of progress, to the other side of the balance sheet. An overview of the costs will provide us with the material we need to suggest a diagnosis of what has gone wrong with late industrial cultures. From here we can identify 'the metaproblem', i.e. the sources of global problems which can be located firmly in the foundations of the industrial worldview itself.

The costs of industrial progress

Before the Second World War, it was possible to look around and see a long, steady process leading to a kind of Utopia, a heaven on earth, where all people would be well-fed, happy and at ease. Many literary utopias explored this vision in compelling detail. But as we all know, this is not what happened. In the early decades of the present century the dream died and utopia turned sour.

Part of the reason is that industrialisation had observable costs and impacts from the start. Forests were felled to provide charcoal. Rivers were dammed for lakes. Native peoples, birds and animals were repeatedly displaced to make room for the new order. To be sure, earlier peoples had modified their landscapes, felled forests, sent other species to extinction. But that had all happened when the human population was relatively small and nature seemed vast and inexhaustible.

During the 19th and 20th centuries the whole process speeded up and changed scale. It is this, perhaps more than anything, that gives rise to concern. For, in many ways, our habits of thought, the assumptions built into our institutions, come from this earlier time. This helps to explain why we act as though we lived in a less fragile, less damaged world; why, therefore, we tend to just let things happen without considering the consequences.

But there have been consequences. In parts of Eastern Europe, the former USSR, in many Third World countries and on many islands, the landscape has been devastated, it would seem, beyond repair. The forests have vanished, the soil has been washed away, the ground water depleted or polluted. In the USA a dust bowl was created where there was fertile soil and a rich grassland ecology. More recently the songbird migrations have been growing sparse. With their habitat compromised and new poisons and dangers to avoid, many species of birds and animals are declining; the odds too heavily stacked against them.

The world's oceans have not escaped the impacts of industrialisation. Tetraethyl lead, added to petrol, is universally distributed throughout the world, along with a witch's brew of other pollutants: cadmium, DDT, PCBs, plutonium and the rest. No one knows when, or even if, some essential link in the ocean food chain will be severed by this treatment. But using the sea as a sewer for industrial waste is not a wise or far-sighted way to use it. Seals in the North Sea, Beluga whales in the St. Lawrence Seaway, penguins in Antarctica all show the effects of toxins in their environment.

The whaling industry has hunted many of the big whales to the edge of extinction. Japan, in particular, still operates under a medieval code in this respect. Other countries have allowed their own, or others' fishing fleets to exhaust whole fisheries, by treating them as a short-term resource. On land the continuing assault upon tropical forests is eliminating birds, plants and animals at a frightening rate. The overall effect is to impair the earth's ability to support life. Forests store carbon (in trees), re-cycle oxygen and host genetic diversity, all of which is beyond value in money terms, but they are being exploited beyond their ability to regenerate.

The impacts of humankind are now operating at the level of a natural or geological force. For example, the composition of the atmosphere is changing, with CO_2 being partly responsible for a steady increase in mean temperature – the so-called 'greenhouse effect' – with all that that entails. The widespread use of CFCs for industrial and domestic purposes is thinning the earth's layer of protective ozone. While production will be phased out completely by the year 2000 it will take a further century for the substance to be eliminated, and no one knows what the full effects will be in the meantime on humans, plants, birds, fish and plankton.

Apart from these costs to natural systems, we should not forget the human costs, particularly to native peoples across the world. Many were visited during the period of colonial expansion and experienced the 'fatal impact' of new cultures, technologies and diseases. In later times, pirates, explorers, missionaries, soldiers, miners, foresters, ranchers, whalers, and others added their impact and destroyed forever the viability of such peoples, and even of their ecosystems. Today native peoples exist as remnants at the margins of the global mega-culture. While some have maintained a sense of identity and pride, most have never recovered. This too is a loss to the whole human race because cultural diversity is, perhaps, the greatest source of inspiration and insight into the different ways human society may be constituted. As with the genetic diversity in the forests, we shall need this knowledge in the years to come, but we are nowhere near valuing or protecting it sufficiently.

So the old image of the 'dark satanic mill' with its gloomy atmosphere, smoke and human misery, is only a part of the story. More important is the total impact of industrialisation as a global force. The impacts may be local, but many also tend to be regional or global. Acid rain is no respecter of national boundaries. Plutonium, with its half-life of 250,000 years, is not a local, temporary problem. Wildlife extinctions are forever. For a barometer of how things are going on this wider scale, one cannot do better than turn to islands.

The plight of islands

There are countless islands in the world which attest to the impact of industrialisation. But I want to close this account with a group of islands I happen to know well: Bermuda.

Bermuda is situated some 700 miles south of New York in the north Atlantic. It was formed by volcanic activity in the distant past. The volcanic islands were eroded away, and the present islands were created by limestone deposition and solidified sand dunes in a later era. They are not spectacular, the highest hills being only a few hundred feet in height. But primeval Bermuda was a natural wonder.

To begin with, millions of sea birds: petrels, shearwaters, terns, herons and so on nested around the rocky shores. Spanish sailors dubbed the place 'the devil's islands' because of the unearthly keening of the birds at night, and Shakespeare wrote this detail into *The Tempest*. Besides the profusion of birds, there were turtles and fish of many kinds. The shallow bays were filled with mangroves where herons nested and, fringing the cliffs and coves, there lay a mysterious forest dominated by cedar, palmetto and olive wood trees. Here the tiny white-eyed vireo evolved shorter wings than its mainland cousin.

The canopy was high, blocking out all but the most persistent of the sun's rays. Ferns grew in profusion in the shade and a clean, peaty odour rose from the soil. The only land vertebrate was the innocuous rock lizard, or skink. Thus the sea birds were free to nest along the cliff-tops, in the soil and on the clean, sandy beaches.

The destruction of this natural wonderland began when Spanish sailors left pigs on the islands for an emergency food-supply, in case of shipwreck. It continued when the first settlers arrived, bringing cats, dogs and, most destructive of all, rats with them. All, that is humans and animals, saw the birds as natural food resources, and, within a few decades, the bird-hosts of the past were gone. At a later stage, the forests were cleared to make room for farmland. Attempts were made to grow tobacco and, more commonly, staple foods such as potatoes and corn. As time went by and a small community grew, so a local craft industry developed, based on the durable and fragrant wood of the cedar. By the beginning of the 20th century, this small group of islands was sprinkled with a scatter of white, lime-washed houses.

The change of scale I referred to earlier also occurred in Bermuda. Despite the early destruction of the bird colonies, here would have been a point at which a viable balance could have been maintained between human use and natural wealth. But that point of balance was completely overwhelmed during the present century. For a while Bermuda was a quiet destination for rich and discriminating tourists, and also a market garden for New York. But as the tourist industry developed, and as the lines of communication, travel and commerce developed around the world, so Bermuda become integrated into this world-wide network.

By the time I arrived there in the late 1960s, the islands were a thriving metropolis. The population had increased rapidly. Hotels had been built. Cars, formerly forbidden, were imported *en masse*. And all the problems of civilisation were springing up in this former paradise. Oil stained the coral sands. The tiny roads were jammed at peak hour. Young people were looking around and trying to make sense of it all. Amid the afflu-ence a great deal of despair was beginning to show. And the islands were crowded. With only 20 square miles in total area, and a resident population of 50,000 there were on average 2,500 people per square mile. Most families lived in a house. Many had a car, a stereo system, a washing machine, a power mower and so on.

Thus, the islands had moved from one state of existence to another. A veritable tidal-wave of people had sought a place in the sun and done what people do – that is, shape their environment to suit their needs and wants. The result for Bermuda is, in my view, a social and ecological disaster. Today, the islands remain relatively prosperous in an economic sense due to income from tourism and their status as an off-shore tax haven. But the soul has departed from this place. The spirit of primeval Bermuda has been extinguished by modernity: it has become a powerful metaphor for the entire globe under late industrial conditions.

The metaproblem

At this point it is useful to introduce an aspect of critical futures thinking. Having considered some of the origins of the western industrial world-view, the achievements and the costs, it is appropriate to turn to a deeper analysis. This means that we can stop considering 'world problems' as if they were somehow separate from the systems of value and meaning which created them in the first place. We can, instead, begin to focus on the underlying breakdowns of meaning which have occurred (and are occurring) within all cultures affected by industrialised epistemologies and assumptions. Once again, it is important to re-emphasise that focuss-ing on 'the breakdown' could be misconstrued if it were taken to be merely an attack on existing ways of life. However, this is not my purpose. It is a necessary diagnostic step. It is important to re-emphasise that knowing what has gone wrong constitutes an important step in putting things right.

I am here concerned with 'constitutive understandings', i.e. those which have shaped our views of the world at a very basic and powerful level; understandings which have been expressed through (and embodied in) our social, economic and technical systems. As such they have taken tangible form and led to the kinds of consequences outlined. These consequences are already evident in our past and present. Others are being displaced into the future and represent challenges created by one generation, but which future generations will have to grapple with, and solve if they can. An example may be useful here.

The SDI (or Strategic Defence Initiative) was an attempt by the Reagan administration to purchase some degree of protection against the possibility of nuclear attack by the USSR. It involved the expenditure of huge sums of money for the construction of a nuclear 'shield'. This 'shield' involved placing military lasers in orbit programmed to destroy Russian missiles before re-entry into the earth's atmosphere. However, despite some very compelling graphics, the system was technically unworkable. Had it been otherwise, a whole new era in the militarisation of space would now be under way. But for what end?

The fact is that there is not now, nor has there ever been, a valid reason for beginning such a project. Moreover, the mere deployment and testing of the system would have exacerbated the already serious problem of 'space junk', thereby further threatening all future attempts at space exploration. (In 1986 there were some 7,000 large objects in known orbits and over 40,000 smaller ones.)

Here is a key point. In a non-critical perspective the SDI could be viewed as a prudent extension of US defence policy. The 'shield' metaphor suggested something benign and protective. But the reality was quite different. Resources which sprang from human ingenuity and the biological productivity of the earth were diverted to wholly negative and destructive ends. In a more critical view, these resources were misused and wasted by the imperatives of institutionalised paranoia. From the point of view of the nuclear state it appeared more 'rational' to turn earth and sky into one huge battlefield than to confront the human origins of its expansionism and fear. Viable futures simply cannot be derived from impulses and assumptions of this kind.

This example could be multiplied indefinitely. It shows why a critical futures approach is essential. Without something along these lines it is all too easy to accept conventional assumptions which later turn out to be disastrous. Given that we have two centuries of evidence to consider, we can draw on that historical experience to identify several aspects of the metaproblem.

The dominance of instrumental rationality (IR)

IR is a powerful cognitive system which matches means to assumed, or pre-given ends. It permits the construction of devices and machines of enormous power: computers, rockets, body-scanners, automobiles and nuclear power plants. The physical infrastructure of our civilisation is dependent upon it. So the point is not to eliminate IR. We could no longer survive without it.

The difficulty is that the way of viewing the world which IR encourages contains certain defects and is wholly inadequate for other non-instrumental purposes. One defect is that it contains no notion of limits. Another is that it provides no rationale for seeing the world as other than a machine, or as a set of inert resources. Since IR is a system which only addresses the physical 'layer' of the world, it cannot supply useful insights about ethics, meanings or purposes. Hence, unless it is limited by some other (higher) principle, its applications can become dangerously over-extended.

Many would now argue that that is exactly what has happened in Western culture. Taken alone, IR is a recipe for disaster. It needs to be incorporated into a wider map of knowledge (see Chapter 10).

Reductionism and loss of the transcendent

Reductionism is the tendency to take something with a diverse range of qualities and to disregard many of them. The standard ploy of reductionism is to say that if something cannot be measured, it does not exist. Economics has fallen into just this trap such that, for example, housework is literally regarded as being without value. Similarly, markets operate wholly on the basis of past experience. Leaving aside the 'futures market' (which is a risky exercise in ecomonic gambling), markets have no methods by which to exercise prudence or foresight. They are crude mechanisms which use signals derived from past and present to govern their operations. As such they effectively make the future vanish. They reduce temporality to a narrow band of self-interest in the here-and-now. This is ethical and ontological nonsense.

Reductionism is endemic in industrialised cultures. It says of phenomena 'this is only . . . ' and then picks out some convenient characteristic. Hence, ecosystems basically provide 'services'. People are simply 'consumers' or 'human resources'. Religion is either useless or mere 'therapy'. The possibility that there could be spiritual or transcendent realities of a completely different order is simply overlooked. So far as IR is concerned, ethics, spirituality and futures all have less reality than ghosts.

Science and technology for irrational ends

It was Lewis Mumford who once said of modern weapons systems that the means were rational, but the ends were entirely mad. He saw, as many others have, that once certain technical means become powerful enough, they become ends in their own right. This can be seen with modern information systems which are expanding very rapidly, not out of some clearly defined 'need' or 'purpose' but from the compulsive dynamism associated with competing capitalist economies and enterprises.

The present period has even been called 'the information age'. But it is by no means certain that this label fits. Information as such is not valuable. Nor is it to be confused with knowledge or wisdom. The dynamics of expanding information systems are such as to lead toward ends which are largely unpredictable. In this process, means and ends tend to be confused. Similar criticisms can be made of nanotechnology (see below). Here the threat of competition is used to fuel technical developments. But again, the ends are problematic. If successful, nanotechnology could well undermine the physical integrity of our world. I contend that such an end is indeed irrational.

The key point is this: when powerful technologies are linked with inadequate worldviews or with primitive human impulses they become irredeemably subversive. If science and technology are to help us move towards humanly viable futures they will need to be reconstructed on a different, non-instrumental basis. Hence, if there is a way out of the present cultural trap it will clearly not be via science and technology as they are presently constituted. It may well be that the only lasting solutions will be through the re-establishment of truly human ends which are expressions of the highest human motives and capacities (see Part 3).

The de-sacralisation of nature

In most traditional cultures there were strong injunctions to protect nature from over-exploitation. Such injunctions draw power from belief systems which endow the environment, and all that lives within it, with specific values and meanings. Many of these entities are sacred. That is, they occupy a higher ontological level than that of mere use. They are not simply 'resources'. They may be worshipped, consulted, propitiated. They become sources of inspiration, metaphors, art – the substance of lived experience.

But Western cultures developed according to the very different dynamic provided by Bacon and Descartes. The result was a culture which felt itself to be separate from nature and also 'above' it. In this view, the Christian injunction to 'subdue the earth' could be completed. But at the price we have noted. For the earlier cultures which animated nature (and made it in some sense holy, or at least possessing intrinsic value), in a real sense 'knew' what they were doing. They retained access to a much richer symbolic world while also protecting their own long-term well-being.

The de-sacralisation of nature meant that all the world and its creatures were no longer special, no longer protected. Whales could be rendered down into oil and corset stays, whole forests could be burned or wood-chipped, the atmosphere just became a sink for all the noxious products of human machine culture. The results are now obvious.

Having substituted for being

Depending upon how one views the world, commerce can be seen as a source of wealth or as a prolific source of misinformation about many things. Or both. Like instrumental rationality, commerce is not inherently 'bad'. But its over-extension is certainly proving bad for the earth. The mercantile influence in modern cultures has become very powerful and, in order to sell goods, the advertising industry uses all the tricks and manipulations available to it.

This would not be a serious problem if there were countervailing forces to keep it in check. But there is plentiful evidence that commercial interests have overstepped the mark. They have marketed many items which were better not used, or at least used in moderation, (cigarettes, alcohol, fast cars). They have debased human sexual responses and pro-moted many forms of mystification and reality-avoidance. They have inscribed false, non-viable values upon the consciousness of entire popu-lations. They support surrogate worlds (through mass entertainment) which 'lock up' the human perceptual system in closed, unproductive loops, leading ever further from an active engagement with the world. They have promulgated the falsehood that possessions are superior to human qualities.

In a state of 'being' one rests secure in the richness of one's human and wider cultural inheritance. It is a poised and dignified state, not under threat. One lacks nothing essential because all the essentials are already given: life, consciousness, awareness. There is no inner scarcity. By contrast, the 'having' mode is permanently at risk. Needs multiply and become demands. The 'being' mode is fundamentally self-sufficient, but the 'having' mode begs to be supplied with an endless series of substitute satisfactions. It is all to the good that these are substitutes, for this means that nothing will ever really satisfy. The state of 'having' requires an endless stream of merchandise. This suits those who supply the goods.

But there is a catch. This only works in a world which can sustain escalating demands. Ours cannot. Yet five billion people are now exposed to this diminished ethic. It is a huge confidence trick. We presently use about 40 per cent of the biomass of the earth. When our numbers double will we need 80 per cent? What of the bald eagle then, or the platypus? What kind of world does the 'having' mode lead to?

It is a desperate and diminished one. Once again, this is not a viable path into the future.

In order to come to grips with the 'metaproblem' we will need to re-negotiate some aspects of the prevailing social and epistemological order. To do so will mean intervening in processes of cultural editing and consciously drawing upon other, hitherto marginalised, starting points, values and assumptions. But before attempting to redesign the world-view, we need to look a little more closely at the ways some of our major institutions are presently malfunctioning.

CHAPTER 2

Looking Around

The argument outlined above is essentially that some important aspects of the Western industrial worldview are defective and need to be replaced. In this chapter I look more closely at this process as it affects some of our major institutions. If this argument is right, the latter will show features that are systemically related to that worldview, yet which are also, in an important sense, 'out of sync' with the needs of our time in the 1990s and beyond. If this can be clearly demonstrated, a substantial part of the case for implementing foresight much more widely than hitherto will be revealed. Then, in Chapter 5, we will be in a better position to explore the difference that foresight can make.

In what follows, I look briefly at politics and governance, economics, education, commerce and the media. Two caveats need to be borne in mind. First, I am aware that these are not the whole picture. For example, I am not looking at science, the judiciary or the church, important though they may be. Second, this is not an academic critique. My intention at this stage is to draw attention to fairly obvious defects without turning this book into a sociological treatise.

Politics and governance

The purpose of politics is to make decisions, to administer and oversee the everyday operations of a society. To this end, ways have been found to select people for this role and to check that their work is of a reasonable quality. Of course there are some societies where dictators and oppressive regimes retain power by open force. These are subject to a different set of defects which are beyond my present scope. They would, in any case, have little use for foresight.

By contrast, liberal democracies select their leaders through the ballot box via elections. But what kind of leadership do they actually get? The people who go into politics tend to have strong personalities and often a striking public profile, but are not necessarily the brightest or best. If the USA can select a second-rate actor of low intellect, but good stage presence, for its president, we can be sure that there are problems elsewhere too. So one issue is the calibre of the people chosen to lead. It is not as good as it might be. Perhaps we could think again about the qualities we require of leaders. One thing is certain: most politicians are not, in fact, leaders at all.

One of the characteristics of a leader is that he or she has a vision of a better future and more than a passing idea on how to bring it about. But the political process is mainly focussed on the present and short-term future up to the next election. The electoral cycle, then, is one of the main stumbling blocks to a longer-term view. Yet the decisions made in the political arena may have very long-term repercussions. Here is an important clue: the time-frames of conventional politics are inappropriate for the long-term processes that they directly affect. I will suggest in Chapter 5 that there are other choices.

A further defect in politics and governance is that the units of area under consideration are often too limited. Local politics, the politics of the town hall, are geared to local problems and needs. There is no easy way to take a wider view. Similarly at the national level, the tendency is to regard the nation state as primary, and the global system (of trade, communication, environment) as secondary. But this is the wrong way round. In an indivisible and interconnected world, local and national politics should be firmly located in their wider contexts. Means are needed to enable this. Moves to form local trading blocks and economic areas are possibly a step in the right direction, so long as they are indeed moves toward greater global co-operation, and not new bases of power and exclusion.

Finally, politics tends to be dominated by 'issues of the day'. Whereas, a few government departments (often defence and economic institutions) and many private corporations have instituted detailed systems of environmental scanning and detailed prospective analysis, governments themselves tend to be somewhat 'rudderless', uncertain of their direction or ends – unless it be simply staying in power. And this brings me to the last point. The motives for going into, and staying in, politics need to be re-assessed. It is not enough to ask MPs to reveal their bank accounts and private interests. Given the difficulties of the times we are in (and also heading toward) we need to make sure that politicians are much more alert, able and ethical than hitherto. We will have to find ways to ensure that politics is transformed into a vocation, inspired by the highest motives possible, not the lowest.

Economics

Economics, the 'dismal science', is important because it is about wealth, trade and the material foundations of civilised life. It is unfortunate, therefore, that the discipline has such an abstract and diminished view of reality that it measures the wrong things, gives the wrong signals and helps to speed the process of social decay and environmental destruction upon the earth.

When systems of national accounting were set up some decades ago, a certain view of what was important was taken, and this has remained largely unchanged since. Thus, an economy is a system of interactions, buying, selling, investing and so on, which, while entirely dependent upon the natural environment, still considers it a mere 'externality'. Similarly, women's work in the home was regarded as of no value – it was simply assumed to be unimportant.

A further error is embedded in the notion of GNP, or gross national product. This is so constructed as to count accidents, disasters and costs of many kinds as positive contributions to the economy. Thus the Alaskan oil spill, which was one of the greatest environmental disasters of recent years, actually served as a stimulus to the economy of that state. This is crazy accounting.

Unfortunately, however, governments tend to rely overmuch on economists and to be drawn into their abstractions to the point where they make national policy very much in the light of economic considerations. But economics is not life. It is frequently a crude abstraction. Worse, policy decisions are often made on the basis of market signals. Now of all entities to give signals to governments, markets are not the best. For one thing they are heavily weighted toward existing agendas and priorities. For another, they are actually leading us in the wrong direction (see Commerce, below). Finally, it is frequently overlooked that market signals are retrospective. Markets do not contain a sufficiently strong forward-looking component because the future is constantly discounted, made to be infinitely less important than the present. This is a mistake, a cultural error. Under different circumstances the future could be considered *more* important than the present, though the latter is part of the route there.

National economies are themselves increasingly open to international forces, to 'globalisation', and there is a flood of 'how to' books telling executives how to expand and prosper. Yet few of them consider the long term. It is mainly critics of mainstream economics such as **Fritz Schumacher**, **Hazel Henderson** and **Susan George** who think outside the standard economic paradigm. If one cares to consider their work, it becomes evident that there are many ways out of the trap: new indicators, new concepts, new methods for making economics responsive to our biological heritage and the long-term future.

But at present, most of these innovations lie ignored and untried. It may take an economic collapse of terrible proportions to give habitually short-termist societies the motivation to reinvent their economics. That, unfortunately, is the price of greed, short-term thinking, and the long habit of social learning not by thinking ahead, but by crude experience.

Education

Education is the sum of formal and informal structures and arrangements instituted by a society to ensure its renewal. However, it tends to be identified with the formal structure of the education system. For brevity's sake alone, I will follow this convention for the time being.

Formal education exhibits a major paradox. On the one hand, it developed in a time of rapid industrial expansion to serve the needs of a factory-based society. Its curriculum and map of knowledge are derived from older medieval models based on the classics, mathematics and philosophy. Generally speaking, it has subjects which look back (history, human geography, geology, economics) but none which look forward except in an implicit, undeveloped way (design would be an example).

Let us consider this for a moment. The educational system of any country costs very large sums of money to run. Its teachers are highly trained. It is a labour-intensive and difficult job. Its purpose is to prepare successive generations to participate in the running of the society, its preservation and development. Here is the paradox: an educational system is from the past and is intended to prepare for the future – yet it turns away from the future in the way it is conceptualised, structured and taught. While futures have been taught explicitly in schools, colleges and universities for over twenty-five years, perhaps 99 per cent of the teaching profession world-wide are unaware of the fact or its significance. This brings me to the next point.

As indicated above, change in the real world over the last two centuries has been rapid, profound and structural. The world we now live in is different in many key respects from anything that has ever existed before. Yet schools have no systematic way of monitoring, describing or even noticing this fact directly and clearly. On the whole, the culture of teaching, while displaying some very fine features, remains inward-looking, parochial and isolated from the wider world. This means that adaptive processes that could be taking place are not happening, or are not happening fast enough. While progress has been made in areas such as peace studies and environmental education – both important fields – the future in schools remains a missing dimension, a blank and largely empty space.

This helps to explain why many young people feel anger and despair. At some level they instinctively know that the future is important. But, on the whole, the messages they get from school, commerce and media (see below) are not helpful.

Commerce

Commerce is an ancient and, in many ways, an honourable activity. It brings variety and stimulation to our lives. Yet in the 19th century, and even more in the 20th, something went wrong with this important human activity. Buying and selling became too important, too compulsive and too damaging to the environment.

Modern marketing now comes equipped with all the tools and know-ledge of this technology-obsessed era. These techniques are now turned upon us to persuade, cajole, even to seduce. The point, as is well known, is to stimulate sales, to increase turnover, to maintain profits. But at the heart of modern marketing and merchandising lies a diminished view of humanity and personhood. Nothing makes this clearer than the emerg-ence of sleaze into the marketing mainstream. If pop stars can peddle their fantasies of sex, power and debasement to millions, we will no doubt see many more people following suit. I am not a moralist, not offended by nudity and not against non-violent erotica. But the market-ing imperative is now penetrating into deeply personal areas where it never went before. It will continue to do so until enough people con-sciously choose limits and stop it.

Commercial interests have exerted profoundly subversive effects within industrialised cultures. On the whole, they have sold materialism so successfully that people more easily think about what they have, instead of what they are or might be. I referred to this as part of 'the metaproblem', above. The constant media assault recommends what are, in fact, a whole series of false solutions to the problems of being in the world: consumption, distraction, gratification of the unreconstructed ego. These false solutions have led on to the creation of what **Ian Mitroff** and **Warren Bennis** have called 'the unreality industry'. And there is much more to come.

Though few consumers are asking for it, we are being prepared for the commercial application of virtual reality, which one day will provide a complete substitute world. The danger here is not just in the nature of the medium itself. More importantly, just as the actual world is reaching a most dangerous and unstable condition, when we are at the point where it is essential to pay attention and 'steer' very, very carefully, people are 'tuning out' in unprecedented numbers. I would venture to suggest that those who understand the implications most clearly are more likely to be readers or writers of science fiction than those involved in public or commercial life. For it is in fiction that the wider social implications of such futures have been most thoroughly explored.

Materialism, consumption, ego-gratification, distraction. Isn't it obvi-ous that these are taking us in the wrong direction? It seems clear that we need a good deal less marketing and a great deal more careful thought – followed by action – about the kind of ethics and worldview that underlies commercial activity. A gilded deception is being exerted here upon entire populations. But we need a different view of commerce. A view that stems from different sources, takes a benign long-term view and participates in a larger and more worthwhile human project.

The media

The media are often castigated for the ills of society and perhaps made to serve as a scapegoat for many projected ills and motives. I do not want to add to this shrill critique. But I do have to make some criticisms.

In the late 20th century the media have become a multi-dimensional industry of very great symbolic and cultural significance. They powerfully affect what, how and why people think. They create a kind of ersatz reality with its own rules, images and dynamics. One might say that while the media are certainly owned by particular individuals and companies, they belong to no one. There is a kind of anarchic variety abroad in media as diverse as papers, books, magazines, journals, films, TV, video, computer games, bulletin boards, e-mail and, soon, virtual reality. They support every conceivable interest group, such that broadcasting is rapidly giving way to narrowcasting, the tailoring of media to personal or group requirements.

Within all this complexity and diversity, it is difficult to make generalisations. But it is important to try. On the whole I believe it is true to say that the powerful news media are attracted to the dramatic, the visual and the negative. They go to any ends to photograph an accident, a siege or a naked princess by a pool. In this latter respect it is hard not to be drawn willy-nilly into a kind of weak, second-hand voyeurism. Even mass market women's magazines have moved in this direction recently.

But there are some subjects that provide a real challenge to the media. I am thinking of good news, things that are routine, but working well and reliably, and social innovations. My reading of the futures literature suggests that for every major problem or dilemma we face, there are considerable numbers of potential solutions waiting to be tried or applied. Unfortunately they are not always dramatic or newsworthy. Ideas circulate in esoteric publications like the journal of the London-based Institute for Social Inventions. They are seldom on the news. This is one of the subtle biases which conditions late 20th century life and contributes to its downbeat flavour. Why is good news so unpalatable?

For young people there is a different problem. I have examined a range of young people's media, looking for the ways in which they represent futures images and ideas. After looking at many examples and checking surveys of young people's views of futures, I came to the following conclusions. First, the images of futures in these media tend to be dark, violent cityscapes dominated by machines, and robots. It is amazingly difficult to find images of future people, particularly people who demonstrate that they too have moved on and evolved in some tangible way. Such futures are often represented in compelling detail and may arguably provide the means through which to consider fears of depersonalisation and so on. Yet what they do not provide is material which can be used to actually create the future. In other words, much of this material is disempowering.

The second conclusion I reached was that young people's media was confused. What I mean by this is that there seem to be a number of fundamental 'category errors' widely reproduced in comics, videos and films, for example. Good and evil, right and wrong, science and magic seem interchangeable. Where, then, is the material through which to interrogate the world, test out its meanings, negotiate rites of passage? With the exception of the 'good' books which fewer young people read, there seem to be not many points of clarity among the confusion. Much of the mass media seems to be little more than a strategy of distraction, driven by too-powerful a marketing imperative.

Why our institutions are out of step with the times

By way of a summary, I want to conclude this chapter by suggesting a number of reasons why some of our major institutions are failing us. They are as follows.

1. They had their beginnings in an earlier age and therefore still reflect that safer, slower, less threatened world.
2. The interests embedded in these institutions are not universal interests supported by clear and high-level values or motives. Instead, they tend to be limited, partial, frequently exploitive and driven by low-level values or motives.
3. Changes within systems and institutions tend to be slower than those outside of them. So it is easy for the former to become rapidly out of touch and unresponsive to current needs. People are often well ahead of the institutional contexts in which they work and this can cause great stress and frustration.
4. Turbulent times pose very severe problems for leaders and those in charge of enterprises. Many are not aware of the tools and other means by which they might see ahead more clearly and achieve a more deliberate, strategic stance. Many so-called leaders are just administrators or caretakers with little awareness or understanding of the wider picture.
5. The Western industrial worldview contains a number of assumptions that are faulty, unhelpful and which directly impede useful responses. One of these is a chronically short-term view, based on Me, Mine and Now. Another is a conception of time that sees the present as a fleeting moment. This helps to cut us off from the universal process in which we are immersed. Other assumptions have served to legitimise the present assault upon the life-support systems of the planet.

'Looking around' at some of our major institutions suggests that this past-oriented culture is attempting to move into the future without a futures perspective – that is, without sustaining and viable notions of how they might be constituted. In the default view, the future is an empty space. It does not exist. It cannot be studied. Yet intuitively this feels wrong.

If that were really the end of the story there would be no point in writing (or reading) this book. We would be 'locked into' a process we could neither foresee nor affect. Fortunately we are not in that dangerous and diminished position. Human beings are born with the capacity for foresight. We need to learn how to mobilise and apply it more effectively. That is, to re-constitute this capacity at the social level. This one development would do much to help us see clearly how industrialism has already breached certain key limits. It would also begin to reveal some of the many options for moving in more life-affirming directions. It follows that late industrial cultures need to adopt the foresight principle as part of their 'software', their underlying assumptions, their *modus operandi*. Without it they will be thrown back on mere experience and that, by itself, is very dangerous indeed.

CHAPTER 3

Looking Forward

Chapter 1 provided an account of what has gone wrong with Western Industrial culture. Chapter 2 showed how some of these inherited defects affect our major institutions in the present. This chapter begins the process of looking ahead. It asks some key questions. What can we know about the future? What are the real megatrends? How can one study futures? When these questions are answered we will be in a better position to extend the notion of foresight to new areas and uses.

What can we know about the future?

From the point of view of empirical science, we can know nothing whatsoever about the future. It does not exist, therefore, it cannot be studied. Yet, as noted above, intuitively we know that something is wrong with this view. It is true that the future is not an object, nor can it be the subject of experimentation. But that does not mean that it does not exist. There are many things that are very important to people which cannot be studied, measured, or even detected, from an empirical perspective. How much is music worth? What does an ethical principle weigh? How long is the present? None of these questions make a lot of sense because to ask them in this form involves category errors.

A category error arises when criteria for truth, reliability etc. are taken from one domain and read onto another. The domain that futures questions are situated in is not the same as that occupied by empirical science, so the criteria of the latter do not apply to the study of futures. We need to look elsewhere for such criteria. And fortunately they are close at hand.

In his work *The Art of Conjecture* **Bertrand de Jouvenal** suggested that studying futures was not, in fact, a question of knowledge and facts at all, but one of conjectures. As his title suggests he likened it to a work of art, in part because it was an expression and a creation of the human mind. So, in this view, the act of studying futures is a construction within the present which takes place in the richly-endowed environment of human minds.

Later observers have debated this issue at great length. Some have attempted to increase the accuracy of forecasting. Others have stressed a range of other methods for coming to grips with the future. Scenarios can give a very clear idea of different future alternatives. Delphic surveys

tap expert opinion of developments in a particular area. Futures workshops encourage people to feel empowered to create aspects of desired
futures. And so on. I do not want to undervalue these activities here. All
are important, all have their place. But in this context I want to take a
different tack.

James Ogilvy has argued that instead of attempting to emulate the
physical sciences, futures study and research should instead align with
developments in the humanities. Further, that such developments actually lead towards, and imply, a need for futures work – which for him
means normative (or value-laden) scenarios. I want to support this view
because I too have found major correspondences between developments
in linguistics, semiotics, critical theory, hermeneutics etc. and the futures
enterprise. It is easy here to diverge into a discussion of these theories
and their importance. But this book is not the place for such a discussion.
Instead, I want to summarise the implications for futures study. This will
show more clearly what kind of enterprise it is and in what sense the
future can be said to be a domain of knowledge.

The dominant (mainly American) tradition of futures work has been
largely empiricist in outlook. That is, it invested a lot of time analysing
time-series data, performing elaborate calculations and producing forecasts, time-lines, decision trees and so on, to guide present-day decision
making. Some of this work was of very high quality. Yet, to my mind, it
overlooked many of the deeper questions – questions to do with language, meaning, fundamentally opposing interests and, most importantly, the social construction of reality. In passing over such questions
this dominant tradition seemed to me to miss the point. One cannot
discuss 'world problems' without giving due weight to the traditions,
epistemologies and communities of discourse which arguably gave rise
to these problems in the first place. This helps us to understand why
many early futures books, with their repetitious description of 'world
problems' and solutions, were so unsatisfying. They missed out the
most important 'layer' or domain, i.e. that which is concerned with
constructing, negotiating and maintaining meanings.

The upshot is that the developments that Ogilvy, myself and others
had noted in other areas had immediate and practical use within the
futures enterprise. In other words, instead of seeing futures work as
something drastically different from other fields, it really has a great deal
in common with them. In this view, the essence of futures study is not
prediction, nor even forecasting – but scholarship. The same general
rules that apply to any non-quantitative field apply in futures: clear
argument, fit with the evidence, clarity, fruitfulness, applicability etc.

The futurist may be distinctive as regards subject matter – i.e. the
future – but not entirely so as regards methods and approaches. So, at
one level, futures study is simply scholarship applied to futures prob-

lems. Where have we come from? Where are we now? Where do we want to go? How do we get there? These questions overlap with those being asked in many other fields and areas. However, it is also the case that futures study frequently involves a number of specifically futures-related methods and approaches (see Chapter 6). What emerges from this discussion is a view of futures study as being partly common with other fields and partly distinctive as regards subject matter and methods. This makes it easier to specify what kind of knowledge is being sought.

It is very clear to me that futures people are unwise to try to predict events, let alone particular scenarios or the future of a social system. Predictions have been widely misunderstood, but they have two key uses. First, they can be applied to technical or physical systems which can be measured and understood. Engineers must be able to predict the stress limits of a bridge or the range of an aircraft. The physical infrastructure which surrounds us must be reliable, and hence it tends to be predictable. Interestingly enough, disasters occur when the assumptions embedded in technical predictions turn out to be wrong, or when the non-technical aspects of such systems are minimised or ignored (as at Chernobyl). Equally, planetary movements can be predicted for many years to come because the mechanics are clear. Second, predictions play a ubiquitous and informal role in everyday life. They underlie all the many assumptions people make, as well as the intuitive exercise of foresight (see below).

Social systems are just too complex to be approached in this way. They are comprised of many qualitative elements which include: values, beliefs, ideologies, presuppositons and so on. Furthermore, any success-ful social predictions would logically rule out the active role of human beings as agents and creators of history. If accurate prediction were possible, there would be no choices and hence no point in futures study. What futures people can do is much more modest, but very useful. By looking carefully at the past and present, they can derive an informed overview of present-day structures and processes. Careful use of this material makes it possible to create a broad brush picture, or account, of the near-term future.

I want to stress that it is not a detailed, or a complete, picture. It is provisional, unproven, yet – and this is important – grounded in a clear set of understandings and propositions. It is clear why scholarship is important. Far from being a problematic enterprise that tests one's cred-ulity, futures work of the kind described here actually calls for the very best work, the very highest standards (of clarity, insight, care etc.) the most careful and under-stated expression of any field of study.

One result of such work is what I call a 'decision context'. It spans past, present and aspects of possible futures. The context is created much as the first three chapters of this book have been created: the look back, the look around, the look forward. In each case there is a mixture of analytic and interpretative elements. The latter becomes more important in the forward look, but there are also strong analytic elements there too.

It follows that knowledge of the future is not empirical knowledge, but interpretative knowledge. What futures people do is to look back and to derive insights, data and knowledge about the past. They interpret that knowledge and use it to approach their understanding of the present. Within the present they look carefully at structures and processes. On the basis of these observations they look forward and create provisional knowledge about futures. They are helped with the study of processes in the present by the work of many other people. In other words, futurists are habitual skimmers. Another way of putting this is to say that they are always scanning the environment for significant signals, interpreting them and then using them to modify their work.

It therefore becomes clear in what sense we can have knowledge about futures. It is logically barred from us that we could ever have future facts about human and cultural systems. So we move to the next best option. That is a provisional, but fairly detailed and grounded picture, or view, of the terrain ahead. This view is continually informed and updated as events occur and our interpretations of the world change. Such a view can never be totally reliable. Yet it tells us much that is useful in the present. Indeed, the thesis of this book is that a carefully constructed forward view may be the single most important thing that we need in order to steer a sane course into the 21st century.

How can we study the future?

The notion of 'steering' into the future can be explained very easily though a simple analogy. We have all stood at a busy street corner waiting for the lights to change. At each side of the street a small crowd gathers. A few people can't wait. They glance both ways and dash across through the traffic, risking life and limb – and occasionally losing both. Most wait for the signal and two groups of pedestrians move toward each other across the road. The two groups pass through each other and reach the other side. How is this possible? How is it that there are not more collisions? The answer is simple, yet the implications are profound.

Each person is the owner of a superbly-tuned brain/mind system. Each one automatically scans ahead before they move. Is it safe? Are there any hazards to watch out for? When they begin to walk the scanning continues in an active loop. It is a feedback process of scanning, detecting the movements of others, interpreting the information and then acting. Even young children can understand this process. They can watch two people walking toward each other along a street. They can see the way that each accommodates the others' path. They can see the result. This is a simple physical analogy of futures study. But there is one huge difference. We are, on the whole, running our complex, powerful, world-shaping societies without a broad understanding of this capacity, and without it being systematically utilised at the social level.

Institutions and processes of foresight remain largely marginal to the key decision-making and policy-making arenas of the world. Hence, unlike the pedestrians in every country, we are attempting to steer into the future blindly, without foresight, without scanning and, on the whole, without being aware of what is at stake.

What can we do about this? The answer is deceptively simple. We can build a foresight capacity into every major institution and government. This is a practical possibility because we already know how to do it. The problem is that this knowledge is simply not being used. How could it be? Well, in a sense, I've already covered that above, so let me summarise here. As I've said, the future cannot be predicted. However:

- some things will continue (so we study continuities);
- some things will change (we monitor events and processes);
- from these materials pictures of future alternatives can be constructed (through scenarios, stories and novels);
- in the light of the above, choices and alternatives can be discussed.

The whole point of studying futures is not to predict but to understand alternatives. This understanding provides a decision context from which emerge options and choices. It is another loop, very much like those used in everyday life: scan, interpret, choose, act. In one sense this is quite simple. But in another it is not. The reason why this is so was explained in chapters 1 and 2: we live in a culture that has lost sight of the human significance of the future and which tends to find it more congenial to look back rather than to look forward. This has meant that futures study and research has been illegitimately dismissed, particularly in higher education. This has been a big mistake because it has slowed the improvement and application of the field. Since universities act as the gatekeepers to what is regarded as valid knowledge, their failure (with some exceptions) to understand the significance of the field has meant that it has taken longer to permeate education at other levels. Hence it has taken longer to become more widely established.

Yet the futures field is a potent cultural resource. So another part of the answer about how we can study futures is to consider this field. What is it? How does it work? What does it offer?

The futures field

Futures is an interdisciplinary field of inquiry. The fact that it is richly interconnected at the margins with many other enterprises and fields means that the boundaries cannot be defined clearly. However, the idea of a core takes on greater clarity. The model presented in Figure 3.1 is made up of several identifiable overlapping layers or elements. For analytical purposes it is convenient to separate them. However, in reality they are interconnected and functionally inseparable. At least six layers can be distinguished, as outlined below.

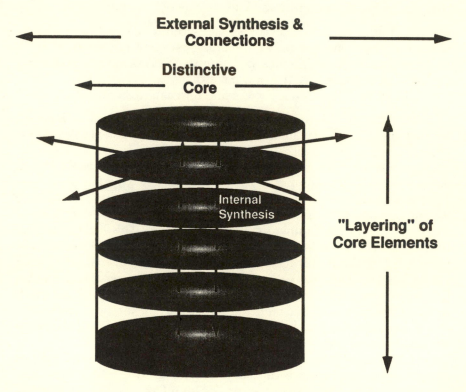

External Synthesis & Connections

Distinctive Core

Internal Synthesis

"Layering" of Core Elements

Figure 3.1 A model of the core of the futures studies field

Language, concepts and metaphors

The language, concepts and metaphors of the futures field can be regarded as primary intellectual and symbolic resources. The very concepts of 'future' and 'futures' point toward one of the distinguishing criteria which provides the possessors of a human brain/mind system with a unique vantage point in time, i.e., one that is not restricted to the 'creature present' of other species. Concepts such as those of 'alternatives', 'options', 'agenda for the 21st century' and 'sustainability' provide the means to think with about futures. They are building blocks for understanding which, when developed and explored, permit otherwise vague and provisional 'schema' about the future to take shape and form.

Metaphors have particular applicability in futures because they organise and shape our conceptual structures in particular ways. Thus, for example, the future can be likened to a dice game where chance plays a big part. It can be like a river, in which case its course is pre-determined, but we can watch out for hazards. It may be like a roller-coaster, suggesting a challenging, but tightly-constrained route. Or it may be like an ocean where we can strike out in any direction. Metaphors tend to invisibly shape discourse, but they can be used deliberately to further our conscious intentions.

Theories, ideas and images

The symbolic building blocks outlined above can be assembled into structures of great power and insight. For example the idea of a post-industrial society, an information age or a wise culture bring with them a whole series of possibilities for attempting to understand – and perhaps distinguish ways beyond – contemporary reality. The field as a whole generates a web of interconnected theories, ideas and images which serve to contradict the popular notion of the future as an 'empty space'. One of the basic propositions is that, far from being, in some sense, inert, unapproachable or deeply problematic, the future is a principle of present action and present consciousness. In this sense, it presents human beings with a wide range of options, alternatives and dilemmas. Some of these can be explored through theories about evolution, progress, chaos, stability, permanence and new forms of society. Some are best approached through imagery, either visual or literary.

Images of futures are both ubiquitous and yet under-studied. They are being continuously negotiated at all levels of society. They are consciously deployed, for example, in the attempts to gain social support for major projects. But they may also be unconscious or obscured by ideological uses. Images of futures in the late 20th century tend to be either technophilic or dystopian. Both can be usefully explored, critiqued and compared with, e.g., those emerging from speculative fiction and art. As noted below, the futurist ignores these at his or her peril because, properly understood, they complement and extend the mostly rationalist operations of professional forecasters and the like.

Literature and practitioners

The elements outlined above come into productive relationships in at least two key ways: in literature and in the people who use (and create) it. The futures field has a very rich literature. Familiarity with the latter provides access to the field. Obviously, this literature can be studied like any other. It can be critiqued, explored and extended. One could not be a futurist without some knowledge of at least part of it. One could not train students to become professionals in the field without it. So teaching and research is heavily indebted to the literature.

There are two main branches. The core of the professional futures literature resides primarily in about 200 key books by authors from around the world, but predominantly from Europe and North America. Many of them are listed at the end of this book. The journals are also very important. When people have inquired about the intellectual foundations of futures studies, I have sometimes suggested that they consider some back issues of *Futures* or, more recently, the Australian based *21C*. No one could consider such publications without coming away with a clear impression of substance and quality. While there are only a handful of core futures journals (and more are needed), they certainly help to sustain the field at its present stage of development.

The other branch of futures literature is that of speculative writing, or science fiction (SF). This tends not to be produced by futurist writers *per se*, but the corpus of written (and pictured) SF is very important for the field. Whereas non-fictional futures work is based on rationality, logic, extrapolation and scholarship, SF draws on different sources – primarily imagination, game-playing (such as 'what if ... ?' games or alternative histories) and creativity. As such, and at its best, it fills out the medium, and the long-term, future with a wide range of possibilities. **Professor Ian Clarke** has shown in detail how this speculative literature has affected social, cultural and technological processes over a very long period. It remains an important resource for those looking beyond the near-term future.

Futures practitioners create, refine and use the formal knowledge which finds its way into non-fiction books about futures. Estimates of the numbers of people working full-time in futures vary, but there are enough to sustain a wide variety of networks and organisations (see below). If it is language, concepts and metaphors that provide the symbolic foundation of futures, it is the practitioners who supply the human, intellectual and applied energy. It is they who are energised by this powerful idea of 'future' and who use it to pursue numerous projects and possibilities in the present. The outcomes of futures work affect social processes in countless ways, but most importantly through projects, enabling structures and social innovations (see below).

Organisations and networks

There are a number of core organisations and networks in the futures field. Two are centrally placed. The US based World Future Society (WFS) and the World Futures Studies Federation (WFSF). According to 1992 figures the latter had 531 individual members and 53 institutional ones. Both are distributed widely across the globe and thus the Federation is a true international network. It has an activist, cultural, political tradition and a broadly facilitative outlook. The WFS, on the other hand, is perhaps an order of magnitude larger but is more popular, conservative and corporatist in orientation. The quality of its publications varies somewhat (from the ever-useful *Future Survey* to the over-popular *Futurist*) and its status as a privately-owned company affects its character in fairly obvious ways. Together, these two organisations cater for the broad interests of most practising futurists through publications, projects and meetings. They both have local or national branches in a number of countries.

In addition, there are a number of more specialised organisations which fall under the heading of 'institutions of foresight'. They include the Millennium Institute (Washington DC), the Club of Rome (Rome), the Network on Responsibilities to Future Generations (Malta), the Secretariat for Futures Studies (Germany), the Institute for Social Inventions (London), the Robert Jungk Futures Library (Salzburg) and the Australian Commission for the Future (Melbourne). In the view outlined here, such organisations – and there are probably a hundred or more worldwide – cluster around the core and support a wide range of more focussed activities. They tend to be small, under-funded, and even marginal. Yet they are of great actual or potential importance. They tend to be pioneers, or 'leading-edge' organisations which act as seed-beds for innovation. While the wastage rate may be high, their collective impact is very significant. It is therefore important to build links between them and to carry out careful research into their effectiveness.

Finally, overlapping these near-core contexts are a diverse range of futures-related organisations. These include NGOs, consultancies, government bodies and international groups often associated with the UNESCO or the OECD. Some overlap with social movements occurs here (see below).

Methodologies, tools and practices

The core of applied futures work is methodology. Just as theories create new structures from underlying concepts etc., so methodologies increase the intellectual and applied power of ideas and theories. Basic methodologies include the following.

- Environmental scanning: systematically scanning the environment for precursors, events, signals of many kinds and interpreting their significance.
- Scenario analysis: outlining a set of internally-consistent futures to test hypotheses, explore alternatives, elucidate policy options and choices, prepare for contingencies etc.
- Cross-impact matrices: systematically impacting a data set upon itself or another set in order to study and assess a field of interactions.
- The Delphic survey method: tapping expert opinion in order to reach a consensus about future developments in a particular area.
- Forecasting and strategic management: using forecasts and other methods to inform and influence planning, decision-making and management.
- National and global modelling: the attempt to study the dynamics of complex systems by reducing them to their core components and manipulating them.
- Positive critique and analysis of discourse: probing beneath the surface of discourses to discover hidden agendas, presuppositions, ideological interests, thereby opening up new interpretative options and, by extension, different future possibilities.

Some elements of these are combined in useful sequences to create a more sustained and penetrating methodology. Such approaches arguably include Michel Godet's 'Prospective', Joseph Coates' 'Issues Management' and the 'QUEST' methodology developed by Selwyn Enzer and Burt Nanus (see below). Methodologies of this extended type are in wide use in some government and corporate contexts. Significantly, educators tend not only not to use them, but not even to know about them. Moves are afoot to bring some elements of these methodologies closer to mainstream educational and political processes. But all such initiatives take time.

Futures tools are simple versions of some of the methodologies, or practical applications drawn from them. They include time-lines, futures wheels, space/time grids, simple technology assessment, strategies for responding to fears and so on. Such tools have been developed and applied over a quarter of a century since the first school courses in futures were taught in, or around, 1966. While it is true that the evaluation of futures teaching in schools has been patchy, it nevertheless remains a fact that much of this work has been pedagogically successful. It can be, and is being, emulated in many places around the world.

Social movements and innovations

The extent to which social movements may be considered part of the futures field is a matter of interpretation. However, I have always seen them as closely related to futures work in that they have not only attempted to discuss and theorise about future societies, but have acted in the present to bring about change. Hence, they align with one of the core purposes of futures work. While some may doubt the connection, it is a substantial one. For example, the peace movement brought popular pressure to bear on a number of governments during the Cold War and arguably helped to bring it to an end. It also helped to undermine the legitimacy of the view that nuclear weapons could or should be deployed for purposes of 'defence'. The women's movement has focussed attention on the ways that women are disadvantaged, not least through 'gendered' language, patriarchal institutons and inappropriate socio-economic values. The environmental movement has drawn attention to the destruction of the planet's life-support systems and, while 'Green' political parties have not yet achieved more than minority status, their impacts upon political agendas internationally have been substantial.

Similarly, the animal liberation movement has created a minor revolution in the ways animals are treated in farms and used for experimentation. Linked with this is the campaign of vegetarians and others to reduce the consumption of meat across the board. A less well-known social movement focussing upon inter-generational equity and the rights of future generations is gaining momentum. Finally, let us also recall the many NGOs, such as Amnesty International, Save the Children and Community Aid Abroad. When taken together, the total spectrum of social movements and NGOs adds up to a very powerful and progressive force in the world. Generally speaking, it is they who pick up issues and generate social support for dealing with them. It is only much later that governments get the message and lend them partial support.

Another connection between futures and social innovations is provided by the example of futurist **Robert Jungk**. He played an important role in setting up the London based Institute for Social Inventions which provides a seed-bed and a context for a wide range of positive social responses to change. This kind of 'output' is in part a consequence of the factors noted above in which concepts, ideas, theories, people and organisations act in concert to produce intended higher-order effects. Yet a note of caution is in order: this account does not presume that all intended effects are achieved, or unintended ones avoided.

On the other hand, social innovations are ubiquitous and easy to study.

The process of creating them can be taught and learned. When young people ask the inevitable question 'what can I do?' one high-quality answer is to reply: 'work toward a social innovation' (see Chapter 8).

So what emerges from this overview? I want to re-emphasise that the futures field can be regarded as an identifiable entity when the factors described above are seen as a series of overlays that are richly connected vertically to each other and laterally to other related fields. The undeniable presence of diffuse margins, overlapping traditions, divergent paradigms and so forth do not in any way detract from this view. As Ogilvy and others have observed, there are no foundations in our uncertain, post-modern word, only a series of interconnected networks. So the futures field is not different to others in this respect. From the above, it seems clear that:

- futures work is essential;
- it is no more difficult or problematic than other fields;
- it has become a structural necessity in many areas; and
- if handled well it will be taken up much more widely.

This account of the field may well be incomplete and is certainly capable of further development. The knowledge core is bound to evolve. Yet, as it stands, it provides a rich matrix for exploring some of the central questions of this, or any other, age. What has gone wrong? How can things be improved? Where do we want to go as a society, and as a species? How can we get there? Replete as these questions are with unclear agendas and problematic concepts and assumptions, they nevertheless still remain central. A culture that is not interested even in asking such questions can no longer be considered viable.

The outlook for the next twenty years

So what can we know about the near-term future? There are at least two ways of answering this question. One is to assess the significance of empirical trends occuring 'out there' in the world. The other is to examine underlying ideas that are either growing or in decline. Both are useful. Hence, this chapter considers the former, while the latter is taken up in Chapter 5.

To begin with, we can set aside most of the so-called 'Megatrends'. The term was coined by **John Naisbitt** in the early 1980s and revisited in 1990. It purported to lay out a series of major trends which were shaping the world. However, careful analysis reveals that barely a third of the much-touted 'Megatrends' actually stand up to examination. What counts as one depends upon a lot of things including: the culture of origin, the interests (and capacity) of the observer, the purposes of the work, the level of aggregation and the underlying framework of analysis.

What this implies, in part, is that the idea of a single, monolithic overview of global change is not viable. Such a God-like perspective simply does not exist. The next best thing would be a view assembled from multiple perspectives on a variety of levels. But this is not what Naisbitt has done.

There are several surprising things about both 'Megatrends' books. First, they are both presented as though they were objective and 'value-free'. Second, no theoretical or methodological justification is given for the approach or the content of the books. Third, they avoid dealing with the global problematique entirely. Fourth, they embody a strong corporate, right-wing, free-enterprise bias. Fifth, they relate mainly to the USA. Sixth, their usefulness is mainly limited to marketing. Unfortunately many people have overlooked these defects and taken these books as authoritative statements about the world. This is a mistake. A more productive response is not to rely on such naive, opportunistic and general 'off the shelf' material, but to use the basic idea. This suggests that organisations would benefit from: setting up their own environmental scanning system, developing their own interpretative criteria, creating their own models and deriving their own views of the dynamics of change.

Standing behind the over-hyped products of 'pop futurism' is a much more substantial literature dealing with global change (see Bibliography). One example is a book edited by **Lester Brown** (and others) and called *Vital Signs 1992: The Trends That Are Shaping Our Future*. Among other things, this book takes a careful look at: food, agricultural resources, energy, economics, social trends, military issues and the environment. It provides a wealth of detail about the current status of these areas and concludes that the world is facing a genuine crisis in many of them. The point is also made that societies tend to be alert to the trends of an earlier time, rather than those which are currently shaping the world. This suggests that 'governing by hindsight' may still be more usual than by foresight.

Such criticisms could not be levelled at **James Dator** whose work on the 'Tsunamis' (or tidal waves) of change is as far-sighted as anyone could wish for. Dator looks in some depth at five broad change processes under the headings of: demographics, economics, environment, technology and globalisation. He sees a range of problems in each area. For example, Western (white) civilisation may become less dominant as population growth races ahead elsewhere. Economic problems will worsen as old-style 'industrial' outlooks are read upon a very different context in which, for example, fewer people will be actually needed for production purposes. The environment will continue to deteriorate for similar reasons, and technology will 'change the rules' faster than we are prepared for. Finally, globalisation will hasten the death of the nation state and aid the resurgence of cultures, perhaps including artificial machine cultures.

Perhaps the most useful overview to date is that from the World Future Society's *World 2000* project. This draws on a very wide range of individuals and sources to provide an account of driving forces for global change, critical issues which arise and several broad strategies. These are summarised in Figure 3.2. While these tend to focus on fairly obvious, largely external phenomena, there are some important points. For example, key cultural concerns are broached (e.g. human rights), major organisational developments are signalled (e.g. managing complexity) and several shifts are called for (e.g. in economics, society's relationship to the environment, de-centralisation and collaborative working relationships). While not methodologically comprehensive, such an overview provides a useful starting point for more detailed work.

Figure 3.2 World 2000: driving forces and critical issues

Driving forces

1. A stable population of 10–14 billion people.
2. Industrial output increased by a factor of 5–10.
3. Information technology will permit the 'wiring of the globe'.
4. A continuation of the 'high-tech' revolution (DNA mapping, robotics, new materials etc.).
5. Closer integration of the globe into a single community.
6. Diversity and complexity through ethnic regions, subcultures etc.
7. A universal standard of freedom and human rights.
8. Limited crime, terrorism, war and disease.
9. A resurgence of transcendent values.

Critical issues

1. Making the transition from separate nation states to a global order.
2. Resolving the conflict between economic growth and sustainability.
3. Reconciling economic interests through a new economic paradigm.
4. Understanding and managing complexity at the institutional level.
5. Alleviating the disparities between north and south.

Source: Halal, W. 'World 2000: An international planning dialogue to help shape the new global system', Futures 25 (1) 1993, pp. 5–21.

What emerges from such views of global trends is a world in genuine crisis. It is a world that has already exceeded some important limits, and looks set to exceed others. In other words, it is a world that is steadily moving toward what the Meadows team call 'an overshoot and collapse' mode. To modify this outlook will require the unprecedented exercise of both foresight and wisdom, the twin themes of this book.

In order to show how urgent it is that we re-think our agendas across the board, I want to summarise six reasons why the prospect darkens before it improves. Figure 3.3 therefore summarises six 'negatrends' or reasons why things get harder before they get easier. They help to illustrate why global trends cannot be dealt with at the empirical level. They suggest that we need to 'look beneath the surface' of cultures in transition to expore the cultural 'software' hidden deep in the Western worldview itself.

Figure 3.3 Six 'negatrends' or why things will get harder before they get easier

1. It takes time to identify deficiencies in the western industrial worldview and put them right.
2. The continuing unsatisfactory operation of the global economy.
3. Failure to resolve the global problematique.
4. Continuing technical innovation creates new dilemmas superimposed on older ones.
5. The ethical basis of late industrial social life remains inadequate and unsustainable.
6. There is inadequate investment in foresight.

The worldview problem has been widely overlooked by mainstream futurists. Yet it powerfully affects the ways we see the world (often through unregarded assumptions and taken-for-granted commitments). Yet there is no rule book for reconstituting a culture. One can't discard a particular 'structure of consciousness' overnight. Moreover, as noted, personal and institutional learning lags slow down the process of cultural innovation. Formal education is very much part of the problem, in part because it remains immersed in the past and has not yet taken up the many concepts, tools and techniques for teaching and learning about futures. But many other institutions are also 'behind the times' and these too contribute to social rigidity.

Gross inequalities between nations persist and are worsening in some cases. They appear to be a systemic feature of the global system. Market economies do not have an intrinsic interest in the future, and market signals operate retrospectively. Classical economics excludes the wider world and regards ecological impacts as 'externalities'. Global problems of poverty, environmental deterioration, pollution and loss of genetic diversity also continue to grow. Most people feel that these are too remote to deal with and are outside of their world of reference. Governments have short-term, limited agendas, linked to the electoral cycle. So, on the whole, they try to ignore the global problematique. The time-frames of governance and those that apply to global atmospheric and other environmental systems are drastically out of step.

Virtual reality, the human genome project, nanotechnology and so-called 'artificial intelligence' all raise as many new problems as they promise to solve. The notion of 'control' in this context is problematic.

Technology is often seen as providing new solutions, but this is a naive view. It tends to be over-valued, while questions of language, meaning and conflicting interests are overlooked. On the whole, Western societies have yet to decisively wean themselves away from anodyne, machine-led views of futures that are clearly not viable in the long term.

The still-powerful (but inadequate) industrial-era ethics of pragmatism, utilitarianism, competitive individualism and the marketing imperative have not, and will not, provide a sound basis for individual or social decision-making. There is a spiritual vacuum at the heart of industrialised culture which makes it very difficult for people to resolve the perennial concerns of human existence. A series of substitute satisfactions are readily available, but they merely shove problems out of sight. Yet at deeper levels people are not fooled; they know that a confidence trick is being played. This helps to explain the continuous outpouring of apocalyptic imagery and the largely unnecessary view of the future as a dark and forbidding place. This very dilemma provides the cultural and historical grounds for critical and creative futures work, but too few are working in these modes.

Finally, as noted, foresight needs to be deployed at the social and organisational levels. But in habitually short-termist, past-oriented cultures, there is little interest in doing so. Hence the savings of successful foresight are denied and the risks of 'overshoot and collapse' beyond critical limits continue to grow.

Of all these factors, the key is foresight. If we invested enough time and effort in systematically thinking ahead, all of the problems would be much easier to deal with. So the following chapter looks at how foresight is already understood and used.

Applying and extending the foresight principle

CHAPTER 4

How Foresight is Already Understood and Used

There is plenty of evidence that foresight is not new. This chapter explores the concept in more depth and shows how it is used in everyday life and in some institutions. Barriers to the further extension of the principle are noted, along with the drastic change of context within which it now operates.

What is foresight?

As noted in the Preface, Webster's dictionary defines foresight as an act or power of foreseeing; prescience; an act of looking forward; a view forward, and provident care, or prudence. These are not qualities that late industrial cultures have been well known for. But they could be. Foresight is primarily a part of the rich world of understanding and perception made possible by the human brain/mind system. Moreover, it is subtly woven into nearly everything we do. Therefore we do not need to invent a new principle, merely apply an old one in new ways. It is a defining condition of human life that actions and decisions (hence, understanding in general) are founded both on what has gone before and on what is expected or intended. The former has received ample attention from psychologists and historians, but the disciplines of futures study and research are relatively new. Hence, until recently the futures dimension did not attract similar attention. However, it is now clear that this dimension is at least as central to the human enterprise as the past is commonly assumed to be. The ability to pursue purposes and formulate meanings, to decide on goals and design strategies, to plan outcomes and intend consequences, to take responsibility for the consequences of actions – these all depend upon an open and undetermined future which is continually scanned from within the moving present.

Experience is not merely a product of past events, nor simply a passive record of elapsed time. Experience is a product of the interaction of memory and foresight, of identity and purpose. In this dynamic process the yield of the past is symbolically transformed through being 'read upon' as yet undetermined situations. The foresight principle is called into play by irreducible uncertainties created by the precariousness of life. Foresight is 'common-sense' in that there is obvious merit in seeking to avoid dangers and reduce risks. However, the principle is easier to implement at the individual level than at the social level.

A more up-to-date and dynamic understanding of foresight stresses the process rather than an isolated act. Hence the definition offered in the Preface. In summary, foresight is the process of attempting to broaden the boundaries of perception by careful futures scanning and the clarification of emerging situations. This suggests a kind of vision: a vision of the mind rather than of the organs of sight. As I indicated above, it pushes the boundaries of perception forward in at least four major ways:

- by assessing the implications of present actions, decisions, etc. (consequence assessment);
- by detecting and avoiding problems before they occur (early warning and guidance);
- by considering the present implications of possible future events (pro-active strategy formulation); and
- by envisioning aspects of desired futures (normative scenarios).

The first three appear to perform guidance and/or early warning functions, but the fourth goes beyond these strategic and protective interests to consider what is desired in positive terms. Here foresight intersects with creative and visionary work of many kinds.

As noted above, at the individual level these operations appear to take place effortlessly within the human mind. However, we should not assume that they are simple. The analogy with physical sight is very close. As far as we are concerned, we just see. We are not, on the whole, aware of the highly complex visual processing which reverses the inverted images that fall on the retina and permits us to see so well under a wide range of lighting conditions. Similarly, the kinds of knowledge and understanding involved in planning an overseas trip are equally interwoven and complex. Several varieties of contextual understanding are needed. For example, a 'world map', rules of procedure, a grasp of the dynamics of emerging situations and an ability to act according to reliable decision-making principles. These exploratory and decision-making processes contain elements of prediction, intuitions, hunches etc. as well as a certain amount of conscious and systematic analysis. Together they help to define a personal decision context which makes goal-oriented behaviour possible while reducing the likelihood of more costly types of learning. Such decision contexts inform virtually all human behaviour at the individual level. To construct them at higher levels of aggregation requires first, that the processes involved are clearly understood, and second, that institutional 'shelters' are available. Clearly this is not always the case.

Since foresight springs, in part, from unconscious, or preconscious sources it cannot be reduced to a technique. It is grounded in innate human capacities and needs. Yet its social expressions require specific, rational institutional arrangements. So a balance is implied between the rational and the non-rational, between technique and the wider world of human significance which supports it. It is therefore likely that the most successful foresight work will draw substantially upon this wider framework (perhaps including an explicitly ethical orientation) rather than adopting the narrower focus of in-house futurist expertise or, worse, a prior commitment to the instrumentalities of science, technology and marketing. When the rational, social and ethical aspects of foresight are co-ordinated and in balance, they can contribute substantially to social homeostasis. But such a balance is not easy to achieve and foresight at the level of social process still lacks support for reasons which are discussed below.

I now want to look at traditional expressions of foresight and at some of the ways it is already implemented in present-day social practice. I then consider barriers to its wider use and the radical change of context within which it now operates. Finally I outline a case for considering foresight as a structural imperative.

The traditional role of foresight

It is highly significant that the value of foresight is clearly expressed in a number of traditional folk sayings. 'Look before you leap' is an injunction to engage in some kind of futures scanning before committing oneself to a particular action. It implies that taking action carries risks and that 'looking' may reduce those risks. It indicates a generalised and informal capacity which, in theory, is available to anyone. Clearly, the injunction is derived from a concern for physical safety, but the metaphor has very many wider uses.

'Forewarned is forearmed' goes a step further. It indicates one of the tangible benefits of futures scanning: a self-protective readiness for whatever may happen. The 'armour' here refers to the preparations which can be made in response to foreknowledge. Such 'knowledge' is clearly of great value, even though its epistemological status remains uncertain. This helps to explain why so much attention has been paid throughout history to prediction in all its many guises. The desire to make careful preparation to cater for contingencies involves a need to assess the future by whatever means are available.

'A stitch in time saves nine' outlines the basic rationale of almost any approach to futures work: the saving of effort that would otherwise be expended clearing up the mess. Here foresight can be equated with notions of prudence and conservation of effort. Complex organisms (and, indeed, organisations) simply cannot afford to 'let the future take care of itself'. There is too much at stake, and fatalism can be fatal. In each case the principle is grounded in examples drawn from individual and group experience; but it clearly has much wider applications. Foresight may begin with the individual or group but it clearly does not end there.

In some respects foresight has long been implemented at the social level. There are many examples: the storage of food (in anticipation of drought, famine, changing seasons); the building of defences (as preparation for, or protection against, attack); the design of tools and buildings for a range of future uses. Notions of design, building and invention are themselves comprehensible only when set in a context embracing past and future. However, the needs which these applications address are based on long-term historical experience. They are well understood and universally accepted. Appropriate social mechanisms have therefore evolved to cater for them. It may be concluded that there is nothing particularly controversial or problematic about the general application of the foresight principle in traditional contexts. A brief review of the present-day uses of foresight will make this clear.

Those who live in climates where the weather changes from day-to-day or hour-to-hour utilise foresight in a very practical and immediate way. They listen to weather forecasts or check the paper before venturing out. In Melbourne, Australia, where this book was written, it is said that there can be 'three seasons in one day'. So preparations for the weather may need to embrace several quite different requirements. The question of how you dress for a heatwave, rain, high winds, all on the same day, is an immediate and practical one. Melburnians have long experience in this art.

Foresight comes directly into play at the key transitions and decision-points of human life. Choosing a partner is a major decision that will affect the rest of one's life, or at least a significant part of it. Familiar questions arise. Can I trust this person? How will they act if one of us loses a job or is sick for a long time? Will they be faithful? And so on. Similar questions arise when a decision is being made about whether or not to begin a family. Can we afford it? Who will stay home? Where will the baby sleep?

Buying a home is another important decision with long-range consequences. Perhaps the key question is: can we afford it? But one might also ask, is the house right for us? Is it big enough, in the right area, close enough to schools, work, shops? What sort of shape is it in? Will we have to spend a lot on repairs? Clearly, this is an extensive exercise in using foresight. There are very many contingencies to cover. Taking a course raises similar questions. Is this the right course for me at this time? Can I cope with the work-load? When will I have time for undisturbed reading or writing? How will the course benefit me in the future?

Clearly people become adept at using foresight. Nothing demonstrates this more clearly than the exercise of planning an overseas trip. This is a true futures exercise. Consider: there are an infinite number of options. The first question is probably where do we want to go? Once this is decided, we move on to the next questions: can we afford it, how shall we travel, where shall we stay? There are many items to consider. They include: passports and visas, foreign currency, health precautions, clothing and other gear, insurance and perhaps local maps. (Nor should one forget the temporary care of the cat, dog or canary at home.) The question of maps, and more generally of mapping where one wishes to go, provides a direct link with the work of the futures field.

In general terms, the purpose of futures work is not, as I have indicated, to predict. It is rather to 'map' the near-term future insofar as this is possible with the knowledge of, and from the vantage-point of, a particular point in time. Like any map, including maps of the physical world, there will be much that cannot be represented. But the futures map does try to indicate such things as areas of danger, areas needing attention and a range of directions, options and alternatives. Given that people have had so much practical experience in foresight, no-one should have too much trouble 'reading' this futures map.

Fragmented foresight at the social level

As noted above, some social arrangements do cater specifically for future contingencies in traditional areas. For example, the insurance industry developed to indemnify people against a wide range of risks and dire events. The security industry provides a range of services and devices to guard against robbery, theft and violence. Similarly, police forces, fire brigades, emergency services and the armed forces are all kept in various states of readiness to deal with a range of threatening or destructive events. Hospitals too have carefully-designed emergency plans to cope with different types of disasters. Past experience has shown that the lack of a quick-response capacity can be very expensive in terms of life and property.

Preventative health care is another area where forward-thinking has become standard practice. In many developed countries, campaigns drawing attention to diet, exercise and lifestyle have successfully reduced the incidence of heart disease, lung cancer and other conditions. An important shift here has been away from treating sickness to promoting health and well-being. It is a good example of the benefits to be derived from implementing foresight. Nor should we overlook the practice of injecting weak strains of pathogenic organisms into babies and children. The reason? We know that by so doing we will stimulate their immune systems to produce antibodies which will protect them against such diseases as chicken pox and diphtheria. Here again, a little short-term pain, and even a slight degree of risk (since some children have adverse reactions), is chosen in order to deliver long-term benefit. This principle can be applied much more widely.

So, on the whole, we are quite good at applying foresight to familiar, close-up problems. We are not yet so good at applying it to wider concerns. Yet even here there are positive signs. The story of the human and institutional response to the thinning of the ozone layer is instructive. In summary, the process went something like this:

1974: The first scientific papers were published suggesting a possible problem.
1978: A law was passed in the USA forbidding use of chloroflourocarbons (CfCs) as propellants.
1984: The first scientific evidence was obtained of an 'ozone hole' over Antarctica.
1987: The Montreal protocol was signed, freezing production of the most common CfCs at 1986 levels and progressively reducing them thereafter.
1990: Representatives of 92 countries met in London and agreed to phase out CfCs entirely by the year 2000.

This shows that the global community can mobilise to act in concert when the need is clear. Yet there is also a sting in the tail of this success story which is highly significant. It took 13 years from the first scientific paper to the signing of the Montreal protocol. It will take about the same time for the latter to be fully implemented. In other words, the human/ institutional response time in this case is about 26 years, or roughly a quarter of a century. Beyond this, it will take another century for the ozone-eating CfCs to be eliminated from the atmosphere. What this demonstrates very clearly is that the implicit time-frames used by most governments and decision makers (say from 1–5 years ahead at the most) is out of step with the dynamics of the life-support systems of the earth. Because of the long delays, the long-term processing periods, the time it takes natural systems to recover from damage or abuse, the time-frames applicable to our environment must be measured in decades or centuries.

Here, then, is a great challenge for habitually growth-oriented, short-termist and resource-intensive societies. How can they begin to deal with this opposition between short-term and long-term? How can they apply systematic foresight to the big issues of planet management now, and in the 21st century? If they continue to regard only the short-term as significant, then it is quite clear that planetary limits associated with resources, pollution and life-support systems will be exceeded. They will then be moving into a period which the systems modellers call 'overshoot and collapse', which is not a pleasant prospect.

Perhaps the only way to avoid this prospect is to understand that, by virtue of its power and impacts throughout the natural world, our globe-spanning industrialised culture is already in the future! The effects of actions, decisions, pollutants, wars and so on are not fully expressed where they happen to originate. Just as it took many years for DDT to silently ascend the food chain, and just as it will take over a century to cleanse the atmosphere of CfCs, so too are there many other substances and impacts presently working through the entire global system. Clearly, we do not just need a long-term early warning system to tell us about things that are already in the pipeline, as it were; we must begin to think ahead on the scale required. While the exact time-scales will differ for different systems and purposes, the above examples suggest that, at the social level, our foresight needs to extend to something like one hundred years into the future.

The prospect would be less daunting if we were simply to apply what we already know about foresight. But, unfortunately, there are a number of barriers or impediments to its wider implementation. These will extend the time, and hence increase the risks and the eventual costs to all forms of life on the planet.

Barriers to the wider use of foresight

There is a saying which declares that 'one person's good idea is another person's workload'. This usefully reminds us that however worthy the notion of foresight may be, someone will have to do the work and someone will have to pay for it. Since all social innovations must run the gauntlet of vested interests, dated attitudes, entrenched bureaucracies and (initially at least) lack of public support, it is necessary to consider impediments and barriers. I will mention only six in the present context. There are certainly many others.

The practice of future discounting

This suggests that because the future has not yet happened, it is inherently less important and can therefore be discounted. The rate of discounting used tends to conceal judgements about the value (or lack of value) of something or someone (i.e. future generations). In practice, a high discount rate suggests that the future is too remote to be worth anything much and can safely be ignored. A low discount rate would be an indication of value or importance. The major problem is that these judgements tend to be inexplicit and made by default.

The empiricist fallacy

It is a dated, yet common empiricist view that the most important subjects for disciplined enquiry are those that can be measured, weighed or otherwise empirically verified. Since there are few or no future facts, the only sources of useful knowledge are those found in the past and the present. Future uncertainty is too great to permit us to say anything much of value about what may lie ahead. Therefore we should stick to what we can know directly and let the future take care of itself.

A sense of disempowerment

Many people feel that the problems are too great and individuals are too insignificant to have any real impact. The difficulty is exacerbated when experts disagree in public. People take the view that they have neither the power, nor the opportunity to help solve major problems. The availability of reality-avoidance industries, including the surrogate worlds of mass entertainment, provides some relief from the resulting tensions. But there remains a sense that one is out of touch, and events are out of control.

The idea that time and space perspectives are fixed

It is assumed that human beings have natural interests in the short-term which cannot be extended very much. These limits create boundaries which cannot be changed. In this view, it is unrealistic to imagine that people will ever be prepared to look more than a few years ahead.

Fear of foresight

It must be acknowledged that foresight can be wrong, badly timed and biased. It may even complicate decision making. The practical difficulties of making long-term policies and decisions based on provisional knowledge can be seen as insuperable.

The cost of foresight

Foresight is too expensive. Organisations are already hard-pressed to cope in difficult circumstances. The last thing they need is a new set of costs. They should stick to what they know and leave others to indulge in idle speculation.

Objections similar to the above clearly carry weight in many contexts. But perhaps that 'weight' derives less from intrinsic validity than from habits of thought and perception which spring from an earlier world view; a view which itself has lost legitimacy and is seriously in doubt. Underlying it are assumptions which persist through inertia rather than through appropriateness or 'fit' with current circumstances or needs. Yet each of the fallacies I have identified should be taken seriously. They indicate issues which foresight work ought not to ignore. Indeed, each can be re-framed as positive agenda items, opportunities for clear and incisive work. Such work is now being carried out in many places. But a lot more will occur when the implications of the new context are more widely understood. We now turn to one way of illuminating the huge difference between the need for foresight in earlier societies and our present, very different, requirements.

From horse and cart to superhighway

Foresight takes on added urgency during periods of rapid change and uncertainty. Such conditions are not entirely new. However, during much of history it is safe to assume that foresight was not felt to be an urgent priority due to relatively slow rates of change, more diffuse populations and the limitations of more primitive technologies. The underlying model for learning was to take the lessons of past experience and apply them within a fairly stable present. But in modern times this stability has vanished. The taken-for-granted present of Western linear time has become fractured and unlivable. Moreover, a new dynamic has become established which has subverted traditional wisdom in very many ways and seemed to outstrip the capacity of societies to respond.

The 'technological trajectory', or direction of technical developments, resulting from such assumptions is by no means a natural feature of the world. Yet it has seemed to many to be both natural and unstoppable. It is therefore useful to explore some of the foresight implications of this shift through simile and metaphor.

Imagine driving a horse and cart slowly along a country lane. It's a fine day and the horse is on familiar ground. There's no need to concentrate. Quite the reverse. A simple flick of the wrist conveys all that is needed. The creature ambles along. There's all the time in the world to dream, meditate on the week's events, idly watch birds gliding across

Source: *The Age*, Melbourne, 14 December 1989.

Figure 4.1 Defensive and anticipatory driving

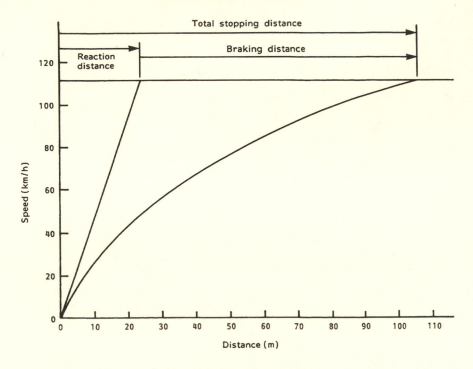

Braking distance increases with speed.
Source: G. Shanks, *Science and the Road* (Victoria, Australia, Roads Corporation, 1981).

Figure 4.2 Defensive and anticipatory driving

the landscape. You can afford to relax because there is no urgency, no danger and no penalty for not being alert. You've done the trip before so your mind wanders.

Contrast this idyllic scene with the demands of driving a fast car. Now you can't afford to relax – at least not completely. It's too easy to have a serious accident. So you concentrate, look ahead, focus and try to antici-pate situations as, or before, they develop. You learn to read the signs as they appear: speed, direction, momentum, road surface, weather, visi-bility, braking distances – all in split seconds. This kind of driving.quite literally takes the human nervous system to the limits of its capacity, and perhaps beyond them (see Figure 4.1).

Note that in both contexts an increase in speed can take one well beyond critical thresholds. Stopping distance increases proportionately to speed. You necessarily put greater effort into anticipation (see Figure 4.2).

Such comparisons are not without drawbacks. Societies are not motor cars and the technological trajectory is certainly not a road. The illustration I have used may even appear banal to professional futurists for whom the principle under discussion is certainly a familiar one. But futurists are very much in the minority and I imagine all would agree that greater public understanding of their work is vital. Perhaps such analogies have wider uses.

I want to suggest that this is indeed the case. By applying traditional and commonplace understandings to modern conditions we can utilise shared experience (at least the experience in developed countries) to highlight an aspect of the principle of foresight. When futurists talk of forecasts, scenarios and cross-impact matrices they speak in a foreign tongue. But every driver understands foresight and anticipation in its familiar practical guise. So, it is not necessary to establish a completely new principle. If it were we would be in even greater danger, because the learning path would be harder to discern and the lags more serious.

Modern conditions clearly make unusual (non-traditional) demands upon present-day people, institutions and structures. They require that we extend the framework of our concerns from the local to the global level, from the here-and-now to a wider temporal span and from simple person-to-person interactions to systemic ones mediated by a range of powerful technologies. Hence we are challenged to exercise our foresight capabilities in new ways. But at least it is clear that we can base the extension of perception and concern on a principle already in wide use.

How a Changing Worldview Can Help Our Institutions Become More Far-Sighted

While we cannot, and should not, try to predict the future, we can create a structural overview that provides us with a usable, broad-brush picture. Such a picture will never be complete or finished. Since it is part of a process of scanning, interpreting, acting and evaluating, it will be continuously revised in the light of new events and knowledge. What, then are some of the starting points for such a picture? Some key empirical trends were considered in Chapter 3. Here some of the implications are set out at the level of ideas and worldview assumptions. It is then possible to see more clearly how our institutions could become more far-sighted.

I suggested in Chapter 2 that our major institutions tend to reflect the past and present, but do not address the future. This is more than a simple mistake. It is a systematic malfunction that invisibly diverts these powerful social formations from some of the most important work that they might undertake.

A trite aphorism from the 'self-improvement' literature states that 'if you don't have a goal, you're sure to miss it'. Strange then, that key institutions lack a long-term view, or vision, of the future. I am not speaking here of an organisational vision, corporate plan or strategy, important as these are in their own contexts. What I am referring to is an informed and collective view of the macro future – the so-called 'big picture'. Without this, more limited outlooks tend mainly to reflect fragmented aspects of the past.

In a sense, the search for a view of 'the big picture' could be mistaken for aiming at the impossible. One of the distinguishing features of the so-called 'post-modern' world is that no single, over-arching interpretive framework can be found. This leads to a host of genuine theoretical problems. And yet the lack of such a framework is not an insuperable barrier. One response is to encourage diversity in our scanning, interpreting, etc., and then pool the resulting insights as openly as possible. Such a process can reveal much of the 'broad-brush' picture as well as areas of controversy.

Until recently such an enterprise might have been considered too difficult, or even impossible. Despite evidence from Cold War scenarios, and increasingly clear messages from the global environment, people have doubted if the future could be studied in any great depth. At first sight it seems contradictory: if it hasn't happened yet, how may one study it? Chapter 3 was devoted to answering that question; but it may take a while before the sheer practicality of futures study becomes more widely appreciated. Meanwhile, the world moves on rapidly and the need for a systematic futures view becomes more urgent.

From trends to ideas

As noted above, the futures literature is rich in accounts of the near-term future and this material can be regarded as a useful cultural resource. Some of the conclusions to emerge include the following.

- Local affairs are increasingly interconnected with global ones.
- The pursuit of old-style material growth is generating major costs and contradictions.
- Chronic problems from the industrial era have not been resolved, yet a new generation of difficulties can be clearly seen emerging.
- Development pressures in the Third World seem likely to grow.
- The demands of marginalised people around the world will also grow and continue to spark a range of protests, some of them violent.
- The environmental carrying capacity of the Earth is being eroded at an unprecedented rate, while the numbers of people inexorably increase.
- New technologies are creating new problems even while they promise to solve older ones.
- Fossil fuels will eventually become more expensive, stimulating the transition to renewables and 'soft energy paths'.

A list of such trends could be extended at length. Yet even these few carry a range of critically important messages for all human societies, including the following.

- Our current institutions are failing to engage with the emerging world picture of the late 1990s and early 21st century.
- It is becoming increasingly vital to take a hard look at the futures now in prospect and use the insights so gained to 'steer' much more carefully.
- Many business-as-usual assumptions and practices no longer work.
- Human societies are entering a time when various social and environmental sub-systems may 'overshoot and collapse'.
- There is a need to establish sustainability as a central socio-economic-political goal, and to set in motion the means to achieve it.

These observations emerge from the futures literature and reflect a world in transition. It is a transition out of the late industrial era and into a period of very considerable uncertainty and change. Institutions which attempt to cling on to the old industrial certainties (growth, unqualified optimism, nature as a resource, science and technology as primary concerns etc.) may well not survive. In fact, as Chapter 2 suggested, they may be impeding the social learning process.

However, it is the thesis of this book that foresight is an active principle which can supply part of the motivation to initiate a series of adaptive changes. Without the insights it makes available there is little, short of direct, crude experience, to initiate system-wide change. On the other hand, the careful use of foresight means that the near-term future can be clarified sufficiently to become an active force in the present.

However, it is not enough to monitor the external trends about such issues as population, resources and the environment. This is perhaps the cardinal error of the dominant American tradition of futures work. Empiricism works well enough in limited contexts, but has neither the depth nor insight into complex systems to guide public policy and reform the big institutions. So, before turning to the ways that a renewed worldview with foresight can help, I want to briefly consider some of the changing ideas that are implicated in the present transition.

Ideas in decline, ideas that are growing: outlines of a renewed worldview?

Figure 5.1 provides a summary of ideas in decline, and ideas that appear to be gaining ground. For example, the notion that the technically advanced nations can still be characterised by the term 'industrial' no longer seems adequate. In virtually all such countries the information sector employs many times more people than are employed in manufacturing industry. Similarly, the ideal of full employment, a distinct class structure and simple unilinear technical development have all given way to a more complex reality, sometimes dubbed 'post-modern'.

The view that nature is 'only' a resource, a collection of things which exist solely for humankind to use, was one of the fundamental assumption of the industrial order. But it has lost legitimacy. This instrumental view is, as I have argued above, a consequence of viewing the world in certain, limited ways derived from the old world picture. The latter has been overtaken by quantum realities as well as by developments in other areas of life and culture (see below). Again, the word 'progress' cannot now be used without irony. In the decades since the image of the future darkened toward Dystopia, it has been impossible to sustain the unqualified optimism of earlier generations. Equally, the consequences of untrammelled material growth have become increasingly clear in many

Ideas in Decline, Resurgent Ideas

Ideas in Decline	Resurgent Ideas
Industrial worldview	Renewed worldview
Full employment	Re-define employment
Nature a resource	Nature a community
Development = progress	Development problematic
Growth is good	Qualitatative growth
Exploitation	Sustainability
Technology is neutral	Technology has embedded social, political interests
Dominance of nation state	Decline of nation state
Subject/object	Unity of subject and object
Fragmented reality	Unitary reality
Loss of sacred	Recovery of sacred
Short-term thinking	Long-term thinking
Lack of foresight	Wide implementation of foresight

Figure 5.1 Ideas in decline, resurgent ideas

parts of the world: polluted landscapes, clear-felled forests, lost species and so on.

The view that technologies are neutral tools, linked with some clearly-articulated notion of human well-being, has also been challenged. While naive accounts continue to promote the notion of neutrality, I doubt that it can be sustained. As J.K. Galbraith, **Langdon Winner**, **Morris Berman** and **Jaques Ellul** (among others) have noted, technical systems seem to exert their own requirements or imperatives upon the societies that use them. They make new demands, create new dependencies and exert new costs even as they deliver new options. The simplest way to express this is to say that new technologies 'change the rules'. Hence, they cannot be neutral. This idea will emerge again in Chapter 7 in relation to a foresight institute for nanotechnology.

A further idea in decline is that of the sovereign nation state. While the world is still politically divided, the boundaries involved are profoundly breached by a range of dynamic processes. These include: trans-border flows of capital (particularly Electronic Funds Transfer (EFT)) and communications, the global impacts of environmental and atmospheric change, rapid and efficient international transport and, powerfully effective at the symbolic level, the view of the Earth from space showing it to be one indivisible whole. In a very real sense, we are indeed 'all in it together'.

Yet the decline of old ideas does not produce a vacuum. There are always new, or renewed, ideas clustering at the margins, emerging through social movements, bubbling up from the hidden foundations of culture. Again, this is a very dynamic process. It powerfully affects what happens, indeed what is considered possible, in the 'real' world, yet tends to be overlooked. The idea of a sustainable society is one that continues to attract support, despite the evident difficulties involved. The insight that the species is living beyond its planetary means is gaining ground. With it comes a new willingness to consider how societies may be restructured for the longer term future. In a very real sense 'sustainability' is challenging the old notion of 'growth' to the point where the climate of public opinion is moving toward the former.

Along with sustainability comes a number of other notions. One is that of a stewardship ethic: the view that we may not be here simply to use, consume, let alone destroy the earth – but perhaps to care for it. If this proposition continues to make headway (and it appears likely) then it may powerfully reinforce the present move away from industrial thinking and psychology. Linked with it is a growing awareness of obligations to future generations. If taken seriously, this may also help to undermine the old 'use it up and throw it away' mentality and help to usher in what Schumacher called 'the economics of permanence'.

As suggested in Chapter 1, one of the great conceits of the European enlightenment and all that followed was that of dualism, the assumed split between the observer and the observed. Clearly, that split has now been breached (though it will take decades or longer before the split disappears from human consciousness) and everything is connected to everything else. Instead of the old dichotomies, there are interpenetrating systems and flows of energy, materials, significance. Meaninglessness, the view that we are stranded in a dead and uncaring universe, is seen as the product of a radically impoverished view. In the new view it seems that meaning and reality are found everywhere we look. The notion of design is appearing in unlikely places (such as cosmology). It is impossible to be certain about such things, but I suspect that this 're-enchantment of the world' (to use Berman's term) is another principle of great cultural power.

In this context, we rediscover that the sacred was not something that could be locked away in churches or other privileged sites. Quite the contrary. The sacred was, and remains, a hidden dimension of everyday life. This is most certainly not a new insight. However, it was lost to industrialising cultures with the early success and immense practical power of science and technology. Now it seems that the world's native peoples were right all along to resist the simplifications of the industrial view. The sacred, thus, now re-appears as part of the innate hierarchy of human existence, recently re-discovered by science, but pre-dating it by centuries.

Finally, the foresight principle itself is emerging as part of the new world picture. For the reasons given, it becomes a *sine qua non* of a livable world. We need it in order to exercise our responsibility, to 'steer carefully during a difficult time and to consider those whose lives grow from our own, but who yet have no voice. In this view, foresight is not merely prudent, it corresponds to a growth of ethical awareness.

Such concepts and ideas may appear insubstantial, even problematic, at first sight. But, as has been said before, there is nothing so powerful as an idea whose time has come. Taken together, they suggest paths that lead beyond the decline of industrialism. While many people and institutions are caught up in the breakdown process, it is of enormous value to consider some of the possible seeds of innovation and recovery. In time they may permit a whole new, or renewed, worldview to emerge from the ruins of the old. Here, then, is a basis for seeing 'light at the end of the tunnel'. It is a heady prospect. But it is not enough to be inspired by these sources. Beyond this lie the tasks of institutional and cultural reconstruction. I therefore now turn to some of the ways that new thinking about a changing worldview informed by foresight may help us to re-invent some of our institutions. This overview of the potential for institutional change prefigures the theme of Part Three: cultural recovery in the 21st century.

Re-inventing politics and governance

Politics during the industrial era became cynical and often destructive. But if we look ahead at the real choices we face, it becomes clear that politics is challenged to change. A technically powerful, but ethically moribund culture with weak political leadership is quite literally a recipe for disaster. Like the proverbial bull in the china shop, industrialised cultures have been ransacking the earth and wrecking the global commons without thought for the future. But the picture is now quite clear. A continuation of the major industrial trends leads on to a sick and devastated world. A world, moreover, that becomes progressively less able to support life, including human life.

If this is in fact the case, then we may collectively see the point of accepting, and responding to, the powerful feedback that is rebounding upon us from a devastatingly unpleasant future. Yet let us not forget, it is a future that need never happen. This is so because such insights may persuade us to change course. Politics, then, can either respond to what is foreseen and institute its own internal innovations or, more likely, be forced to do so by other vocal and insistent constituencies. Either way, for there to be a future worth having, some real and substantial changes are needed in the framing of the political process. These may well include the following.

Adopting a range of time-frames for different purposes

It is tempting to just ask politicians to 'think long-term'. But this is really too simple. As noted above, a more sophisticated view suggests that we begin to match different aspects of the social and political process with appropriate time-frames. For example, if a building is to go up with a projected lifespan of, say 100 years, then the time-frame is clear. Interest on the cost of the building may be calculated accordingly. On the other hand, if a marsh is to be drained for development, the applicable time-frame might be related to the length of time the marsh had been there and the time it would take for the ecological services it provided to be regenerated elsewhere. Or, if toxic substances were under consideration, the time-frame might be anything up to 250,000 years. This is the time it takes for plutonium to decay.

Such time-frames greatly exceed those that have become traditional in governments around the world. However, it is useful to remember that earlier people, such as the American Indian nations built wisdom and foresight into their governance. They not only appointed stewards to look after specific areas of land and required their chiefs to have a range of specific human qualities. The Great Law of Iroquois stated in part that:

> self-interest must be cast into oblivion . . . (They shall) look and listen for the welfare of the whole people and have always in view not only the present but also the coming generations, even those whose faces are yet beneath the surface of the ground, the un-born of the future Nation.

The fact that Western governments change every three or four years has been taken to imply that a longer-term view is impossible. Yet this is not the case. What is needed is a range of small, efficient institutions of foresight to stand alongside governments and to carry out a variety of work in the public interest. Some examples are given below and in Chapter 7.

Institutional innovations

The outlook revealed by foresight in the light of the new world picture suggests a number of institutional innovations. As discussed below, a wide range of measures can be taken to enable politics and governance to become more explicitly oriented to futures.

Briefly, the world of politics and governance can begin to tap the very best environmental scanning and futures expertise available, and build this into all relevant structures and processes. The aim should be to create high-quality information and decision-making systems that are sensitive to emerging issues and responsive to the futures now in prospect. This will not be an easy task, yet it may well be helped by some of the measures outlined here.

For example, **Lester Milbrath** has proposed a Council for Long-range Societal Guidance. This would carry out long-range impact assessment, develop scenarios and make detailed recommendations to Congress. Some progress toward this was made by **Albert Gore**, now vice-president of the USA, who proposed a Critical Trends Assessment Act in the US Senate. All nations would benefit from participating in a programme of 21st century studies. A substantial body of inter-disciplinary knowledge is being assembled under this heading. This knowledge is practical (how to carry out a successful 21st century study) and theoretical (developing an inter-sectorial view of future options). A closely-linked effort is already underway to address the rights of future generations. The idea of an ombudsman to speak on their behalf has been proposed, though it has not yet been taken seriously. In the UK a Council for Posterity was formed. This attempted to raise the profile of longer-term concerns through a variety of publicity-generating events. As will become clear below, there is a range of methods for engaging in foresight work at the institutional level.

Along with the need for politics to reach out into time and space is the need for political leaders and representatives to consult citizens and to listen to their views. Every attempt must be made to increase participation, so that people can feel that they have a genuine stake in the future. Yet to achieve this, a different kind of politician will certainly be needed.

A new generation of politicians

In the old world picture, a successful politician could proceed on some fairly primitive drives such as ego-gratification, the search for power or even the pursuit of wealth. Such motives are no longer adequate to the new world picture or the choices revealed by foresight. In their place we urgently require not new motives, but higher ones.

A new generation of politicians may emerge from the ranks of those who have successfully made their own personal transition out of industrialism, and who have found new sources of strength, insight and power. By 'power' I do not mean old-style coercion, but symbolic, ethical and organisational power based on motives such as stewardship, transcendence of ego-needs and service to humankind as a whole. Some may emerge from older traditions, such as those inspired by Mahatma Ghandi and Martin Luther King. Others may be shapers of a new one, inspired by well grounded social activists such as **Robert Jungk**, **Joanna Macy** and John Seed. Those individuals who can tap some of the deeper sources of wisdom (such as the 'Perennial tradition', i.e the universal spiritual insights of humankind, see below) and be alert to all the many signals provided by systematic foresight, may find it easier to truly lead our global society toward a different future.

Foresight and wisdom are the twin themes of this book. Each is powerful in its own right. But taken together they open out whole new worlds of possibility for politics and governance, as indeed for social life in a truly post-industrial context.

The economics of permanence

The prospect of an 'economics of permanence' sends shock-waves of terror and uncertainty through the economic establishment. How can we provide jobs without growth? How can we afford to clean up the environment? How can we make our industry leaner, improve competitiveness, without more growth?

Foresight suggests that conventional economics is very much part of the old industrial paradigm. It follows that there will be enormous resistance to the kind of changes outlined here. But it now seems likely that many of the axioms of classical economics will need to be abandoned, revised, reconceptualised or re-chosen. In consequence the significance we attach to terms such as 'growth', 'wealth', 'security' and so on is also likely to change.

In the new world picture, we may come to believe that rapid or exponential growth in material throughput is no longer a viable goal. Even if humankind should one day mine the asteroids and find new sources of power in space, the resulting dramatic increase in the scale and impact of human activity would still be environmentally unsustainable. So the challenge is not, as is frequently assumed, one of simply removing certain limits by scouring the universe for energy and resources. Instead it may be more pertinent to re-define our individual and collective purposes, our notions of human needs and ways of fulfilling them.

The dominance of economics in social and cultural affairs needs to be re-considered. Why should everything be submitted to a diminished accounting of dollars and cents? Why should wealth be understood mainly in relation to material possessions? The environment can be re-valued not just to reflect the range of services it provides, (i.e. use value and exchange value) but its intrinsic value. Deep ecologists such as **Bill Devall** and **George Sessions** have much of interest to say on this issue. There appears to be no good reason why the well-established trend of 'doing more with less' should not apply in some ways to human beings. For it seems that many human powers and capacities have been passed over, forgotten, lost or de-valued amid the pressures of late industrial life.

Western society has held itself up as the model for enlightenment and progress, only to find that its particular trajectory cannot be sustained. Therefore it will find it salutary to approach other cultures with respect and to metaphorically 'sit at the feet' of those wise persons and traditions that still exist at the margins of the global mega-culture. By so doing, processes of cultural editing will become increasingly obvious. These are not simply of academic interest. They reveal many cultural alternatives, understandings, beliefs and practices. A combination of foresight, critical thinking and cultural learning will show that there exists a vast range of options for re-valuing and re-constituting economics on a more permanent basis.

For example, Japanese economist Kaoru Yamuguchi has proposed what he calls a 'Mu Ra Topian' economics for the information age. 'Mu Ra' literally means 'village'. 'Mu' also means 'nothingness' a basic concept of Buddhism. 'Ra' means 'being naked' or without possessions, which stands in stark contrast to the predatory materialism of the industrial age. It is essentially a non-materialist approach which is grounded in both information theory and in aspects of the new worldview. In part it is a response to the growth of more fluid, less material products such as software and services.

One consequence of such developments may be that a post-materialist view becomes established. If so, the environment and all of its species may be re-valued. They may, in Berman's evocative phrase, become 're-enchanted', special, no longer subjected to careless exploitation. The prospect of a devastated world (in stark contrast with one that has recovered from industrialisation and moved on, see below) will stimulate perceptions of the sacred and cosmic in every aspect of daily life. Thus, it will be remembered that the very oxygen that we breathe is itself a product of life, almost sacramental in significance. The atoms that comprise our bodies were forged in stars. Our roots are ancient and our actions reverberate throughout ages yet to come. This is the basis for the notion of an 'extended present', discussed below.

It may only be a matter of time before work is no longer exclusively linked with payment in money. According to **James Robertson** and others, a rich variety of types of work and types of reward, including intrinsic reward, may flourish. The long dole queues of today may be replaced with a wide range of cultural, artistic, caring and stewardship activities. There is really no shortage of work to be done. The extent of the damage of the whole industrial saga – in both human and environmental terms – could well require another two centuries of healing and restoration.

An economics of permanence will focus on such long-term issues as desertification, salination, deforestation, soil erosion, over-grazing and so on. It will use tools such as permaculture, conservation, genetic engineering and ecological restoration to halt, and then reverse the great extinction now underway as tropical forests disappear and islands are over-run. Though hubris remains a constant threat, it may well be possible to improve on nature in some ways. That is, to re-design ecosystems, re-animate vanished species from fragments of DNA and restore previously ravaged areas. Here, then, is one of the great projects of the next millennium.

Foresight suggests that economics will become more useful when it is equipped with a long-term view. Future-discounting (the practice of reducing value as we look further ahead) can be drastically reduced or eliminated altogether. The practice of imputing value and importance to 'me', or 'us' and 'now' may belong to the past. Instead it is likely that we will begin to see ourselves as part of a (very) long process of change and development. In that process, the unborn future will be re-valued, not discounted. We may one day reach a point when the collective awareness of our role as the temporary guardians of life may cause us to look more kindly upon life as a whole, and therefore more willing to conserve and enrich its own innate ends.

Foresight and educational innovation

The real business of education is not the past, important as this is, but the future. Equipped with the insights provided by careful, systematic foresight, educators may come to see their work as much more directly related to the mainstream futures enterprise. Futures study and research could be seen, therefore, as a core disciplinary area and constant inspiration to practice.

Futures concepts, ideas, tools and techniques may become as common in educational discourse as geography and history are now. Experience shows that once the threshold difficulties are surmounted, people – that is students and teachers alike – find futures approaches stimulating and useful. One major consequence of good futures work in schools is a distinct increase in empowerment, i.e., the sense that one counts and can make a difference. Another is the way exposure to 'the big picture' can give people a chance to review their lives and work in a different light. Finally, a futures view in education permits us to reconnect the latter with the wider world. All three consequences have positive implications for the further development and evolution of education itself.

A range of innovations can already be seen in practice. For example, the wide use of futures concepts in education provides a rich symbolic resource. The best futures concepts are structurally simple, but they may be elaborated in depth when needed. Concepts such as those of 'alternatives', 'options', 'an agenda for the 21st century', 'sustainability' and 'the 200-year present' (see below) all provide 'the means to think with' about futures. They permit vague and unfocussed ideas to spring into focus, thereby enabling a true futures discourse to take shape. The steady emergence of such a discourse from our schools, colleges and universities would go a long way towards enabling some of the wider shifts of understanding and perception discussed here to take place.

At present young people are fearful about the future. Yet there are many ways to help them deal with such fears and turn them to advantage. Some are described below in Chapter 8. Similarly, the theme of social innovations opens up many options for creative work. This is considered in Chapter 9. There are many ways of implementing foresight in education. One of the simplest is to design specific modules, packages or courses. Another approach is to re-shape a school's modus operandi according to futures ideas and principles. This was done quite successfully at the Montclair Futures School in New Jersey for several years. System-wide projects also have a useful role. For example, the Australian Bicentennial Futures Education Project (or BFEP) was able to achieve a broad impact through careful use of communications media, publications and a number of widely-scattered 'lighthouse schools' which received special assistance.

Finally the role of futures workshops should be mentioned. Elise Boulding, Joanna Macy and Robert Jungk have all developed different types of workshops which provide contexts for people to actively engage with futures concerns. When properly done, these workshops can be a powerful means through which individuals may empower themselves and their communities. They provide a flexible way of dealing with futures problems, nurturing images and exploring the implications in a small group context. This theme is taken up again in the following chapter.

As we look ahead, it is clear that education will not necessarily continue to be identified exclusively with schools. But we can be sure that the role of foresight as a principle and a catalyst will be an active one. If properly integrated into educational theory and practice, it may help to transform this child of the early industrial era into something much more in line with our individual and collective needs of the 21st century.

Commerce for human needs in a fragile world

The view of people as mere consumers was never satisfactory because it only addressed a part of human beings. As **Erich Fromm** showed with great clarity, material goods may provide the means to live with, but they were never able to supply anything to live for. This lack of purpose has dogged us during late industrial times and helped produce the spiritual vacuum that lies behind the marketing glitter. **Victor Frankl** is one of those who believe that people need meaning and purpose more than they need products. The insight is not new. Long ago it was said that 'man does not live by bread alone'.

So the first priority of commerce in the 1990s and beyond, may be to recover a broader vision of what human beings are and the nature of their real needs. This would be considerably more difficult were it not for the role of foresight. This tells us that on the one hand, the people of the affluent west are suffering from a lack of meaning and purpose, while on the other, the poor of much of the rest of the world are suffering because their basic material needs have not been met. As is well known, the contrast between the two is a breeding-ground for endemic violence, hatred, jealousy and anger. Again, this is unsustainable in a closely interconnected world. It can only be borne now because of the protective role of short-term thinking and future discounting. When these are removed, our eyes look out on a fragile, interconnected world steadily slipping into profound crises. Yet a wider, long-term vision suggests that both sets of needs can be addressed as part of a successful transition to a safer, saner world.

The logic seems inexorable. The rich West is challenged not only to reduce its material consumption and the impacts of its polluting waste on the global system, but also to help the less well-off to improve their own lives. This reversal of current trends is substantially helped by the power of foresight. From within the confines of a rapacious, materialistic culture, commercial imperatives have 'constructed' whole populations as mere consumers, overlooking their innate potential for meaning-making and also overlooking the limits of the global system. But as our view extends forward and we clearly perceive the logical consequence of the old system, so we discover a new stimulus and rationale for change. This idea has been lucidly articulated by **Susan George** and her colleagues at the Transnational Institute. Their book *The Debt Boomerang* clearly shows how the debt crises in the Third World rebounds on affluent populations through several routes: environmental deterioration, the drug trade, abuses of the banking system, lost jobs and markets, immigration, conflict and war. It is a powerful argument which is founded directly upon the foresight principle and derives much of its force from it.

Commercial interests therefore need to think what has hitherto been unthinkable: how to function in a way that is consistent with what foresight reveals, in the context of the new world picture. In this challenging context, old certainties could well be turned on their head, old principles abandoned and old priorities changed. Out of this difficult process of cultural and commercial innovation may emerge a different ethical foundation for commercial activity based on low impact, long-term use and sustained yield. For example, ethical investing suggests a way of supporting genuinely progressive enterprises. Sophisticated new bartering systems may complement or replace cash transactions. New forms of co-operatives may re-invigorate local economies. The value of intact ecosystems may go well beyond the tourist income they could generate to the licensing of access to their genetic resources. In this respect what have been dubbed 'the genetic super-powers' may not always be among the world's poorest nations.

People may come to be viewed not so much as 'consumers' than as 'layered beings' with a range of material and non-material needs. According to writers such as **Ken Wilber** and **Duane Elgin** the latter view may one day be seen to be primary. If so there will be new opportunities for those who will work to nurture people's sense of significance. Here there is scope for endless non-material growth and development. It is possible that a renaissance of the arts and humanities could occur. There may be well-made, long-lasting products and an ever-evolving range of subtle and sophisticated services. Some tantalising images of what may occur can be gleaned from the work of the best writers of speculative fiction. For example, the cloud sculpting and sonic sculptures described by **J.G. Ballard** in *Vermilion Sands*, or the semi-sentient totems in **Terry Dowling**'s *Rynosseros* and *Blue Tyson*. But perhaps the most fascinating depiction of a post-materialist culture is that described by **Ursula le Guin** in her novel *Always Coming Home*. Here we see a culture that has consciously chosen a distinctly non-Western path. Such glimpses provide both a challenge and a series of contrasts to late 20th century life. Are these merely stories, or are they the first hints of a very different future trajectory?

The media in transition

As noted above, the mass media are right in the middle of a major upheaval, the outcomes of which are impossible to foresee. However, even during this process a number of different emphases may be proposed. Three are discussed here.

Focus on processes

As suggested, the media tend to respond to the dramatic, the visual and the negative. Like human beings, they respond to events much more readily than to processes. Yet an understanding of the latter is essential. Discrete events by themselves tell us little. It is only when those events are seen in a broader context that their implications begin to emerge. Over the last twenty years a series of technical developments have occurred that make it feasible for mass media to depict processes in great detail. Improvements in graphics, software, remote sensing, data processing and so on mean that visually-elaborate overviews of global processes can be easily constructed.

The 'ozone hole' over the Antarctic was vividly depicted through graphics derived from satellite data. Similarly, remote sensing makes it possible to monitor soil loss, deforestation, algal blooms and so on anywhere in the world. This means that up-to-date information on vital processes can be delivered to any point on earth: to private homes, universities and classrooms. This is only the beginning. The material published in *Vital Signs 1992*, published by the Worldwatch Institute, need not be available only through print on paper pages. It could also be rendered into graphics and made available at regular intervals through TV and satellite. Beyond this lies the notion of 'global embassies' which could be situated in every town and city. These would summarise global processes and project the information graphically in holographic images. Such a use of the mass media is almost unheard-of. Yet, given a move away from entertainment and advertising, they could begin to serve the deeper interest of humanity in many new ways.

Tell the good news

Another major bias of modern media is that they exhibit a strong preference for bad news. Yet, accompanying the breakdown of the industrial paradigm, and standing behind the stories of disaster and despair, there are many others of courage, hope and, indeed, of optimism. These stories should be told more often. For example, social innovations provide a way of sharing the 'good news' more widely. The newsletters and magazines of many social movements, as well as the collected work of organisations such as the Institute for Social Inventions, provide numerous starting points and stories. Similarly the proposals of constructive social critics such as **Hazel Henderson** deserve wider attention. Hazel's work on a new generation of social and economic indicators is a good example. Bill Mollinson's concept of permaculture is another.

A more positive, process-oriented outlook by the mass media would perhaps lead to a greater emphasis on success stories and achievements. For example, I wrote in Chapter 1 of the plight of islands, using Bermuda as an example. However, even here there are signs of hope. Twenty years ago, Bermuda's conservation officer, David Wingate, initiated a project called 'the Living Museum'. It involved re-planting a whole island with native vegetation and re-seeding it with native birds and animals. Today Nonsuch Island is much more than a museum. It is a living example of the ability of people to restore their environment and to re-create what had been lost. If taken up and applied more widely, such work holds out great promise for the future.

Explore alternative futures

With the capacity of modern media to manipulate images, process data and present ideas to whole populations, it is surprising that futures concepts and themes have so far not been well-presented. As I noted above, when young people's media deal with futures at all, they tend towards superficiality and incoherence. Yet it should not be difficult to dramatise a set of linked scenarios, showing how in each case certain decisions moved events in one direction rather than another.

A different source of material lies in the many alternative world stories that have been produced by speculative writers. These portray worlds that differ from ours by virtue of an event in the past that worked out differently. Several are mentioned in the following chapter. They show, as few dramatic forms can, how history is full of branching points which lead in different directions. This, in turn, leads us to think more carefully about options and decisions in our present and the range of future implications they imply.

Finally the rapid evolution of communications media is creating a whole new series of niches for specialised material. There is no reason why some media should not focus explicitly on futures. The World Futures Studies Federation (WSSF) has already used e-mail for this purpose. An expansion of the hypercard concept may soon make it possible to explore a wide range of alternative routes through a rich 'problem landscape'. Indeed, this may be one of the constructive uses of virtual reality. As more options appear, and global electronic networking becomes a reality, so ideas, concepts and proposals about futures can be shared and debated among increasing numbers of people. In time there may be a series of parallel, and overlapping, 'global conversations' about re-forestation, sustainability and the possible shape of a viable human future. The hardware exists. It now needs to be turned to new purposes.

To summarise, nearly everyone knows that the world is changing. But the insights to be derived from foresight have not yet permeated the often-redundant institutions and organisations which surround us. These are still marching to the rhythm and imperatives of an earlier time. So there is a painful gap between our perceptions and the contexts in which we live and work.

Yet the human brain/mind system, aided by a whole range of futures-related methods and approaches, is neither helpless nor blind in the face of the future. We see clearly enough, and understand well enough, to know that the present course of global change is towards a devastated and imperilled planet. This is incontrovertible. Hence the challenge of foresight: to make the view of what is sought or what is to be avoided real enough to stimulate the right kind of responses. We need to envision sustainable, human futures in compelling detail. We also need to study disaster precisely to bring into being the policies, changes, counter-pressures and so on that will lead our global culture in a different direction.

For both to be possible, we will need to upgrade our notion of foresight and then begin to implement it effectively at the social level. These twin concerns form the subjects of the following two chapters.

CHAPTER 6

Extending Foresight Through Analysis, Imagination and Social Imaging

As noted in Chapter 4, foresight is primarily a human capacity. As such, it can be developed and applied in a number of ways so that its symbolic and practical power can be increased. This chapter looks at how foresight can be extended through analysis and imagination. Chapter 7 considers the case for creating and sustaining specific contexts where foresight can be deployed in the public interest.

Analysis, an aspect of the power of reason, provides a number of tools that are important in foresight work. In general, these tend to draw material from past and present to elaborate a decision context that also embraces aspects of possible futures. Thus it is possible to create a number of scenarios, or alternative futures, in order to reveal choices in the present. An example is given below. But future uncertainty dictates that reason and analysis cannot take us very far into the future. So, at the point where the curves look problematic and our time-series data ends, we need a different approach: imagination. The latter is not tied to facts, the past or the here-and-now. It is a true time traveller. While the human body is restricted to the 'creature present' the imagination (some would also say spirit) is free to roam at will across time past, time present and time yet to come.

So the key to extending foresight is not to invest significance in analysis or imagination. Rather, it is to use both for what they each are able to deliver. In what follows, I look at examples of analytic and imaginative approaches, and examples of some approaches which combine both.

A divergence map with outline scenarios

Figure 6.1 shows a simple divergence map. That is, a map in which aspects of the present steadily diverge to create scenarios of different social futures. These are not in any sense predictions, but contrasting pictures which provide a framework for considering alternative futures.

The BREAKDOWN scenario is one in which something important went wrong. Possible causes or triggers include:

Divergent paths to alternative social futures

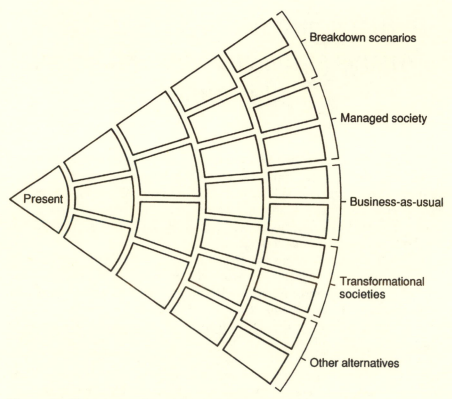

Figure 6.1 Divergent paths to alternative social futures

- an acceleration of soil loss, salination or desertification;
- nuclear accident(s) or conflicts;
- ecocide (the loss of whole ecological systems);
- a chronic rise in social conflict, crime and morbidity; and
- chronic depletion of essential resources.

This is clearly a depressing picture. That is one reason why breakdown scenarios are seldom considered by governments or other quasi-official bodies. Yet they are clearly possible and certainly provide one type of possible future to consider. Moreover, as we have seen above, such scenarios provide important guidance and warnings which can help to stimulate corrective social responses. They thus contribute to the process of feedback through foresight.

REPRESSIVE (OR OVER-MANAGED) SOCIETIES are clearly seen in our collective past and present. Despite the crumbling of the old Soviet empire, they could be part of our future too. Possible causes include:

- adoption of a *Nineteen Eighty-Four* ideology (war is peace etc.);
- the rise of right-wing ecological governments;
- the use of information systems for invasive purposes;
- scarcity used as a tool of control; and
- overpopulation.

Fascist futures of this kind are permanently possible so long as the tools of oppression and the social systems that give rise to them exist. Hence, given the emergence of new global limits, with their powerful constraints on human activity, scenarios of this kind should be kept firmly in mind.

BUSINESS-AS-USUAL is a very interesting case because it represents the implicit expectation of very much official literature and thinking on futures. Its possible features include:

- increased inequalities within and between nations;
- growing dilemmas in the areas of energy and ecology;
- the steady growth of resource constraints;
- further development of reality-avoidance industries; and
- a downward spiral into irresolvable crisis.

This characterisation of business-as-usual futures assumes that there are real and unavoidable problems which such an approach cannot solve. If this is in fact the case, then scenarios of this kind either become break-down scenarios or bridges to some kind of breakthrough. Either way, the option is unsustainable in the long run. It is important to note that this interpretation stands in direct contrast to conventional assumptions.

The ECOLOGICAL DECENTRALIST world looks very different from the one we now have. Here:

- humans are subordinated to nature, or seen as part of it;
- benign 'soft energy paths' are developed and applied;
- real limits to growth are recognised and implemented; and
- a stewardship ethic becomes established, and with it a deep commitment to ecological restoration.

Such a scenario is certainly an option, but it would represent a very major and substantial change of direction for a civilisation which has adopted a strong and aggressive ideology of economic growth. Hence this kind of shift would not be easily achieved.

TRANSFORMATIONAL SOCIETIES are more difficult to characterise, in part because they could develop through at least two distinct routes: through some new stage of human development or through the benign operation of a new form of technology. Possible features therefore might be:

- an acceleration of human development into new modalities;
- the transcendence or dissolution of conventional problems;

- the development of subtle and sophisticated person/machine interactions;
- new approaches to healing, psychic clarity, conflict resolution; and
- economics becoming subordinated to higher ethical imperatives.

Though somewhat improbable at first sight, these scenarios probably
hold out the greatest hope for real human progress and cultural development. While it would be a mistake to think that any of them could be
quickly achieved, such futures are of immediate interest and value
because they provide clear contrasts to dominant, implicitly technocratic,
views of futures. They also provide a challenging series of potentially
powerful guiding images (see below).

Each of these five contrasting groups of scenarios have roots in our
present-day world and could emerge from it. They are all possible, but
not all of them are desirable. Taken together, they provide the beginnings
of a framework for making choices and designing policies. As such they
form part of the 'map' which the futures field provides.

The QUEST technique

The QUEST technique was developed in the early 1980s by **Professor
Burt Nanus** and Selwyn Enzer. It was intended to help organisations to
look ahead, assess alternatives and explore a number of strategic options.
The process is of interest here because it provides a way of exploring the
near-term future without overdue reliance on forecasts or predictions. It
constitutes a useful and flexible foresight technique which can certainly
be applied widely at minimal cost. (Readers who are not interested in
the details may skip this section.)

Figure 6.2 provides an outline of the QUEST process. Five stages are
identified. They are preparation, an environmental scanning workshop,
intermediate analysis and report, a strategic options workshop and,
finally, follow-up work.

Preparation

This stage is important. If it is done well, the rest of the process runs
much more easily. It begins with the initial contact and subsequent
briefing, during which any foreseeable ambiguities and problems should
be ironed out. A team from the organisation is chosen from among the
top management. An ideal number for the team is about ten, including
the CEO and at least one individual from each major division or area.
The team should be briefed about the nature of QUEST and what it can
and cannot do. Three points can be made. First, it is prudent to avoid
'over-promising'. Nanus has described this as the single most important
error to avoid. Second, it should be stressed that QUEST is not predictive.
It explores an array of futures using different assumptions. Third, QUEST

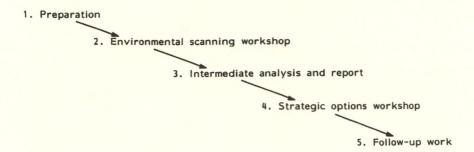

1. Preparation

2. Environmental scanning workshop

3. Intermediate analysis and report

4. Strategic options workshop

5. Follow-up work

Figure 6.2 Main stages of the QUEST process

should not be seen in isolation, but as a so-called 'front end' process which leads on to further work within the organisation.

The other main aspect of preparation is the compilation of a notebook containing information about the organisation and its environment. That is, information about trends, events, opinions, policies, competitors etc. Statistical summaries of key indicators of performance are also useful here. The entire team is asked to review this material prior to the first workshop. It provides a common base from which to begin the exercise. While some users of QUEST have dispensed with this step, most would agree that it is a useful starting point, particularly if there are likely to be significant time pressures.

Strategic planning workshop

It is unlikely that there will be any difficulty defining the organisation since many people will already be familiar with a 'SWOTs' (Strengths, Weaknesses, Opportunities, Threats) analysis. However, the identification of future external trends and events which may affect the organisation is more demanding. Perhaps 100 or more will be derived and written down. But before the top ten trends and events of greatest potential impact are voted for and used further, it is important to clarify entries and to make them more precise without becoming bogged down in long discussions. Once the trend/event set is agreed and clear, a simple voting process (such as the nominal group technique) yields perhaps ten items which the group collectively decides are the major ones. These can be assessed for probability or they can be entered directly into the cross-impact matrix. The matrix provides a systematic 'picture' of the inter-action of the chosen trends and events. It can also be useful to impact the top ten trends and events against key performance indicators since this provides additional insight into the way external factors may affect the internal dynamics of the organisation.

It is essential that the matrices are completed by the end of the first day. However, this is demanding work and it is likely that the participants will be tired at this stage, so the process needs careful handling.

Analysis and draft report

The intermediate analysis and report is normally produced over a period of weeks and fed back to the team for comment and revision. It will outline areas of disagreement, possible omissions and inconsistencies and, most importantly, draft scenarios for the second workshop. The latter are drawn from the matrices and the full list of trends and events. They depict contrasting future environments which accord with clusters of trends and events. It is important that the scenarios are clear, internally consistent and plausible. When the time between workshops is reduced, shorter versions may be used.

Strategic options workshop

The second workshop uses each scenario as a starting point for the identification and refining of strategic options. The team divides into groups. Each group works its way into a particular scenario and poses a key question: 'If this occurred, what strategic responses could we make?' Once a list of options has been produced, discussed and refined it can be impacted upon the strengths and weaknesses identified on the first day. This is a very fruitful exercise. It is at this point that the QUEST begins to repay the effort involved, since new insights about the organisation and its options now begin to emerge.

The pattern of options impacted against strengths and weaknesses models a set of judgements and interactions which are extremely important to the organisation in terms of its present self-understanding and the evolution of its strategic planning. Equally, at this point some of the judgements may appear questionable. If so, they may be discussed and revised.

The next step is to select the most robust options for further work. Those which are deemed 'robust' are options which seem to apply across the range of scenarios. In other words, they represent a distinct 'pay-off' regardless of which path events take.

Follow-up work

If the most productive use is to be made of QUEST then the options which have been identified need to be redefined in terms of work tasks, specific responsibilities and personnel, and explicitly incorporated into a strategic planning cycle. If there is insufficient time during the workshop the options may simply take the form of key ideas for further work. The important thing is to feed the early results of QUEST directly into the structures and processes of the organisation. Finally, it is good practice to provide the organisation with clean copies of the workshop materials, along with a final report summarising the major conclusions.

QUEST clearly represents a very fluid and adaptable approach to the problems experienced by organisations: change, complexity, and environmental 'turbulence'. It has been used in a wide variety of organisations. These include: financial institutions, manufacturing corporations, health care organisations, international airlines, universities, colleges and schools, government agencies and non-profit organisations. Given this diversity, it is hardly surprising that QUEST has taken a variety of forms. In less than a decade, it has spread to several countries. This suggests that the claims made on its behalf are not exaggerated. The most widely-reported benefits and outcomes include the following.

- It provides an opportunity to develop a shared view of future options and eventualities.
- It permits the clarification of the underlying mission or purpose of the organisation in relation to specific environmental changes.
- It promotes a greater awareness of the dynamics of the environment and of the key variables involved.
- There tends to be an increase in strategic thinking.
- Shifts toward more 'proactive' attitudes and practices are experienced.
- The process promotes team-building and a stronger organisational identity.
- It strengthens commitment to the strategic planning process.

It is clear that none of these results are dependent upon a 'hard' notion of forecasting or prediction. This lends weight to the view expounded above that a major purpose of futures work is not to make confident assertions about 'the future' but to elaborate understanding in the present (however defined). But is this all? Is QUEST simply a flexible, multi-faceted technique which helps organisations to plan effectively?

The significance of QUEST as a foresight technique

The apparent success of the technique may partly be found in the novel way it circumvents and resolves the ambiguous desire of human beings to 'know' some aspects of the future ahead of time. It seems to me that forecasting and prediction *per se* have been accorded undue prominence within the field. But it may be a mistake to regard them as dominant, paradigmatic foci since they are highly specialised activities which only embrace a small part of the spectrum of futures work.

The so-called 'crisis' in forecasting has only partially been resolved by improvements in methodology. It has been repeatedly shown that expert opinion may not be more accurate in the end than common speculation, and that forecasters have missed many of the key shifts and events of our time. How could they do otherwise? As I suggested in Chapter 3, futures scanning in a social, cultural or economic context cannot be considered primarily as a technical issue. No technique or method can imitate history and come up with future facts unless they are about inherently predictable physical systems such as planetary motions, lunar cycles, tides etc. Most matters of deeper human and cultural concern lie almost entirely beyond measurement and calculation. Of the hundreds of futurists who gathered in Beijing in September 1988 for the tenth annual conference of the World Futures Studies Federation, not one, to my knowledge, harboured the slightest suspicion about the tragic events which would occur there a scant nine months later. Such 'system breaks' have regularly confounded forecasting and prediction, and they will continue to do so.

However, foresight work is not limited to reason and analysis. Futures can also be intuited, imagined and envisioned. Their outlines can be constructed through imagination, stories, myths, scenarios and the implementation of practical policies and choices. The key point is that it is the search for forecasting accuracy which generates the basic ambiguity. This search is a Will-O-the Wisp which can produce useful insights in some fields, but misses the point in others. The point, after all, is not to foresee the future (singular) since this is an impossibility. It is rather to provide a context in the present for the choices and decisions which will help to create some aspects of the future (and avoid others). That is why some organisations have realised that the focus of planning has changed from forecasting accuracy to responsiveness to change.

It is precisely this shift which QUEST facilitates. It explicitly recognises that 'accuracy' is not a criterion which can be readily sustained in the face of future uncertainty. Instead of going all-out for the 'correct' snapshot, it provides a systematic way of creating a broad-brush picture which is divergent, relevant and helpful. So QUEST appears to embody an important shift of perception. It is a shift away from the contradictions of attempting to 'predict the future' toward dealing with those of its challenges which are visible in the present via a range of iterative and exploratory processes. QUEST has been widely adopted partly because of its structural simplicity (arising from two standard futures tools), partly because its procedural complexity makes it inherently flexible but, most importantly, because it is free of the forecaster's conceit (i.e. to 'know' the future) and is therefore more useful. It is this practicability and relevance to the unique dynamics of an organisation which is, perhaps, its strongest attraction.

Time travel through the speculative imagination

In the old industrial worldview it was common to hear the phrase 'forget it, that's just speculation'. In this view, to speculate was regarded as of little or no importance. And yet, if we pause to think, to reflect not just on what is, but on what might be – this is one of the things that makes us human. It is also one of the foundations of foresight.

The speculative imagination has an important role to play in releasing our species from the prison of a fractured and fleeting present. How long is the present? Well, as noted above, it depends. The default present that has developed in late industrialism is brief and unknowable: 'as soon as you notice it, it's gone'. But if we cannot be 'at home' in the present, where, or when, can we be so?

The question, 'how long is the present?' relates to the discussion of time-frames in Chapter 5. And, as noted, there is no single answer. What we mean by the present depends upon who we are, what we are doing and the kinds of questions we are asking. If we are interested in a long-term historical overview, stretching from the distant past to the distant future, then we will need to venture out of the minimal present through the speculative imagination. This is a literary, scholarly, imaginative and creative task.

An example is **David Darling**'s outstanding book *Deep Time*. Here he traces the origins of the Universe in the big bang, follows though the stages of stellar evolution, describes the formation of the Earth, traces evolution to our time and, finally, speculates about the further development of life and the cosmos in the distant future. Through the disciplined use of the speculative imagination, Darling does more than tell a story, he tells *the* story. It is a powerful and heartening one. For it turns out that the universe appears to be designed and that life, far from being a cosmic accident, is integral to the whole. Moreover, he posits the necessity of there being an observer (us). In one short book this writer sketches in aspects of the new world picture through an imaginatively constructed narrative. It is an inspiring, visionary book.

On a different level, in *Wonderful Life*, science writer **Steven Jay Gould** harnesses his fertile imagination and intellect to the exploration of some fossilised remains in the Burgess Shales of Canada. It turns out that more types of basic body plans can be found in these ancient sediments than ever survived to our time. In other words, many lines (or Phyla) were extinguished, seemingly by chance, over the millennia. This has enormous implications for the human race. For, necessary though life may well be in our newly-enchanted universe, it need not have been human life as we know it. So, on the one hand we may feel somehow 'special', while, on the other, the actual form we inhabit might well have been very different indeed. These are the kinds of insights to emerge from such work. They paint a picture of a universe that is far more subtle, yet also more challenging and meaningful, than the bland billiard-ball universe described by Newton.

In the new quantum universe more things are possible, not less. This frees the imagination to look anew upon history. Is our present as 'solid' as it seems? Could we have been living in a very different world? The answer seems to be 'no' to the first and 'yes' to the second. This line of questioning has been carried forward by many people, but not least by writers of speculative fiction. One branch of the latter looks back and considers how the present world might have been different if key historical events had worked out differently.

For example, **Keith Roberts** wrote a novel called *Pavane*, in which Elizabeth I was assassinated in 1588. Philip II, King of Spain, therefore also became the King of England. Protestantism was crushed and the Catholic church grew in power to the extent that the Industrial Revolution never took place. Slower technological change meant that by the 20th century in this history, steam-powered traction engines ply the roads and communication is by semaphore towers.

Another book in this genre is **Ward Moore**'s *Bring the Jubilee*, which speculates upon a modern USA in which the South had won the Civil War. More imaginatively resonant still, is **Phillip Dick**'s masterwork *The Man in the High Castle*, which describes a USA under the double heel of Germany to the East and Japan to the West. In this impressive and sustained work of imagination, Dick creates a present which is certainly related to our own, but which is also alien from it. A more recent book in a similar vein is **William Gibson** and **Bruce Sterling**'s *The Difference Engine*, speculating on social implications of the success of this early mechanical computer.

Works of this kind cannot be dismissed as 'mere fiction'. For, not only does social reality look more and more like 'fiction' (in that it is non-objective construction), but these alternative world stories highlight something that is very pertinent to foresight, i.e. historical contingency. What we take to be the present is by no means as settled and monolithic as we tend to believe. It could well have been very different indeed. This 'unfreezing' of historical perspective is not simply for entertainment. It opens our eyes to the extensions of contingency and choice in the range of future alternatives now before us.

Imaginative writers have long explored future time. During the earlier part of the industrial era, and before, many writers turned their hands to the writing of utopias, perfected future societies. More recently, several outstanding authors have explored distant futures through the device of future histories. Isaac Asimov, Frederick Pohl, James Blish and Larry Niven are among those to have experimented with this form. But some of the most powerful works on futures have taken the form of separate novels.

Olaf Stapledon was a lecturer in philosophy at the University of Liverpool, and he produced what are still outstanding works of speculative imagination. In *Star Maker* he speculated about the role of a future humanity in the cosmos. And in *Last and First Men*, he traced the development of humanity though very many stages of future evolution. The perspectives in these works are stunning. Having read them, no one could ever again misconstrue the future as an empty space!

But, as I have mentioned, for me one of the most powerful works of this type is **Ursula le Guin**'s *Always Coming Home*. It is not a novel as such; more a tapestry of culture. But this is not a culture like our present one. It has made some very different choices. For example, it has chosen to situate relationship, ritual and meaning at the heart of the social order and to de-centre the machine. The result is a fascinating and convincing evocation of a way of life that stands in clear contrast to our own. As such it is a primary resource for the speculative imagination and for foresight in general. A lesser, but still interesting, example, is **Kim Stanley Robinson**'s *Pacific Edge*, an account of a near-future society built around the politics of sustainability. Other examples could be cited. However the point is clear: imaginative explorations of the distant past, parallel worlds and alternative futures broaden our understanding of where we are from, where we are, and where we may be going. They provide imaginative and symbolic content to an area that, in an earlier view, had almost none.

In the light of all the many products of the speculative imagination, we can clearly see why the old view was wrong. The future, like the past, is part of the natural playground of the human mind and spirit. The prison of the minimal present was never convincing. The full flourishing of people and cultures will necessarily involve insights and understandings gleaned from this broader arena. For, in truth, it now turns out that this was always our true home.

Imaging as a social or group process

Futures, and images of futures, play a much greater role in our lives than we usually imagine. Far from being distant abstractions, futures concerns in general are an essential part of our common humanity. Without a forward-looking temporal context we could not create plans, purposes, goals, intentions ... or meanings. Human life and culture cannot be described or explained simply by referring to the push of the past. It is also profoundly influenced by the pull of the future. Sir Karl Popper, scourge of historicism, put the point clearly and with emphasis. He wrote:

the open future is, almost as a promise, as a temptation, as a lure, present; indeed actively present, at every moment. The old world picture that puts before us a mechanism operating with causes that are all in the past – the past kicking and driving us with kicks into the future – the past that is gone is no longer adequate to our indeterministic world ... It is not the kicks from the back, from the past, that impel us, but the attraction, the lure of the future and its attractive possibilities that entice us: this is what keeps life – and, indeed, the world – unfolding.

Images of the future present us with options and possibilities from which we can select and choose or with which we may argue and debate. Either way, they are active, shaping components of human consciousness. The main purpose of considering futures, and images of futures, is not to predict what will happen in any hard or precise sense, nor even to select from alternatives, though this is important. It is, perhaps, to discern the wider ground from which images are constituted so as to take an active part both in creating and nurturing those which seem worthwhile.

Imaging is by no means a specialised or impersonal activity. It plays a central guiding role in many creative vocations. Consider the writer. He or she may well begin with just one central image. If the image is a compelling one it acts like a magnet and, over time, draws toward it the other details from which a story can be woven: context, characters, plot and so on. Similarly an architect or an interior designer is likely to begin a new project with a series of sketches or 'roughs'. These evolve into detailed blueprints and plans. The artist or sculptor often works in the same fundamental way: first comes the concept or image, next the process of refining it; finally there is the hard work of translating images and concepts into a finished product. Social imaging seems to conform to this general pattern.

Imaging is a social process with a very long history. If we consider some of the major works of antiquity – the Parthenon, the pyramids, the Great Wall of China – it is evident that they would never have been built without a strong guiding image. The stupendous labour involved could not have been undertaken if this image had not been capable of marshalling a powerful social effort to turn an 'image-ined' reality into a real and tangible one. So, at the social level, the right image can act as a cultural force to bring new projects to fruition.

Such images may be visual or they may be more abstractly symbolic. Consider Martin Luther King's 'I have a dream ... ' speech. Or John Kennedy's 'We choose to go the moon ... ' Both helped to define and focus a collective effort to realise major social goals: in one case social justice for black people in America; in the other a largely technical effort to realise culturally significant goals (self-confidence, leadership over the

Soviets). However, for the reasons given above, grand visions have become relatively rare in the 20th century.

Contemporary views of futures tend to be not so much about the things we want to achieve as about the things we want to avoid: pollution, the greenhouse effect, the loss of tropical forests. Outside engineering contexts, it is hard to find grand visions to compare with those which provided coherence and direction in other cultures at other times. The late 20th century equivalents of the Great Exhibition of 1851 seldom represent the triumphant expression of a clearly expressed vision, so much as a national marketing opportunity and an attempt at reassurance. Behind the slick technology and laser light shows there is a seldom-acknowledged lack of confidence and vision. As Umberto Eco observes in *A Theory of Expositions* 'the basic ideology of an exposition is that the packaging is more important than the product'. That is partly why the big international expos draw more heavily upon the mass entertainment values of Disneyland than the assured and optimistic cultural values such as were expressed and displayed at the Crystal Palace. But then, this is a very different age.

The contrast between expo as marketing or escapism and expo as confident statement is fairly stark. It expresses a decisive shift in our views of the world – and the future – during the present century.

Beyond utopia and dystopia

The attempt to imagine ideal societies has a long and honourable past. For over four hundred years writers, scholars, and speculators of many different persuasions put pen to paper and tried to imagine how the ills of their societies could be overcome and new possibilities created. From Sir Thomas Moore's classic *Utopia* (1516) onwards there was a vast and varied outpouring of such material. It prepared the ground for many social innovations which we now take for granted: health insurance, democratic government, courts of law and the emancipation of women, to mention only a few.

Perhaps the last great utopia was **H. G. Wells'** attempt to write what he called *A Modern Utopia* (1905). It was a bold vision based on the assumed benefits of science and technology. But there was also a darker side to the picture. Wells not only saw the rational organisation of human affairs leading to an era of peace and prosperity. He also foresaw the armoured land tank and nuclear weapons. There is a powerful description of the latter in one of his later books. He worried endlessly about what he termed 'human folly'.

Four years after the publication of Wells' Utopia, another writer produced a powerful story which considered the dark side of Wells' vision. The writer in question was **E. M. Forster** (*A Passage to India, Howards*

End) and his story was called 'The Machine Stops'. It was, and remains, a powerful vision of a world in which all human life is dependent upon machines. It is a repressive, high-tech future in which people have forgotten how to control 'the machine' and have also forgotten that technology takes away even as it provides.

So at the beginning of the 20th century we see the long tradition of utopia giving way to anti-utopia (or dystopia). The twin extremes represent two poles of our destiny: progress and disaster. As the present century has passed, so it has become progressively easier to imagine dystopia and harder to believe in progress. Utopia has even been subjected to negative reversals which suggest that notions of social improvement are 'unrealistic', pie-in-the-sky or oppressively overbearing. There have certainly been many dystopian images and events to draw on: overcrowded cities, polluted seas, dying animals and birds, stark images of famine, war and decay. The use of nuclear weapons at the end of the Second World War, the growing fears for the environment and a pervasive sense of uncertainty and loss of control has made the future appear increasingly problematic.

The implications are far from obvious because the impacts of such shifts frequently take place in hidden, unregarded ways. If we take the view that people are symbolic creatures who pursue meaning, then we can see why change often hits us hardest at the symbolic level. In tearing apart symbols which have provided our lives with meaning and continuity, it wreaks a kind of invisible, but very painful havoc. Here is another important source of the sense of fragmentation and meaninglessness found in post-modern cultures. Terms such as 'work', 'leisure', 'wealth', 'health', 'defence' and 'progress' no longer mean what they once did. In the place of simple, taken-for-granted understanding, we see a symbolic struggle of epic proportions.

Yet in popular culture we have become so accustomed to moods of cynicism, violence and despair that we no longer think them unusual or unacceptable. The great dystopias of the century (Huxley's *Brave New World* and Orwell's *Nineteen Eighty-Four*) clearly articulated widely-felt concerns about depersonalisation and other threats to our well-being. So far, so good. But they were succeeded by entire industries which now permeate the global village. In the 1990s it is almost impossible to contemplate an evening's TV viewing or the week's films without noting references back to familiar dystopian themes of disaster, decay and dissolution. Clearly our pre-occupation with bright new technologies has not fooled the collective unconscious: something important is missing. This sense of loss is faithfully reproduced in the mass media. Yet the media reveal little awareness either of the proliferation of negative futures imagery or of the human implications of ersatz surrogate worlds. A number of observers have commented on how the latter misrepresent social reality in various ways. In other words, the distortions of the technological screen between us and the natural world complicate the task of understanding it and of acting to preserve it for future generations.

It is not that dystopia is necessarily 'bad' in any simple-minded way. As noted above, breakdown scenarios and dystopias provide important feedback when read as warnings, destinations to avoid. As components upon a map of futures, areas of danger are as important as possible destinations. Such is the power of applied foresight. On the other hand, anodyne or apparently positive images may conceal many dangers behind a seemingly harmless facade. This should alert us to the fact that, like optimism and pessimism, utopia and dystopia are ambiguous. Care should be taken in believing and interpreting them. These simple oppositions have more to do with the preference of the human mind for polar contrasts than with a profoundly interconnected world. The latter demands a deeper approach to the imaging dilemma.

Responding to the imaging dilemma

As we near the end of the 20th century there is an inevitable growth of interest in the year 2,000 and the new millennium. Such transitions are much more than artefacts of a numbering system; they have enormous cultural significance. Hence, projects to celebrate the historical divide are already being conceived. But, at the same time, this is taking place in a context in which compelling images of futures are very few and far between. It might appear that our long-term social imaging capacity is failing at the very time when it is needed most. Yet this is partly a question of perspective. It turns on the fact that we already live in a period which incorporates many of the features that earlier generations thought of as being 'in the future'. Men have walked on the moon. Human hearts are routinely transplanted. We can speak to each other across the entire world and photograph distant planets. But the technical achievements of yesterday soon lose their power to uplift and inspire. Perhaps we should reflect on this hint that today's marvels may not be all they are advertised to be.

Two contradictory factors can be observed. On the one hand, there has been a loss of confidence about our ability to solve major problems and to survive in a world severely compromised by human activity. On the other hand, we have already achieved many of the things which people worked towards when they were only dreams and visions located 'in the future'. We live longer, travel further, and know more than ever before. But the social capacity to imagine new and different futures has clearly declined. What can we do about this? There are a number of options, some of which are outlined here, others in later chapters.

At this point it can be suggested that the apparent exhaustion of our imaging capacity is only temporary. The human and cultural sources of images have certainly not been lost. In some ways they are stronger and more accessible than ever before (see below). While many have been relegated to the cultural margins, they can always be reclaimed and utilised. Similarly, we can revalue counter-traditions that incorporate visionary elements which breach the bounds of everyday assumptions and practices. On a more practical level, it is entirely reasonable to suggest that more effort be devoted to scanning and exploring futures. But to achieve this will necessitate a fundamental shift of perception. This shift is primarily one which revalues the future; which sees it not as an abstraction or an empty space but as a principle of present action.

So it is important to initiate the kinds of social processes whereby people are encouraged to participate in imagining the kinds of futures they would like to live in and pass on to their children. Such processes are not particularly easy to create and sustain. But we certainly know enough to make a good start. A culture which can invent wonder drugs and place machines in orbit should not shrink from such work simply because it is human and cultural, rather than scientific and technical. As we saw above, that very partiality (towards the assumed dominance of science and technology) is itself a long-standing continuity which frames our present dilemma.

So, while pessimism certainly seems uppermost, there are grounds for re-establishing more constructive views. Those grounds can be explored and developed almost without limit. They can be likened to a set of tools waiting to be taken up, elaborated and used more widely. To be more specific, both 'positive' and 'negative' images can be critiqued. Futures workshops can help people to establish different images and use them as 'magnets' for personal goals or social innovations of many kinds. Nor need the directives and imperatives set by technology fads and international capital be passively followed. As will be seen below, other alternatives can be consciously cultivated.

Futures workshops

Futures workshops provide a flexible way of dealing with futures concerns, nurturing images and exploring their implications in a small group context. Some workshops are exploratory and open-ended, some are more highly structured. Some combine both approaches. Among the most highly structured are those developed by Boulding and Zieglar. One of their workshops is called Envisaging a World Without Weapons. Over a weekend, or several days, people elaborate a vision of a future that works for them. The group supports and validates this work. The links back to the real present are then traced. This reveals points of leverage, action contexts, needs, resources and so on. It is a very effective approach which by now has been taken by thousands of people around the world.

Similar in philosophy, but not in approach, are the futures workshops developed over a number of years by Robert Jungk. They can be run in a day, a weekend or longer. They deliberately intertwine rational-logical and intuitive-emotional strands. They are intended to provide forums in which people can reflect on issues of concern to them and from there produce a plan for action which may result in a social innovation or other creative change. They have been held in a number of European countries with evident success.

A different approach is to use a guided fantasy to elicit images of futures. Noel Wilson of South Australia uses this method with teenagers in Australia and the UK. He works from a prepared script to take the participants through several stages. First, there is a relaxation stage. Next, they are taken on a journey into the clouds. Finally they return to earth in some future time and draw what they see. From numerous examples, Wilson was able to create a clear composite picture. It was a largely bleak future dominated by computers, robots, huge impersonal buildings and devastated landscapes. Most of these futures were dehumanised and devoid of humans.

It is clear from this work and that of many others that young people tend to have very negative views of their likely futures. The question is, how can teachers and others help them to move away from the pain and anguish involved and explore other options? Are there ways of moving out of the depression and learning to respond to the fears? Chapter 8 deals with this question in detail.

Resources for dealing with fears

Joanna Macy is a leading practitioner in this area. Her *Despair and Personal Empowerment in the Nuclear Age* offers a rich compendium of strategies which deal directly with feelings of helplessness, anger, grief and so on. She articulates five principles:

1. Feelings of pain for our world are natural and healthy.
2. This pain is morbid only if denied.
3. Information alone is not enough.
4. Unblocking repressed feelings releases energy, clears the mind.
5. Unblocking our pain for the world reconnects us with the larger web of life.

Much of her work takes place in workshops and retreats, in locations around the world. These workshops can be very powerful since they elicit human responses at fairly profound levels. This occurs not simply because of her grasp of group processes, but, more importantly, because she herself has explored some of the richest grounds for cultural innovation and the recovery of meaning. She is a practicing Buddhist and draws on this (and other traditions) for insight and understanding. Hence, Joanna Macy's workshops are based on more than technique. They are founded on a deep understanding of the human predicament, on a substantial involvement with the theory and practice of deep ecology and on a vision of an interconnected and indivisible world.   Such an approach must be deployed with care and sensitivity. Yet when it is done well it has the effect of reframing issues and concerns and then linking the human response to powerful cultural resources at the levels necessary for insights and resolutions to occur. This can be seen in an exercise called The Council of all Beings. It is a deeply moving ritual in which people identify closely with different creatures or features of the environment and speak as if from that perspective. With this in mind, two further principles can be outlined:

1.   The critical factor in dealing with fears is the nature of the human response to the situation(s) from which the fears derive. I call this 'the empowerment principle'. A group context means that a wide range of potential responses is available.

2.   The resources deployed to deal with fears must be adequate to the task and will therefore tend to be grounded primarily in cultural and spiritual traditions, and only secondarily in technique or psychology. This helps to explain why more instrumental, goal-oriented approaches can be less productive.

Yet this does not mean that one must spend years practicing the Eastern arts before acting or facilitating workshops. Simpler approaches are not without value, so long as their limitations are acknowledged. Some of these are discussed below.

This chapter has explored some of the ways that analysis, imagination, and social imaging can expand our ability to develop and apply foresight. The capacity to imagine other, and different, futures is one of the defining characteristics of humankind. When properly harnessed toward shared ends it provides many of the keys to our predicament. Redundant assumptions can be discarded, values can be renegotiated, oppressive and destructive systems can be dismantled. In their place the open future is waiting to emerge. Once we give up the impossible task of trying to predict the future and instead begin to participate in creating it, the foundations of informed optimism and empowerment become very much clearer.

So, while it remains true that violent, cynical and otherwise negative images continue to dominate existing views of futures, it is also true that all the resources, the tools, concepts, methods, etc. of the futures field, along with an impressive array of non-industrial cultural resources and the inspiration and energy of people of goodwill, provide the where-withal to change this otherwise depressing picture. The exhaustion of a particular worldview and its inherent possibilities in no way signals the end of human aspiration or ability. Rather, it directs us back to some of the most fundamental questions about the constitution of the social order: questions about people, nature, purpose, meaning and responsibility. Close attention to the shifting foundations, in fact reveals a fascinating picture which can be taken as the outlines of a new (or renewed) cultural synthesis. Here are the most durable grounds for recovery and hope. They are discussed further in Chapter 9.

The basis for qualified optimism is not an illusion. It lies in the steady emergence of a 'deep consensus' about necessary changes and adaptations, in the creative potential of futures imaging processes and in the richness of cultural resources which have so far hardly been called into play. The upshot is that despite all the major challenges and crises facing us, the 21st century really could be worth living in. The transition to a sustainable society and a global culture will not be easy, but it no longer seems like an impossible dream.

Why We Need Institutions of Foresight

After what was said in Chapter 2, it might seem strange to be discussing institutions. Surely they are part of the problems carried over from the industrial past? Well, yes. Except that, as argued in Chapter 5, there is enormous potential for our institutions to be improved. But, more specifically, why institutions of foresight? This chapter looks at seven examples and derives a number of conclusions. These include outcomes, costs and benefits, and the grounds for what might be called 'the foresight imperative'.

It was suggested above that foresight is first and foremost an attribute of the human brain/mind system. Further, that all normally equipped people already use foresight in their own everyday affairs. But then we run into a major structural problem. For there is not yet an effective social equivalent to the neural processing that takes place in individuals. In other words, we have foresight at the individual level and, in some cases, at the organisational level. But foresight at the social level is almost non-existent. This is a grave oversight.

What it means is that late industrial societies are plunging blindly toward a most challenging and unstable period without the tools of understanding, the insight or the institutional capacity to make good, long-term strategic decisions. The historical context can be summarised by referring to Figure 7.1. Here five broad periods are identified. First, the two-hundred or so years during which the industrial system took shape. Clearly this was an era of expansion and growth. Second, the relatively short period of 'high industrialism' for the mid-19th Century to World War 1. Third, a period of greatly increased uncertainty and the emergence of the global problematique. This covers the century or so from World War 1 to the early 21st Century. It is the pivotal century, the period of choice, the time when foresight became essential. In this view, it is followed by what I have termed the 'catastrophe' period not because I believe that it must necessarily *be* catastrophic, but because if systemic problems are not resolved the underlying dynamic of that time may be very like that of a mathematical 'catastrophe surface'. In that case, environmental and cultural systems could 'flip' very suddenly from one state to another. The instabilities so generated would make civilised life all but impossible. The final period is that of a 'new system state'.

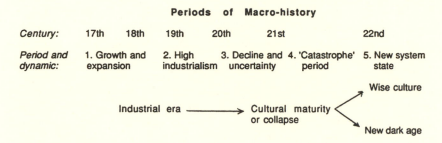

Figure 7.1 Periods of macro-history: wisdom or a new dark age?

Figure 7.1 portrays this as a stark choice between a wise culture and a new dark age.

It might be objected that there are always more than two choices. Quite so. But I want to dramatise an underlying reality of this 'new system state' period. It seems to me that by then, our species will either have turned the corner and will be living very differently upon the earth, or our children and grandchildren will have inherited the unresolved problems created by several previous generations. They come in the form of ruined ecosystems, mined-out resources, planetary pollution, disease, violence, decay and entropy in all its many forms. This is the abyss mentioned a number of times above: a planet so ruined by a long period of thoughtless, short-term exploitation and damage, that its ability to support human and other life has rapidly declined.

It is necessary to look into this dark future and to see the end of a civilisation that mistook technical power for wisdom and thereby squandered its inheritance. It has happened before in limited areas of the Earth, so it follows that a short-sighted global culture could, indeed, devastate the entire planet. Indeed, it is already doing so. There is no logical, rational way to impress upon our minds the horror and degradation that would occur in this terrible future. However, one choice open to us is to look afresh upon the catastophes of our day and to see them not merely as happening to 'someone else' but to ourselves, and our children in the near-term future. Another option is to consider stories and novels that evoke the many varieties of Dystopia. *Brave New World* and *Nineteen Eighty-Four* are two familiar examples, though by now they are dated. There are other, more powerful and recent works that are informed by subsequent history – particularly threats to the environment. For example, **John Brunner**'s *The Sheep Look Up* is set in a chronically polluted world. Several of **J.G. Ballard**'s novels also fit the bill: *The Drowned World*,

The Wind from Nowhere and *Vermilion Sands* come to mind. There are many other post-catastrophe novels and stories to be found on such themes. Some are worthy of study, not simply as warnings, but as providing part of the imaginative charge to propel us into a different *modus operandi* in our present.

On the other hand, it is a mistake to constitute the near-term future in stereotypically disastrous terms. When Rose Macaulay wrote *The Pleasure of Ruins*, she did so knowing that they appealed to part of the human psyche which takes pleasure in the dark delights of entropy and decay – a reflection, no doubt, of human mortality. Yet, if we are to deal with highly-charged negative material, it is important to be able to balance it with more hopeful and empowering views. This is attempted in the three final chapters. Here I only want to note that foresight brings us face to face with both sides of the coin. On one side, disaster and decay. On the other, a renewed vision of life and a re-enchanted world. Both convey important messages to the people of the 1990s.

It follows that we require foresight at the social level in order to carry out a number of vitally important tasks: scanning, warning, direction-setting, determining priorities, educating decision-makers, informing and involving the public and so on. Such tasks are too important to be left to chance. They should be undertaken systematically and with wide social, cultural and political support. The institutions that carry them out can be metaphorically likened to the headlights on a car, the radar in a plane or the skilled judgement of a ship's pilot. They are needed in order to develop sophisticated and useful views of the 1990s decision context. That is, to put as much structural detail as possible on the grainy picture of the near-term future. It is only by so doing that we can begin to see clearly enough to steer away from disaster and toward a more viable way of life.

Before turning to pointers for future work in this context, it is useful to consider some examples of existing institutions. At present they tend to be culturally marginal, even experimental. But, for the reasons given throughout this book, they are highly significant precursors of what, in later times, may well become standard equipment for all human societies.

Seven institutions of foresight

In recent years there have been a number of concerted attempts to broaden temporal boundaries and to implement foresight activities of one sort or another. Some are government sponsored, others are private. Some exist as distinct institutions, others take the form of voluntary networks, associations or councils. A brief review of several examples will make the picture clearer.

The Congressional Clearing House on the Future (CCF)

The CCF was founded in 1976 to provide information about emerging issues to senators and representatives of the US congress. It is basically a non-profit, in-house think-tank which attempts to raise the profile of issues and to introduce new ideas and methods. According to the director, Rob McCord, the CCF takes special interest in issues which are of growing interest, which lend themselves to redefinition and which initiate new ideas or arguments.

The kinds of issues under consideration include: the information age, aging, housing, biotechnology, the economy, civil rights, and the press. The CCF publishes a number of items including a newsletter called What's Next?, a range of Forecast Critiques and Emerging Issues briefs. It also produces topical videos, often with the assistance of congressional members.

In order to perform its role, the CCF engages in systematic environmental scanning. It stays in close contact with state planning agencies, uses a professional journal abstracting service and also seeks information from corporations and businesses. Serious networking with other think-tanks, institutions and individuals means that the flow of information is both steady and high-quality.

The effectiveness of the CCF is enhanced by its association with a sister organisation, the Congressional Institute for the Future (CIF). The latter is a private sector organisation with separate funding from a number of sponsors and a wider range of projects. For example, it has co-operated with the Office of Technology Assessment (OTA) and the Carnegie Corporation on the policy implications of new technologies. The CIF frequently republishes material produced by the CCF and distributes it more widely. According to the director, the outlook for both organisations is good despite the loss of the Critical Trends Assessment Bill in 1985. While this was certainly a setback, three factors are identified which will ensure a continuing role: increasing overseas competition, rapid technological innovation and the approach of the third millennium. These will ensure that congress and the informed public will continue to look to the CCF and the CIF for informed commentary on emerging issues. In this context at least, it would seem that despite the difficulties, the role of foresight is well established at the heart of the American political process.

The Foresight Institute

One of the most stimulating and provocative books to appear in recent years is **Eric Drexler**'s *Engines of Creation*. Here the author makes an impressive attempt to set out an agenda for understanding and regulating the development and applications of a new technology well before it actually exists. The technology in question has been dubbed 'nanotechnology' to distinguish it from the 'bulk technology' of our time. It is based not on the gross shaping, heating and cutting of conventional materials but on molecular assemblers. These, it is suggested, will allow engineers to make sophisticated new materials and devices from almost anything, thus by-passing many traditional manufacturing problems. According to Drexler, such assemblers will provide a new foundation for technology. When the assemblers become self-replicating, they may enable us to make anything from tiny computers to spaceships at very low cost.

The perspective is stunning: engines will be grown in vats; space suits will be like a second skin but light, flexible and highly versatile; tiny machines will float in human bloodstreams bringing 'long life in an open world'. It is even possible that the ecology will be restored, and advanced cell repair will bring back entire species from extinction. Along with developments in artificial intelligence, nanotechnology may take human-kind another step towards 'the limits of the possible'.

It is tempting to dismiss the above as technophilic fantasy. But there are at least three reasons why such a response would be wrong. First, the author clearly knows what he is talking about. While the book does make enormous leaps, it is firmly based on real science and engineering know-how. Second, and to his credit, he does not try to pull the wool over our eyes. One chapter, called 'Engines of Destruction', explores some of the many possible dangers. Third, he has made an essential connection between innovation and foresight. He argues that the benefits of technology and the pressure of competition impel us forward. But as the pace quickens, so the likelihood of a fatal error grows. Since we cannot slow the pace of change, he suggests, we must do more to encourage the growth of foresight. This will enable us to direct the process of technical change in safer directions.

From this beginning Drexler has vigorously taken the initiative and created the Foresight Institute (FI). The policy of this organisation is given in Figure 7.2. It is a non-profit corporation founded to help prepare for future technologies by research, public education and institutional development. A basic goal of the FI is to help develop several related organisations which will share a common focus on the problems and opportunities posed by nanotechnology. To this end, the FI publishes news, essays and information. It serves as a networking forum and a source of suggestions for projects in a variety of related areas: computer software, media resources, molecular graphics, political action and tertiary teaching, to name but a few. According to the author, the main strength of the Foresight Institute lies in the ideas it proposes about how to make the future work, given the new technologies in view.

Clearly this is a major initiative and an important embodiment of the foresight rationale. In principle Drexler is right: the prospect of such radical and far-reaching changes means that careful foresight work is essential. But there are at least three weaknesses in this application of the principle. First, the FI cannot be said to be working solely in the public interest (however defined) because it has chosen an advocacy role. The FI documents I have seen are as concerned to establish the scientific and engineering basis of nanotechnology as they are to encourage debate about it. This represents a confusion of roles which pre-empts some of the most important questions (e.g. do we really need such a radically de-stabilising suite of technologies?) Second, there is a barely-concealed determinism about Drexler's whole account. He has convinced himself of the 'inevitability' of these developments and wants us to become involved in 'guiding' their application. He begs the question about this apparent inevitability and takes as his frame of reference the present distribution of commercial and political power.

Foresight Institute Policy

The Foresight Institute (FI) aims to help society prepare for new and future technologies such as nanotechnology, artificial intelligence, and large-scale space development by:

• promoting understanding of these technologies and their consequences;
• formulating sound policies for gaining their benefits while avoiding their dangers;
• informing the public and decision makers regarding these technologies and policies;
• developing an organisational base for implementing these policies; and
• ensuring their implementation.

FI has a special interest in nanotechnology: at this early stage, it receives relatively little attention (considering its importance), giving even a small effort great leverage. We believe certain basic considerations must guide policy:

Nanotechnology will let us control the structure of matter - but who will control nanotechnology? The chief danger isn't a great accident, but a great abuse of power. In a competitive world, nanotechnology will surely be developed; if we are to guide its use, it must be developed by groups within our political reach. To keep it from being developed in military secrecy, either here or abroad, we must emphasise its value in medicine, in the economy, and in restoring the environment. Nanotechnology must be developed openly to serve the general welfare.

Source: Foresight Institute, Palo Alto, CA, 1988

Figure 7.2 Foresight institute policy

Given the long time-frames applied to the technology, this represents a clear failure of imagination: the politics are static, the technology rips ahead. In this view, it does not occur that such a prior commitment actually obscures the kind of reconceptualisation which would make the technology itself more problematic, less inevitable. This falls into the familiar pattern of some American futures work: the technology occupies the high ground but the worldview, with its hidden assumptions, commitments and agendas, is tucked away out of sight, unavailable and unregarded.

Finally, we are enjoined to enter the debate – but strictly under the agenda provided. It seems that with nanotechnology there is a real 'problem of nonsense'. We are explicitly warned against 'false ideas', and against 'flakes', 'fanatics', 'extremists' and 'crazies'. But such attempts to circumscribe what is, by any account, an important debate, are self-defeating. They betray an underlying weakness which seems to spring from an unresolved conflict of interests. Foresight and advocacy are clearly uncomfortable bedfellows.

The principle rests uneasily upon a technical foundation. It would fare better, perhaps, with an ethical one.

The Global Network on Responsibilities to Future Generations

The future generations project is based in the International Environment Institute at the University of Malta. It is supported by UNESCO and carries out a program of networking, research and publishing. There is a regular newsletter which contains articles on themes relating to inter-generational equity, bibliographies, international contacts and so on. The aims of the network are:

- to discover, develop, and present facts and insights on the problem of the protection of the interests of future generations; and
- to stimulate the world community to act in specific ways to promote those interests explicitly and actively.

The scope of this work is very wide and involves two major foci. One involves monitoring and assessing issues in at least four major areas: far-reaching technologies, environmental quality, development/underdevelopment, institutions and culture. The other considers the basis for exercising responsibilities to future generations and the nature of those responsibilities. Essays by Tony Macelli outline aspects of the ethical framework and conclude that the present generation needs to develop better forecasting methods and futures studies. These are needed to consider future needs and the impact of present policies.

A 1988 newsletter reprints a statement which emerged from a United Nations University meeting in Goa, India. This considered the growing concern about the deterioration of the world environment and explored the basis for introducing 'a long-term temporal dimension into international law'. Some specific strategies recommended include:

- the designation of ombudsmen or commissioners for protecting the interests of future generations;
- the creation of monitoring systems for natural and cultural resources;
- measures to ensure use of renewable resources and ecological systems on a sustainable basis;
- commitment to relevant scientific and technical research; and
- programs of education and learning at all social levels.

The network itself also runs a 'Future Generations Research Exchange' with contact-persons in many countries. This aims to cover some of the many issues and themes mentioned above and to make the results available to decision-makers, academics, educators and others.

It is difficult to assess such an organisation on the basis of a small sample of its publications. However, three points stand out. First, the work being attempted is clearly significant. The notion that the ethical community to which we belong extends to future generations is one which, if accepted, would alter our perceptions and behaviour in ways which could only improve our individual and collective prospects. Second, the task of working out and implementing intergenerational responsibilities is a difficult one which requires the widest possible participation. It would therefore be desirable for many more people to be involved. Finally, it follows from this example that the foresight principle is centrally involved in one of the most important ethical debates of our time. If this is correct, then we may expect to see more such organisations focusing on this key issue. A recent example is the Institute for the Integrated Study of Future Generations in Kyoto, Japan, led by Professor Tae-Chang Kim and Mr. Katsuhiko Yazaki.

The Council for Posterity

The view that technical invention has outrun social invention is a widespread and depressing one. However, as with any potentially depressing possibility, what matters is not the focus of attention but the response to it. Active responses to technological domination include the critique of technocratic projects of the future, the elaboration of social alternatives, the pursuit of non-technical options and the search for social inventions. The Institute for Social Inventions was launched in Britain in 1985 with the aim of encouraging the public to engage in this kind of inventiveness. Since then many new and imaginative ways for tackling social problems or improving the quality of life have been put forward.

The Council for Posterity was one such idea. It was put forward by Professor Richard Scorer who won the main Social Inventions award in 1988. In his view, the purpose of such councils is to look more closely at our intended, and unintended actions in the world. This is not just a matter of good intentions. It is more an attempt to introduce questions of morality into a context where selfishness and opportunism (two key features of the old industrial system) still operate.

The council acted as an advocate for the interests of future generations whom, it is assumed, will be more numerous than ourselves, yet presently can neither vote nor speak directly to us in defence of their interests. It was governed by about thirty eminent council members whose professions had a direct bearing upon the future. Several initiatives included:

- council statements on matters concerning posterity;
- providing a panel of speakers who will be available to the media and others for informed comment;
- an annual UK Council for Posterity award for a leading article in any particular year;
- an annual Reith-style lecture and dinner;
- support for the formation of other such councils in other countries; and
- the launching of a Posterity Journal.

Figure 7.3 reproduces the Universal Declaration of the Rights of Posterity. It sets out an ambitious agenda for responding to the needs and rights of those who will follow us. While it does not attempt to specify legal obligations, it does define many of the specific areas in which such obligations would have to be admitted. As such, it challenges the dominant mode of instrumental rationality which has become so solidly established in the modern world.

The Australian Commission For the Future (CFF)

The CFF was formed in 1986 as a result of an initiative by the then Australian Minister for Science, the Hon. Barry Jones. While sceptics saw the CFF as a front for government policy, the remit of the organisation was somewhat wider. For an organisation employing only 10–12 people at any one time, and with an annual budget of well under $A1m ($US700,000) it has produced a number of outputs.

Under its first director (1986–1988) the CFF pursued four major programme elements.

- Research and policy analysis (eg. the future of work; education for a technological future; population trends; economic options; the information society; and futures research techniques).
- Education (eg. the Bicentennial Futures Education Project (BFEP) ; the Skilling the Future conference).
- Information and communication (e.g. parliamentary information programme; a series of 'impact seminars'; national conferences on various themes; the In Future magazine; TV and radio programmes).
- Public involvement (eg. the Clearing House on Futures Issues (CHOFI); a science shop; a community science and technology network; and a Future Options discussion kit).

In addition to the above, a number of special projects were initiated. These include: Culture, Creativity and Science; Women's Enterprise; Leadership for the Future; and the Greenhouse Project. Many of these initiatives produced a variety of publications and other outputs.

These are notable achievements. Perhaps the most productive work so far has been through the BFEP and the Greenhouse Project. The former

Those who live after us have no voice amongst us

We therefore declare and determine their right
to inherit a planet which has been treated by us
with respect for its richness, its beauty and diversity

a planet
whose atmosphere is life-giving and good, and can
remain so for aeons to come

a planet
whose resources have been carefully maintained and
whose forms of life retain their diversity

a planet
whose soil has been preserved from erosion
with both soil and water unpoisoned
by the waste of the living

a planet
whose people apply their technologies cautiously
with consideration for the long-term consequences

a planet
whose people live in human-scale societies
unravaged by population excess

a planet
whose future generations have interests
which are represented and protected
in the decision-making councils of those alive today.

Source: The Council for Posterity, London, 1990

Figure 7.3 Declaration of the rights of posterity

went some way toward introducing futures perspectives into Australian
schools by way of workshops, conferences and curriculum materials. The
latter has helped to make the term 'greenhouse effect' a household name.

A change of direction was initiated by a later director away from
processes (means) and toward desired objectives (ends). Five new areas
were identified. They were: Creative Futures; Enterprising Futures;
Healthy Futures; Sustainable Futures; and Australia/Asia Futures. These
new initiatives reflected the director's idealistic view that, by making a

definite commitment to chosen futures goals, their realisation would become possible. Unfortunately, however, this 'soft', campaigning approach was out of step with the times, particularly with the Australian economy sliding toward recession. It proved an unmitigated disaster for the long-term development of the CFF, whose reputation and standing slumped. Yet at least two success stories emerged from this period: the formation of Asialink (now part of Melbourne University) and the journal *21C*.

21C began as an over-designed, large-format, glossy magazine. Yet after a few issues, and under a new editor, it found its feet and began to publish a wide range of reviews, critical articles, interviews and so on. By 1992 it had established a wide readership and was, without doubt the leading mass circulation journal of its kind anywhere. More recently it has returned to a more standard format. During this period, a fourth director began the difficult job of bringing the CFF back from the brink, as it were. She brought a 'hard-headed' business expertise to the job and initiated a series of more carefully researched studies on topics such as: future cities, energy futures and savings policy. However, she resigned in 1993.

A year-long hiatus followed. As this book goes to press the CFF has negotiated an arrangement with Monash University and advertised for a new director. It remains in receipt of core funding from the government. So the outlook is less uncertain than it was. The CFF could still evolve into a world-class institution of foresight if the lessons of its own institutions history, and those of others, are learned and applied.

The Institute for 21st Century Studies (ITCS)/Millennium Institute

The ITCS had its origins in *The Global 2000 Report to the President* (of the USA, Jimmy Carter) in 1980. Following publication, Gerald Barney, the director of the study, began to receive numerous enquiries from people around the world who wanted to carry out their own studies. Three years later, in 1983, the ITCS was established as an independent, non-profit corporation. The term '21st Century Study' was coined the next year.

In the following decade, the ITCS developed rapidly and has played a strong catalytic role in supporting national 21st century studies in many different countries. It has offered at least three kinds of support. First, a series of publications on aspects of study methodology. Second, a number of international meetings. Third, regional training programs for study teams in four continents. These are substantial achievements. But the significance of the ITCS is even greater than this.

What it has done has been to help create what may be the world's first body of international knowledge about how to carry out such a study and, equally important, how to assess its significance. A valuable series of guidelines has been derived from this work, meaning that new studies can be established in the light of lessons learned over the past decade. The broad guidelines for 21st century studies include the following.

- Studies are carried out by a team of nationals, with broad-based support and participation from a cross-section of society.
- Studies cover all key sectors and pay particular attention to linkages between them.
- A long-term perspective of twenty to thirty years is preferred.
- Interactions between national and global concerns is encouraged, particularly as regards the economy, the environment and security.
- Studies look for strategies that are environmentally, socially and economically sustainable.
- Studies examine moral, philosophical and political issues and evaluate national institutions in this light.
- The purposes of a study are clearly stated and carried out using a range of appropriate methodologies.
- Careful attention is paid to implementation in order to encourage public debate, policy formulation and practical action.

Clearly, these are important guidelines. Moreover, they are supported by documentation, personnel and training. So the ITCS may become one of the most effective institutions of foresight in existence. It has a small board of directors, an even smaller advisory council and two offices: one in Washington DC and one in Sweden. In time, the separate national studies will contribute to a detailed international overview of key policy issues over the next two or three decades. This will be a real achievement of great value to all who wish to situate their work in its wider framework. Shortly before this book went to press the ITCS changed its name to 'The Millennium Institute' in order to more accurately project its 'goal of harnessing the emotional energy of the new millennium for a sustainable future for the earth'.

The International Futures Library (IFL)

The IFL in Austria, is located in elegant rooms by the fast, grey river that bisects Salzburg. It was founded in 1985 by Professor Robert Jungk, one of the pioneering futurists of this century. Its goal was to assemble a body of futures-related material from a wide range of sources and to make this available to the interested public.

The central idea was that, in the age of the expert, lay persons needed access to knowledge about the global situation which would help equip them to face the future with hope. So, besides the critical analysis of present conditions, the IFL attemps to show how pessimism about the future is already being countered by a variety of creative ideas, projects and initiatives. The library is financed by the City and Province of Salzburg.

To these ends, the IFL has published the journal *Pro Zukunft* (Pro Futures) since 1987 and books such as *A Catalogue of Hope: 51 Models for the Future*. The latter describes a range of activities and projects which show how people can positively influence their own futures. Other such projects are to be summarised in an on-line data base, provisionally called 'Hopenet'. The IFL organises and supports panel discussions, futures workshops and other events to encourage as many people as possible to participate in the process of designing and implementing humanly-desirable futures. It has developed a strong reputation in the German-speaking world, and beyond.

Sadly, at the time of writing, Professor Jungk lies in hospital following a serious stroke. The future of the IFL may therefore be uncertain. However, the ideas and practices developed there will certainly not vanish. The work of Walter Spielmann (at the library) and of Peter Moll (in developing a new futures clearing house) ensure that foresight work of this kind will continue. Indeed, this is exactly what Professor Jungk himself realised. He regarded foresight contexts as 'seedbeds' of social innovation. As such, the contribution of the IFL to foresight work is considerable. The lessons, work, practices, publications and so on produced in one place are transferable. They can and will be taken up and applied elsewhere, regardless of the fate of individuals.

Before looking at pointers for foresight work in the future, I want to briefly summarise exactly what it is that successful institutions of foresight 'deliver' to the societies which support them.

What do institutions of foresight actually 'contribute'?

This review of several examples of such institutions has revealed considerable diversity. But it has also revealed a common underlying pattern. Broadly speaking these organisations pursue some or all of the following tasks.

1. Raising issues of common concern that may be overlooked in the conventional short-term view, e.g. peace, environmental stability, inter-generational ethics, implications of new, and expected, technical developments.
2. Highlighting dangers, alternatives and choices that need to be considered before they become urgent.
3. Publicising the emerging picture of the near-term future in order to involve the public and contribute to present-day decision-making.
4. Contributing to a body of knowledge about foresight and the macro-processes of continuity and change that frame the future.

5. Identifying the dynamics and policy implications of the transition to sustainability.
6. Helping to identify aspects of a new world order so as to place these on the global political agenda.
7. Facilitating the development of social innovations.
8. Helping people to deal with fears and become genuinely empowered to participate in creating the future.
9. Helping organisations to evolve in appropriate ways.
10. Providing institutional shelters for innovative futures work which, perhaps, could not easily be carried out elsewhere.

These are clearly significant contributions. Like the QUEST process, discussed in Chapter 6, they can help to initiate the crucial shifts of perception, policy and practice which, in no small way, form the pivot upon which this culture now turns.

Pointers for future foresight work

The six examples given above represent only a small sample of the range of existing foresight initiatives. Yet they provide sufficient evidence for some tentative conclusions.

First, it is clear that the impulse to engage in foresight work cannot be identified with particular limited interests. It is arising in many different places simultaneously and therefore indicates some kind of 'sea change' which should be taken seriously. Second, with some exceptions, foresight work still appears to be culturally marginal. However, if it represents a 'leading edge' of social innovation, this is just what we would expect. Given the nature of the barriers involved, and the embedded character of business-as-usual assumptions, a strong shift toward the implementation of foresight will necessarily take some time. Third, there are some obvious mistakes to avoid. They include over-promising, conflicts of interest, superficiality and isolation. A number of general guidelines therefore emerge from this discussion.

- It is clearly essential to build up effective constituencies of support. This implies attention to 'outreach' via public forums, the careful use of media and effective public relations.
- Quality control should form an essential part of the *modus operandi* of any such institution or process – it should apply across the board to staffing, publications, events and to justifications for foresight work. A second rate effort is, perhaps, worse than none at all (since grounds are thereby provided for the illegitimate dismissal of foresight work).
- It is important to ground any foresight initiative in modes of enquiry,

action and communication which are sufficiently robust for the difficult tasks involved; in part this means:

— implementing an explicitly futures-related and interdisciplinary
  perspective;
— having access to a range of critical methods and approaches; and,
  most importantly,
— drawing on a substantive ethical foundation (rather than, say, a
  political or administrative one, or one dominated by the compulsive dynamism associated with scientific and technological
  innovations).

• Communication between foresight contexts is highly desirable to
  avoid duplication, share resources, provide informed feedback and
  facilitate networking. This now happens in a haphazard way but it
  could, perhaps, be systematised via. a dedicated network of electronic
  bulletin boards. This technology has reached the point where a
  system could be designed specifically for these organisations.

• There is an urgent need for in-depth research on foresight contexts.
  Depending upon how they are defined, there may be perhaps a
  hundred or more worldwide. They represent a true cultural innovation, the importance of which can scarcely be overestimated. Since
  their concerns are broadly oriented toward public well-being, their
  work, and the study of it, should, in most cases be seen as a public
  service and funded accordingly. The area is ripe for enquiry at the
  Ph.D. level, for publications to popularise it and for a sub-tradition
  of futures work to emerge from it.

No-one should be surprised if some of the examples considered above
one day disappear from the map. However, this would not mean that
foresight does not work. As noted, these are pioneering institutions, and
a relatively high failure rate must be expected. However, their work,
achievements – and indeed their failures – should not be taken in isolation. At heart they are all part of a much wider learning process. The
point is to use the knowledge gained to move the process on as rapidly
as possible before the wider costs (of lack of foresight) become entirely
unacceptable.

The costs and benefits of foresight

How much does foresight cost, and who should pay for it? These are
two key questions. But they don't have straightforward answers. It
depends upon the organisation involved, the work to be done and the
way the work is approached.

For example, at its peak, Australia's Commission for the Future cost
about $A1 million ($US700,000) a year to run, and was a mere 'drop in
the bucket' in relation to other government expenditures. Milbrath's

proposal for a Council for Long-Range Societal Guidance (in the USA) would be an order of magnitude larger, employing as many as 200 people. This might cost $US20 million to set up, and up to $US1 billion a year for studies and impact assessments. This might seem a lot – until one compares it with other expenditures: $US10 billion for a nuclear power plant, or the $US300 billion needed to clean up hazardous waste dumps. Milbrath correctly points out that the latter would not have been needed if adequate foresight had been in place forty years ago. And that, really, is the point. How does one assess cost in relation to assumed benefits? A simple example will make this clearer.

A couple of years ago I looked at the work of a voluntary youth worker who works exclusively with graffiti kids in suburban Melbourne. Despite numerous applications to official bodies, this dedicated individual could get no funding. So I added up the financial costs to the community (excluding the significant range of human costs) which included cleaning damaged property, prosecuting individuals and jailing them. Depending on the assumptions used, I came up with a figure of between $A315,000 ($US220,500) and $A1,500,000 ($US1,050,000) per year for dealing with forty active individuals after the event. A median figure was $A592,500 ($US414,750). In other words, for an outlay of about $A40,000 ($US28,000) for the salary of this one worker, the state could save in the region of half a million dollars.

Yet the odd thing was, and is, that the transit authorities and police continue to spend far more on prosecutions and clean-up activities – around $A12 million ($US8,400,000) last year. Here, then, is a specific example of the costs of not using foresight in active prevention. The old saying 'a stitch in time saves nine' was proved to be true – though it was nearer 1:14 in this case (592,500/40,00 = 14.8).

Such examples could be extended indefinitely. Indeed, they ought to be extended so that decision makers can begin to perceive the real financial benefits of successful foresight. For, wherever we look, we see short-term thinking storing up increasingly expensive problems and dangers for the future. It is therefore important to assess dangers, to give a full accounting of the associated costs, and to show in particular contexts just what savings can be expected from implementing foresight over a sustained period. The notion of 'foresight auditing' has enormous potential because it can clearly show the magnitude of savings to be derived from successful foresight work. In this respect, it is not unlike energy accounting. Both provide long-term rationales for doing things differently.

Since present-day actions and decisions stretch far into the future, systematic foresight should be built into all our institutions and all aspects of government. It has already proved extremely useful in government at the state level in the USA. Rather than see it as an extra cost, it may well be that existing planning systems can be revised and up-graded to include environmental scanning and foresight.

On the other hand, foresight can be informal and facilitative. The World Futures Studies Federation operates on a tiny fraction of the sums mentioned above. Similarly, the cost of some networks is minimal, particularly when they involve donated time and shared information. So, while it is true that foresight will cost money in some circumstances, this should not be uncritically generalised or used as a reason to avoid using it. As noted, it is possible to show that foresight will save more than will be expended upon it. If one also adds in an estimate of other costs – human, social, environmental – the cost: benefit ratio is even more clear. In short, foresight is no longer a choice. It has become an imperative that the human community must respond to.

This book deliberately explores foresight as an individual and social capacity. It also questions the idea that prediction and foresight are necessarily related. Yet there is one very particular context in which they are intimately connected. Late in 1992 a comet dubbed Swift-Tuttle, came close enough to the Earth to pose a significant threat of collision. The physics are significant. With a nucleus of 6–15 kilometres in diameter, a collision at a speed of some 60 km per second would have released sufficient kinetic energy to destroy civilisation. According to a *Newsweek* report, the threshold for widespread extinction of living creatures is a much smaller object of only 1–2 km.

The earth has experienced such disasters before. For example, it is widely believed that the extinction of the dinosaurs was caused by a severe climate change, following such a collision. In the present century, the so called Tunguska event flattened several thousand square kilometres of forest in central Siberia with enough force to have obliterated a city. The explosion was equivalent to the detonation of a 10–20 megaton nuclear device. But it left no crater and no meteorite fragments were ever found. More recently scientists have suggested that the event was caused by the explosion of a stony asteroid about 30 metres in diameter at a height of some ten kilometres. Only large, iron-rich meteorites actually make it to the surface of the Earth. The rest deposit their energy in the atmosphere. But there is one significant difference between meteorites and comets.

The former fall to Earth, shed their energy and are finished. But comets return. They pass through the solar system, around the sun, and out again into deep space – only to turn up again many years later. Swift-Tuttle is expected back in 2126, when it will pass close to the Earth, and again in 3044, when the risk of a direct hit is thought to be high. Even the earlier date carries significant risks, for fragments of the comet's solid nucleus may break free. If so, a series of random nuclear-sized explosions could well bombard the planet. There could obviously be massive destruction and loss of life. Nor can we assume that this is the only comet to pose a direct threat to life on Earth. There are likely to be many others. So what would constitute a responsible response?

One Australian astronomer was quoted as saying that 'we have reached the stage where we should urgently run an international program to identify (objects) with the potential to cause global catastrophe'. The longer the warning of the approach of a possibly dangerous object, the greater the chances that something could be done about it. As another astronomer put it 'if we can give ourselves 50, 100 or 200 years' notice of a problem, I've no doubt our descendants will fix it. And it will be one of the most important messages this century can send into the future'.

The cost of a three-year program of research into near-earth objects (NEOs) at the Anglo-Australian Observatory in New South Wales was a mere $A50,000 ($US35,000) per year. So cost alone is hardly the issue. It is more a question of psychology, short- versus long-term thinking and, indeed, of applied foresight. This wider dilemma about the vulnerability of the entire Earth to devastation from space sounds like an SF novel. (Indeed, several have been written on this very theme.) Yet the issue is a real one which frames all the others discussed in this book. It suggests that the time has come to put in place the very system the astronomers have suggested: an early-warning system to protect the Earth from NEOs. Such a system is the epitome of foresight applied to physical systems. It is a small investment made in the present to protect against likely future events. As such, it is another step away from a past-driven civilisation to a far-sighted, futures-responsive one.

The foresight imperative

The growth of human understanding and the extension of our concerns beyond the present has the effect of extending the ethical community beyond the here-and-now to our future selves, to our descendants and even to other species. Such an extension does raise genuine problems in many fields and these problems need to be addressed. However, given that our species has dangerously over-extended itself, such developments are entirely justified. Under modern conditions foresight is less a choice than a necessity with all the force of an historical imperative. This is so because a simple continuation of business-as-usual attitudes and practices leads inexorably on to futures no sane person would wish to inhabit. I therefore expect to see foresight work continue to develop in many contexts: in government, industry, business, education and public advocacy.

As noted, adding a foresight capacity to an existing institution can cost money, but this is not the main issue. It is primarily one which depends upon a shift of perception and a fairly straightforward re-direction of human effort into increasingly well-understood channels and procedures. Universities could, and should, play a major part in this process since they have within their walls many talented people and much of the expertise required. UNESCO has put some time and seeding money into encouraging 'future-oriented studies'.

Yet most institutions of higher learning remain structured according to narrow disciplines and still hark back to the Middle Ages and to notions of knowledge in which the past is dominant. In the 1930s H. G. Wells attended the centenary of the University of London and found the scene illuminating. He wrote, 'I realised that these medieval robes were in the highest degree symptomatic. They clothed an organisation essentially medieval, inadequate and out of date. We are living in 1937 and our universities, I suggest, are not half-way out of the fifteenth century'. Clearly this is not a new problem and it will not be resolved overnight. However, in the meantime, institutions and processes of foresight will continue to flourish and develop in other locations.

The human species has compromised the environment to the extent that its future viability can no longer be assumed. It has read upon the world a remarkable variety of short-sighted and untenable ideologies and systems of value and belief which have unacceptable costs in the long term. It has sanctioned the construction of vast armies and weapon systems, complete with large stocks of hazardous materials which, were they ever used, would deplete and pollute the global commons beyond repair. However, the widespread implementation of the foresight principle may provide a powerful stimulus for system change. It sets up a different dynamic to that established during the industrial age: one which helps us to question the accepted wisdom of the past and to participate in the creation (or recovery) of a worldview which interprets the world according to a different epistemology and a non-instrumental mode of rationality (see Chapters 9 and 10).

The outcomes of this process are unpredictable. Yet the outlines of a more sustaining and sustainable way of life are beginning to appear. They are visible in the struggles of minority groups, in progressive social movements and in the coalescing of global networks around common causes. They are also evident in the laudable attempt to clarify just what may be involved in extending the scope of the ethical community beyond the limited interests of a single generation.

In summary, foresight in the 1990s means consciously working to complete the transition to a more sustainable world while there is time to achieve it and the future remains open. Can there be a more pointed and critical challenge to the human species than this?

3

Cultural recovery in the 21st century

CHAPTER 8

Creating Positive Views of Futures with Young People

To many young people the future looks bleak. Their fears and concerns should be respected. They are not illusions. On the whole, they are based on reality. However, there are many ways of helping the young move towards more positive, creative and empowering views of futures for themselves and their society. This chapter explores six specific strategies for young people. Chapter 9 considers more demanding options for adults. Finally, Chapter 10 takes up the question of what a wise culture might look like.

|•|•|•| THREE CAMEOS |•|•|•|

The School Captain 'The Prime Minister and the Opposition Leader are two uninspiring heavyweights slugging away until the final bell on March the twenty-fourth.'

This is not the view of a world-weary voter. It is that of a young woman who would like to see some genuine idealism injected into the Australian political process. Ms. . . , 17, school captain of . . . said Mr Hawke and Mr Peacock should pursue some nobler ideals.

The policies seem to be short term. They're not aiming for the future and they lack a grand vision of what society could be,' said Ms. . . . 'At the moment it's all looking pretty dull. You see a dark tunnel but you need to be able to see some light at the end of that tunnel. Both leaders are biting at each other's necks. They see it as a race, a competition, and they try to make themselves look better by putting the other party down. They're covering up the problems, sweeping them under the mat. We need someone to change things.' (From: 'Leaders Lack Grand Vision, Says Student'. Report in *The Age*, Melbourne, 27 February 1990.)

A Year 9 School Drop-out 'Graffiti is everything. It is the one way I can really control my parents. If I had the choice of looking at a sex magazine or graffiti photos, I would look at the graffiti all night. Graff is all I have. I tried legals but it is nowhere near the same buzz. I went to a pub and was amazed how quickly I got accepted and asked to do a panel with some major people. They are my friends . . .'

'I have two really good look-outs that just watch for me while I panel or piece. I am very, very, careful who I tell about what I do. My parents thought I stopped after the first raid and charges. Now [ten months later and beyond court] they found a note I scribbled on paper and hid in my sock. Mum found it in the laundry and thinks I go bombing. They don't know I panel often. They finally caught on. I sneak out at night.

One time I did it and the wind caught the back screen door and Dad got up to fix it and found me missing from my room.'

'When my friend died in a recent car accident, I was very depressed [and left home for four days]. This is all I have going for me. I tried to get work with a signwriter, but he does not have any opening just now.'

From: Noel Buchanan, a graffiti youth worker in Melbourne, 1992.

The Suicide   'Teenagers in the developed world are now better off and physically healthier and can look forward to a longer lifespan than their parents . . . It should be the best of all possible worlds for adolescents. But the opposite appears to be true. The evidence points to a rising tide of unhappiness and serious problems among adolescents in the industrialised countries. Last week, experts from Europe and America grappled with this phenomenon at a conference . . . (in Switzerland).'

'Professor Rene Diekstra, a Dutch clinical psychologist, moved the assembly of child specialists with an account of one of his patients, a 12-year-old girl whose parents had divorced. Over the years she had written a 5,000-word diary in which she recorded a high level of emotional distress that the adult world had unconsciously conspired to ignore. She had written in a piece of schoolwork, for example, that she wanted to die; her teacher had written on the bottom: "Don't be so silly".'

'She had visited her father and on the balcony of his flat slipped her leg over the edge. When he asked her irritably what she was doing, she replied: "Practicing". One day she and her mother had a row over her intention to go out on her bike to get a snack an hour before supper.'

'She went to the top of a block of flats and threw herself off.'

From: 'Teen Age of Despair', Melanie Phillips, *Sunday Age*, 22 November, 1992.

The dilemma of the young

What the above examples show is that young people are growing up and maturing at a time when many of the old certainties have broken down. They have inherited difficulties from the industrial era which have few or no historical equivalents. The term 'global problematique' (or interlocking set of social, economic, political and environmental problems) was coined by the Club of Rome to draw attention to this. More recently the term 'resolutique' has been used to draw attention to possible solutions. However, it is evident that the latter are difficult to find and even more difficult to implement. In the 1990s there is a sense of things falling apart, of a radical loss of certainty and vision.

In this context it is easy to feel cynical, depressed or fearful. Avoidance strategies are common and many diversions are available through a range of increasingly compelling media. Yet young people continue to have fears about their own personal future. They worry about unemployment, family breakdown, personal security and overall life prospects. These fears arise in the context of wider concerns about the state of the planet and, in particular, long-term environmental deterioration. Young people are aware of living through some fairly powerful, often disturbing, historical shifts. For example, in many places sunbathing is no longer the carefree hedonistic experience it once was; skin cancer has become all too common. Similarly, the AIDS pandemic has introduced new anxieties into teenage sexuality and relationships. Such examples are only the tip of the iceberg. At a deeper level, young people know that there is much more to come.

Living in the interregnum

The problem, as outlined in Chapters 1 and 2, is that we are living through the interregnum, or gap, between two eras. Donald Schon understood very clearly what this meant. More than two decades ago he described how social systems tend not to move smoothly from one period to another. He noted how 'the old' comes apart before 'the new' comes together. However, those trapped within the transition process are often unable to grasp the new picture, only the old one that is being lost. Hence there tends to be great anguish and uncertainty for those involved mainly because it was the old system which provided the basis for identity and purpose.

The era we have left is the industrial era, with its unquestioned belief in material growth, in progress, its scientific and technical optimism, materialism and careless exploitation of natural systems. This world is over – though its effects will continue to be felt for centuries. Yet the era we are moving towards is still taking shape. Many old certainties have gone, but, on the whole, they have not been replaced by new ones. The result is a frightening social and spiritual vacuum which, at some level, is felt by everyone.

It is hardly surprising that many young people turn away from uncomfortable realities to a wide range of avoidance strategies. These include: sport, video, TV, drugs, music and a mostly vapid, often chronically oppositional, pop culture. Within this glittering arena of media and marketing there are many compelling diversions, but little in the way of penetrating insights into the grounds of the condition experienced by young people during this time. With computer games becoming steadily more sophisticated, and virtual reality on the horizon, the technological screen between young people and the world becomes more opaque, more difficult to penetrate, understand or control. It is a confusing time. Powerful forces are at work within the human system and the wider world, but they are often 'out of sync'; they do not add up to a coherent whole. Mystification is rife and some resort to desperate solutions.

One might have expected educators to have dealt effectively with this bleak outlook and, to be fair, some have tried. But, for reasons outlined in Chapter 2, they are up against powerful system imperatives which continue to work in a different direction. While I am keenly aware that many talented and dedicated teachers work hard to serve their students' best interests, they can do little to overturn basic assumptions that are structured within, or inscribed upon, educational systems which continue to be driven by the past, focussed on the short-term present and unresponsive to the future. Such a stance would be appropriate during settled times. Yesterday's solutions would still apply today. Yesterday's structures would still fit current needs. But in unsettled times, when everything is at stake, short-term thinking is very dangerous indeed.

In the early 1990s futures thinking and futures methods are routinely employed in government, commercial and industrial enterprises. Yet, in most cases, educators, even at the highest levels, not only do not use them but, generally speaking, they do not even know about them. While I do not want to paint the entire educational enterprise as a failure, I do believe that it has so far failed to understand the ways in which the foresight principle intersects with every one of its major concerns. This is not merely an oversight. It puts educators in a very weak position to deal with the range of futures-related concerns that are now becoming real social crises: drugs, violence, meaninglessness, unemployment and the rest. But all is not lost. Futures concepts, ideas, teaching methods and so on can be implemented quickly and easily once the threshold barriers (mainly of seeing the point of the exercise) are surmounted.

So, in summary, the great problem for young people is that they have been born in a time of transition. They have inherited a culture which is technically powerful but humanly weak and spiritually desolate. It is a 'thin' culture, one which has lost sight of limits, values, meanings, myths, rituals, commitments and principles, all of which are needed for a robust, healthy and wise society. In the age of 'the fast buck', of compulsive merchandising, legalised insanity, chronic derivative fantasy and the endless fictional rehearsal of disaster, it is genuinely difficult to grow up sane.

Six strategies for young people

Here are six ways of beginning to respond to difficult times. They are explored in more detail below.

- Develop an understanding of the effects of young people's media.
- Change fears into motivations.
- Explore social innovations.
- See the future as part of the present.
- Use futures concepts, tools and ideas.
- Design your way out of the industrial era.

Understanding the effects of young people's media

Young people's media includes books, films, comics, TV and video, computer games, arcade games, fantasy games, simulations and, before long, virtual reality (VR). While there are many fine books for the young, the decline of print-based literacy is matched only by the rise and rise of the image. We are, as J.G. **Ballard** has observed, 'obsessed with the image'. And with the advent of cheap TVs and video machines we have access to a richness and a variety of images that is without precedent.

In a futures context, at least three concerns arise from this media-rich environment. First, representations of futures, whether they be overtly fictional or otherwise, exhibit a familiar and stereotypical constellation of qualities. The first of these is violence. The violence may well emerge from an openly dystopian context and is the dominating dynamic in very many films, videos, comics and games. Second, 'the future' tends to be represented largely through the display of things. That is, computers, mega-cities, robots, space stations etc. As noted in Chapter 2, one must look long and hard to find credible images of people as people (rather than servants of the machine) in these images. The clear message is that such futures are built externally though science and technology – rather than through human decisions. This is a spurious and unhelpful view. Third, the future is not seen as a dynamic field of potentials interpenetrating the present but, rather, as a kind of blank screen, somewhere 'out there' upon which contemporary hopes and fears are projected. The array of alternatives which arise from foresight studies and translate into present-day options and choices, is obscured, and the young are thereby disempowered.

Some of these concerns can be explored through the structuring of categories in futuristic media – that is, the way that basic polarities of life such as good and evil, right and wrong, science and magic, are portrayed. In one study I did of such material, I came to the conclusion that these important categories were irretrievably scrambled at the epistemological level. As will become clear below, I am not arguing that young people are helpless or incapable of responding. What I am suggesting is that a significant amount of popular culture in these modes is trivial, diversionary and, in the first instance, confusing. There is a prima facie case for considering much of this material as detracting from young people's attempts to make sense of the world and to feel at home in it. This contrasts dramatically with the more positive uses of some mainstream literature and, say, traditional fairy stories which arguably rehearsed more viable life strategies.

The point, however, is not to rail against 'the media'. Having outlined the problem we should consider a strategy of response. A central concern, perhaps, is that a very great deal of low-quality material is experienced by young people with minimal filtering, thus by-passing the critical faculties and passing straight into the subconscious. I doubt if anyone knows just what the consequences are – and that alone is cause for concern. Are young people being subtly, and not so subtly, moulded in unknown ways? A lot more research is needed before we can be sure of the answer. However, there may be a surprisingly simple interim solution.

If some of the more questionable material was intercepted before it passed into the subconscious, I have no doubt that most young people would be able to assess its significance, understand its uses and limitations, and begin to develop some critical insight into cultural imaging processes. In other words, parents, teachers and others working with young people can try to ensure that there are plenty of opportunities to actively process media experiences. This would mean that, for example, TV would be less like 'electronic wallpaper'. It could be regarded far more critically as the very powerful symbolic medium that it really is (analogous in many ways to a powerful drug) and therefore used with similar attention and care. Early work in this area has shown some promising results.

Change fears into motivations via the empowerment principle

When the question of attitudes arises, many people tend to think in terms of two polar opposites: optimism and pessimism. This is fine as far as it goes. In general terms it is far better to adopt an optimistic attitude than a negative one. However, optimism and pessimism are too simple to be applied uncritically to futures problems. The fact is that both terms are ambiguous. An optimistic person may believe that there is no cause for alarm, when in fact there may be very good cause for it. Similarly, a pessimistic person may get so concerned about a particular problem that they will get up and do something about it. So the important thing is not a person's starting disposition but what (if anything) then follows. The key to dealing with issues, concerns and fears about futures lies in the nature of the human response. This is known as 'the empowerment principle', and it is an important part of futures education.

Figure 8.1 is a matrix which can be used to explore a variety of responses to whatever may be feared. The matrix has two main purposes. The first is to place negative associations in a wider context. The second is to focus attention upon what may be meant by 'high-quality' responses (see below).

This approach can be used in a workshop situation, as a counselling tool or by individuals working alone. Whatever the method, it is often helpful to begin by listening to the fears or concerns and recognising that they usually have a sound basis in reality. In all but a small minority

	Low-quality responses	High-quality responses
Acceptance of negative images		
Rejection of negative images		

Matrix for considering images of futures. The matrix is a workshop tool for dealing with fears and investigating images of futures. Each cell describes a type of strategy or response. When the matrix is completed, these can be compared. A preferred resolution is normally suggested. Finally, there is a discussion about what resources may be needed.
Source: R. Slaughter, *Futures Tools and Techniques* (1988).

Figure 8.1 Matrix for exploring fears

of cases they are likely to be rational responses to a drastically altered world.

The next step is for students to hold the images, associations, feelings or responses out before them in a relaxed and non-judgemental way. Four sets of responses are then explored by following the matrix.

1. Accept the possibility that what is feared will come to pass, and explore low-quality responses.
2. Accept the possibility and explore high-quality responses.
3. Reject the possibility with low-quality responses.
4. Reject the possibility with high-quality responses.

The acceptance/rejection distinction is not clear-cut in all cases and can generate ambiguities. However, in this context, these are not important and time should not be wasted on them. The first point is that the exercise generates up to four sets of strategies, which can be compared. Possible solutions emerge across each of the four categories. At this point, further questions arise. What appeared to be the 'best' solutions? What resources, changes, commitments and/or support would be needed to put a preferred strategy into practice?

It may be helpful here to consider some of the criteria that may be applied to decide if a response is 'high-quality' or not. To begin with, they can be seen in a wider context; there is always a wide range to choose from. Second, many fears are overstated. It may be that they can be scaled down and given a less overblown status. Third, fears which are linked to images or concerns about futures are both provisional and negotiable. They are not set in concrete, but represent opportunities for engagement, choice and purposive action. It's important to note that concerns about the future depend on human vision, perception and understanding. Therefore, the locus of power lies in people and not in a disembodied vision beyond human influence. Finally, note that a high-quality response is, above all, creative. It has the capacity to go beyond the given and break new ground.

Young people who can begin to move away from a preoccupation with optimism or pessimism, who will view their initial responses in a wider context and who will begin to consider the nature and grounds of high-quality responses, will find that they have started to fashion a fundamental and very important shift of perception. It is a shift away from having things happen to one, to a position where one takes greater control and makes things happen. In other words, this is a big step towards personal empowerment.

Explore social innovations

A social innovation is something that someone has created out of a perceived need. Human societies are made up of countless social innovations. Examples include: courts of law, bike helmets, credit cards, insurance, group therapy, franchising and institutions of foresight.

The best way to begin with young people is to consider local examples of such innovations, and, if possible, to draw on the experience of local people who, perhaps, had a hand in getting them adopted. The actual focus is less important than the principle involved which is that if enough people care about something, there is a good chance that it can be made to happen (or, if appropriate, avoided).

How is it that enough people come to care sufficiently to create a long-term change? Usually it is because one person, or a very small group, made a long-term commitment and worked hard over a period of time to convince others. As suggested in Chapter 3, the big social movements for women's rights, the environment, peace and so on, all started modestly. But given time, they stir governments and alter public perceptions in very major ways. So it is worth taking a close look at such innovations and movements and attempting to understand how they work. It is generally a mistake to proselytise on behalf of such entities, but it is responsible to make sure that they are included on the significant map of knowledge.

Young people can try out the process of social innovation easily and safely. There are basically just a few simple steps, as follows.

1. Get informed about something important (environmental scanning).
2. Investigate the topic for a period of time (research).
3. Develop some initial conclusions about it (analysis and reasoning).
4. Discuss these conclusions with advisers (check for safety and appropriateness).
5. Construct a project and present a proposal (project formulation).
6. Expect indifference, opposition etc., but don't give up (social process).
7. Assess the outcomes (evaluation).

By following this kind of approach, young people can learn about the ways that societies respond to attempts to change them. They will learn about barriers to change, about the uses of power and authority, the importance of clear thinking and communication skills and so on. But the main thing they will learn is that in a very positive sense, people are powerful. If they decide to do something constructive, and do it carefully, there is a very good chance that their efforts will be rewarded. Such grassroots efforts have the potential to profoundly affect the present and therefore the future also.

See the future as part of the present

The tenses of the English language create three distinct 'boxes' for past, present and future. They therefore create false boundaries between them and confirm the illusion that they are separate. It is true that they are different, but it is not the case that they are separate, as Figure 8.2 shows. Here there is a flow of relationships which cannot be separated or assigned to individual 'boxes'.

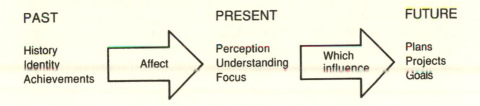

Figure 8.2 Connections between past, present and future

However, the connections are richer yet, since the 'flow' is not all in one 'direction'. For example, hopes or fears about futures may not just affect the present, they may also cause one to reconsider aspects of the past which led in such a direction. Similarly, any projects which one may elect to undertake do not spring fully-formed from the present. They arise from the historical and cultural matrix in which we exist. The most important point is that while the body may be constrained within a fairly narrow present, the human mind and spirit are able to range at will across very broad spans of time and space.

Figure 8.2 suggests therefore, that the boundaries between past, present and future are, in fact, fluid and open. This means that instead of being 'stranded' in a narrow and restrictive present, there are other creative and cultural choices available. In fact, normal living requires a fluid and easy movement between past, present and future. Only brain-damaged people with impaired memories lack this capacity. They are locked into a moving present in which they can neither remember nor foresee. The results are confusion and deep frustration.

Two processes are centrally involved in constructing the present. One is the interpretation of past experience. The other is the anticipation of possible futures. The two processes are not in opposition. One cannot be considered more or less important than the other. They are mutually reinforcing, mutually necessary in supporting normal consciousness. However, the attempt to remain in the imagined past or future for any length of time risks being escapist because it fails to re-connect with the present. In this view, futuristic fantasies and historical novels, films and costume dramas may fulfil the same basic function.

It follows that the present is not a fixed period of time: it varies according to perception and need. However, whatever notion of it is adopted at any time, it is possible to see the present as, in some sense, 'woven' from past and future; that is from memory and prevision, from experience and goals, from identity and purpose. Figure 8.3 makes this clear. The 'here-and-now' may indeed represent a very restricted span of time. However, the materials imported into this arena may come from far and wide. In other words, young people need not be, in any sense, 'locked into' a narrow and alienating present. If they will begin to journey more widely into past and future, they will discover many of the resources they need to survive and prosper in difficult times. The notion of an 'extended present' is a very simple, but powerful one. It is taken up again below.

Use futures concepts, tools and ideas

To be active in politics one needs a political discourse, in economics an economic discourse, and in foresight work – a futures discourse. None of these are exclusive. Yet each tends to develop first in a particular context. Over time, the most useful linguistic, conceptual and symbolic resources subsequently become public property. This is what is beginning to happen with futures concepts. They may have developed in isolation, but they are now being used more widely.

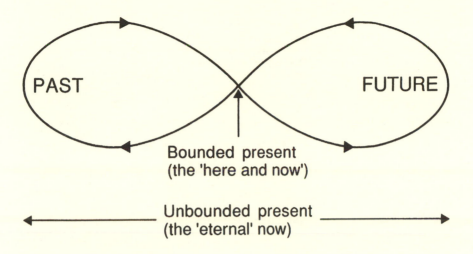

Figure 8.3 Weaving the present from past and future

Futures concepts have been widely overlooked. But, as suggested in Chapter 3, they are important because they provide part of the means by which to consider futures. Like the language and symbols of any area, they give substance to what may otherwise seem vague and unreal. They provide clarity and definition so that hitherto obscured ideas and possibilities spring into sharper focus. In other words, they augment the natural capacity of the human brain/mind system and raise its power to engage in futures work to new levels. Futures concepts and methods are the most important tools for teaching about futures. They are not used merely to forecast or predict 'what will happen' but, rather, to elaborate our understanding of futures in the present. This is a more interesting and educationally productive task. Here are a number of futures concepts and methods in wide use.

The futures field

Chapter 3 provided a brief account of the core, or knowledge base of futures studies. This is one of many possible maps of the area. It may also be mapped through a network of concepts. Figure 8.4 provides an example. Using such maps as starting points, one can begin to locate some of the methodologies, processes and people who work in the field. The work of outstanding individuals represents an accessible way of introducing futures to students. Clearly this is a multi-disciplinary area so it can take a little time to feel 'at home'. Yet this broad structure gives access to a very wide range of conceptual, intellectual, practical and human resources.

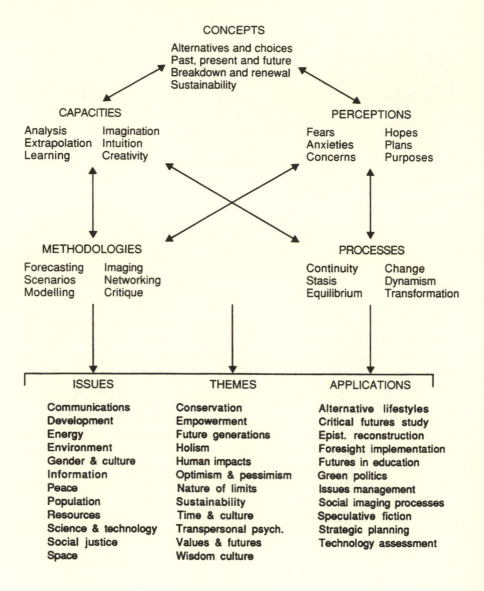

Figure 8.4 Concept map of the futures field

Alternatives and choices

These are two key concepts of the field. They suggest that there is no single, deterministic future, but rather a range of options and possibilities which invite a range of human responses. How can one conceptualise alternatives? Chapter 6 used a divergence map to answer this question.

Alternatives emerge from engaging with the subject matter over a period of time, from looking beyond the obvious, from examining assumptions and, perhaps, using some of the major foresight techniques such as environmental scanning, the cross-impact matrix, cultural critique and the analysis of cycles of change. Since each can be approached at a range of levels, they can all be adapted for educational use.

Creating futures

The central point of using foresight and teaching about futures is to show that everyone is involved; all are capable of pursuing ends and purposes which lead away from some outcomes and toward others. This goes a long way towards reassuring individuals that they are able to contribute to ends which matter and not to feel intimidated by the vast collectivities of power, prestige and profit which may sometimes seem (but are not) overwhelming.

Futures are scanned routinely and informally by everyone. They are scanned routinely and systematically by forecasters and strategic planners. Futures are created or avoided by the sum total of formal and informal processes by which important social decisions are made and acted upon. All these processes can be clarified, studied, subjected to careful and informed analysis. Moreover, individuals are free to participate in them. Governments may be the last to know when a major shift is underway. Many such shifts developed, grew and gained legitimacy because people cared enough to get on with the necessary work. Hence, there is a notion of active and responsible citizenship at the centre of foresight work in general and futures teaching in particular. It is realised, in part, through simple methodologies and tools, some of which are outlined below.

Environmental scanning

One of the keys to implementing foresight is to be sure that one is receiving the right messages from the environment. This means being alert to information about relevant matters. Young people can monitor specific areas over a period and begin to develop the necessary skills. Clearly there is a tie-up here with a number of curriculum areas: philosophy, English, media studies and so on. Environmental scanning is an activity which need not remain the province of large organisations. Individuals too can learn some of the skills involved: being alert for precursors (or early signals); sorting information from propaganda; discerning trends; summarising data and keeping it organised in an accessible and useable form. These skills can all be taught and learned in schools and other contexts.

Futures wheels

Futures wheels are one of the most flexible and useful tools available. Students begin with a large sheet of blank paper. They ask a 'what if' question: 'What if cars were banned? What if the human life-span doubled? What if wars ended?' etc. This possible future event is placed at the centre of the paper. The next question is 'If this happens, what would happen next?' In this way, a ring of immediate consequences is placed around the original event. The ring can be extended by considering secondary consequences. And so on. The result is a pattern of judgements. The pattern is not 'right' and it is not 'wrong'. It incorporates assumptions, both positive and negative which dictate how the pattern could develop. The futures wheel can be 're-run' according to different assumptions. It can be regarded as an end in its own right, or as a starting point for further work. Often the outer edges of the pattern throw up fresh ideas. They can be created with students of any age and level of sophistication. With very young children teachers can write responses on a wall board. With older people the exercise can be developed and extended in various ways.

Critique

I have argued throughout this book that the dominant Western/industrial worldview has at least two kinds of major systemic defects of concern to those working with the young. One is that underlying assumptions (about technology, growth, progress, the environment etc.) are proving to be wide of the mark. The other is that a number of core meanings and commitments are breaking down. This suggests that attention be paid to major shifts in areas such as: work, leisure, health, defence and, indeed, education. Careful attention to each of these areas reveals both a loss of coherence and a number of alternative interpretations vying for attention. As the process of breakdown and renewal becomes clearer and better understood, that is as both sides of the coin are revealed, a new insight dawns. No teacher or pupil need ever feel helpless. In other words, critical worldview analysis and positive critique leads directly toward empowerment. This idea is developed more fully in Chapters 9 and 10.

Acting

One of the commonest early responses to foresight work is a feeling that the problems of the world are too great to be addressed by individuals. Young people may see the point of something but they will often respond by saying something like 'OK, but what can I do?' That is a legitimate question and every teacher or youth worker should be able to answer it.

Figure 8.5 provides one way of beginning to deal with this question. It suggests that when the question is asked there is a wide range of resources to be drawn upon. In relation to foresight, there is first and foremost an individual's own capacities and perceptions. Both can be looked at and consciously developed. Next are futures concepts and methodologies which articulate futures concerns and provide ways of approaching them. Finally there is the study of real-world processes. The latter describes things that are happening in the world and thus provides starting points for an infinite variety of projects.

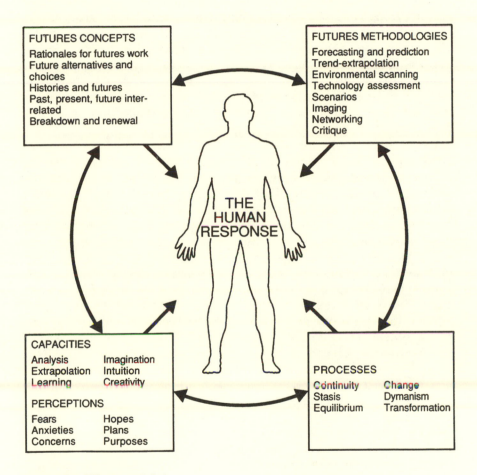

Figure 8.5 What can I do?

If there is a single answer to dealing with the problems of a world in transition then it is this – learning to act effectively and to persist until constructive changes are achieved. So one answer to the question, 'What can I do?' is to reply, 'The answer is a journey'. This short summary statement is useful because it points people in the most promising direction of all: the development of their own abilities and perceptions. It is a journey of inner discovery as individuals come to know their own capacities and purposes. It is also a journey of outer exploration, research and action in the wider world. This twin journey identifies a central purpose of education at any level. But approaching it through the foresight principle gives it much greater force and meaning.

Design your way out of the industrial era

After opening out a new range of alternatives in terms of ideas, visions and options, the next step is to look at other possible changes in the ways things are understood or done. To some extent this is already happening in areas such as energy conservation and re-cycling. However, there are many other ways of applying the notion of 'design'. Figure 8.6 relates it to several key aspects of the cultural environment. In this way the idea of social innovations can be extended, challenging us to find new ways of applying creative imagination.

Design is routinely applied to technical systems and infrastructures. Indeed, there are many uses for it in such places. As we move into the 21st century it will be necessary to re-think and replace many technical systems that were founded on old assumptions (rapid growth, unlimited fossil energy, high environmental impacts). In their place we will need to adapt, re-fit and create new systems based on different assumptions (steady-state, or qualitative growth, energy conservation, low impact and a vast increase in communications). There is scope here for a great deal of innovative design work, some of which can be carried out by young people. However, as Figure 8.6 suggests, the notion of design can also be applied to other domains including: the language system, the spatial system, the regulatory system, the temporal system and the ethical/moral system. There follow some key questions that may be asked in relation to each of them.

The language system

What ideas, images and metaphors from the past are no longer helpful? How can language accurately represent the interconnected global system and the major defects which impair its operation? How can language (and imagery) be used to explore a wide range of futures options and alternatives? What types of humanistic and artistic productions are suggested by the above?

The spatial system

What assumptions about space have been inherited from the past? How has land-use been conditioned by cheap petrol, and city layouts by the

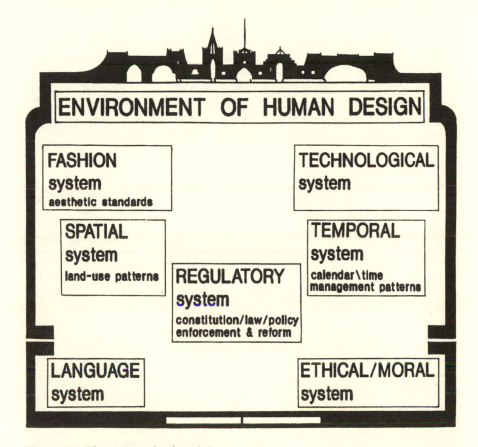

Figure 8.6 The range of cultural design

private car? What changes might be foreshadowed by using different assumptions and different forces of change? Similarly, how do patterns of housing, transport, industry and mining reflect industrial priorities? What kinds of spatial design solutions will be needed in an information, and image-rich, society attempting to move toward sustainability?

The regulatory system

How can a regulatory system based on precedent and past practice begin to deal systematically with new problems and dilemmas? How can it be modified to give a voice to the disenfranchised, and to future generations? Is there a role for an ombudsman for future generations? How can one mediate between a productive system adapted to growth and the need to preserve the integrity of the environment? How can regulation actively encourage closed-loop processing and ecological restoration?

The temporal system

Western cultures seem to pay much more attention to space than to time. Yet time is culture-specific and powerfully conditions the social order. How can time be studied? What models are useful for understanding it? How do linear and cyclic models affect social processes? What is future-discounting and how does it operate to 'make the future vanish'? What are time-frames, and how are they used? How might we use time-frames more consciously, matching them with particular activities?

The ethical system

Our ethics are badly in need of an overhaul. The diminished 'ethics' of marketing and consumerism have become system imperatives, yet they are patently destructive. How can they be changed or replaced? What other sources of value and meaning are available to us? How can they be accessed? What are the grounds of a stewardship ethic? Could this play a more central role in a society of the future? How might we begin to activate the notion of a wise society? What might a wise culture be like, and how would its operating assumptions differ from our present ones?

Such questions can stimulate young people to look beyond the obvious for insights and materials that lead away from feared futures to new, and renewed ways of life.

Limitations of the strategies

The above provide a number of starting points that can be used successfully to deal with many fears and concerns. But I would not wish to pretend that they exhaust the field or that all problems have solutions. Many problems do not, in fact, have solutions on the level at which they are first understood or experienced. A qualitatively different approach is needed for dealing with systemic difficulties and deep-seated worldview assumptions or commitments. In the final two chapters we therefore turn to the twin themes of cultural reconstruction and the notion of a wise culture.

CHAPTER 9

Cultural Reconstruction in the 'Post-Modern' World: Aspects of a Renewed Worldview

Standing beyond the strategies that can be used with young people, there lie a number of more powerful and profound options. These are discussed below under the headings of 'processes of meaning-making' and 'new and renewed worldview commitments'. Taken together, they provide a basis for approaching and grappling with the difficult question of cultural reconstruction.

How can one reconstruct a culture? After all, we have seen the decline of certainty during the present century and the rise of various perspectives which have greatly complicated our view of the world. The idea of cultural reconstruction can all too easily suggest a kind of hubris which is unjustified in post-modern conditions. The construction metaphor itself implies a tangible subject and an assumption of control which may seem inappropriate in this context. So why use it? This is a good time to remind ourselves of the active role of humans in shaping their present and future. If there is a central idea underlying the foresight principle, it is that humans are creators of culture, makers of meaning, conscious agents in the social/historical process. Of course, there are limits to our ability to do any or all of these things. We never have objective knowledge, never achieve perfect understanding and never accurately foresee the full consequences of everything we do. From these objections, some will construct a philosophy of despair, saying in effect, that issues of cultural design are simply too difficult. That is the default stance of the mass media and the educational establishment in the mid-1990s. But it is an unhelpful one.

The post-modern movement has tended to support such a view. The subject (i.e. us) we are told, has been 'de-centred'. There is a frightening gulf between the sign, the signifier and the signified. Deconstruction has torn away many of the old certainties leaving a sense of radical emptiness at the heart of things. Values and other meaning structures are seen as provisional and culture-bound. Some supermarkets have even been given architect-designed cracks – a reflection of epistemological 'cracks' in the worldview, perhaps. A vapid pop culture fills many of the sophisticated, newly-available channels made possible by satellites and fibre optics. Amidst all this chaos, where is certainty?

Yet perhaps too much weight has been given to post-modernism and its fashionable angst. It is, after all, not a culturally monolithic enterprise, but one of several found in the arts and humanities. It cannot speak for culture as a whole, nor be taken as an authoritative commentary on the world. It is an interpretive framework and, as such, has all the strengths and failings of its kind. I conclude that we should feel free to take from post-modernism what we can, and also free to resist its over-extension into other areas. So, rather than share in the prevailing mood of pessimism, I want to complete this book with a perspective that is optimistic, but hopefully not naive.

My starting point is to acknowledge the difficulty of the enterprise suggested by the term 'cultural reconstruction'. There are two points. First, culture is not something we operate on as if it and we were separate. Rather, it is something we are immersed in and deeply conditioned by. So the notion of reconstruction I am using here should not be taken to imply merely an external operation, still less a return to Cartesian dualism. It will necessarily be a process in which people change even as they exert their reason and intentionality upon cultural phenomena. Second, we must acknowledge that there is no clear 'rule book' to guide our attempt to reconstruct late industrial culture. Such 'instructions' as we do have are gleaned from many sources: from our interpretations of the past and present, critiques, non-Western cultures and, of course, from foresight. Such sources are open, provisional, and even problematic.

But rather than take these real difficulties as reason for despair, I want to see them as indicating the need for a certain modesty as we contemplate vast and hidden forces. In other words, we have both to feel free and empowered to renegotiate powerful cultural commitments and structures inscribed within the present and, at the same time, to avoid the over-stated confidence that we know fully what we are doing; for manifestly we do not. The key point is that between the extremes of despair and over-confidence lies a profoundly significant arena of freedom. Its boundaries are uncertain and contested, but the arena is certainly broad enough to provide us with a substantial degree of steering capacity. This is a central pillar of the present work: we cannot possibly know everything, but we are far from helpless.

Given these qualifications, how then can we begin to reconstruct the culture? One answer is implicit in the previous chapters. We can look back, discern the origins of the industrial system, trace the consequences and, finally, look ahead with every means at our disposal to form judgements about the entire perspective. I use the term 'judgement' advisedly. For while technique is certainly part of foresight work, judgement remains primary. That is why this book concentrates on the latter. If our forward view indicates that a terrible and devastated world is likely, then the loop of futures thinking directs us back to the roots of that devastation in the present. In other words, reconstruction begins with a cultural diagnosis. This was the subject of Part One of this book.

The use of foresight lends valuable weight to scenarios that will become more likely if we continue with the business-as-usual outlook. It provides part of the motivation that will enable us to engage in serious system change, redesign, before changes are forced upon us. What, then, are the next steps? Here are some possibilities.

1. Discard aspects of the old world view and re-constitute the social and economic structures that flowed from it.
2. Consciously intervene in some of the processes of meaning-making through which present-day social reality is mediated.
3. Employ the notion of 'design' to develop and implement new, or more appropriate, ideas, principles, practices and structures.
4. Create a shared vision of a future worth aiming for.
5. Institutionalise foresight in order to make the coming transition clearer and easier, and so that such efforts can be monitored and evaluated.

The first point was discussed above in Chapters 1 (under the heading of 'the metaproblem') and 2. The second and third points are taken up in the present chapter. The fourth point is the subject of Chapter 10. The fifth is a thread connecting all parts of the book.

Processes of meaning-making

Using Cultural Editing

Back in 1935 Ruth Benedict published a book called *Patterns of Culture* which took the view that no one looks at the world through 'pristine eyes'. Rather, Benedict showed how we all see it edited by a particular configuration of customs and institutions and ways of knowing. This is no longer a new insight, but its importance has been widely overlooked.

On the negative side, the cultural editing which has taken place within the industrial worldview has had a number of powerful consequences. We have come to view the world in certain ways and these have power-fully affected how we have used and abused it. But foresight tells us that many of the resulting 'habits of perception' are not viable in the longer term. If we want to create a sustainable culture we will have to find ways to 'reprogramme' some our cultural editing processes. This is a very positive option; one which puts back into people's own hands the means to achieve a real cultural transition.

Current dilemmas suggest that we need to reconstruct our worldview – literally change the ways we construe the world. This is an historically unprecedented task. It will not be accomplished overnight. Nevertheless, we can clarify some aspects of the task and propose others which may qualify for inclusion in a renewed worldview. For example:

- a sense of temporal process embracing past, present and future;
- a more conscious and strategic use of time-frames, matching them appropriately to different activities;
- a global and systemic view;
- recognition of the rights of future generations;
- a recovery of participating consciousness; and
- a commitment to higher-order human development.

Some of these are examined in this and the following chapter.

It is not clear to what extent a culture can consciously change its own editing processes. However, looking back at successful examples of systemic change (such as have been to some extent achieved by the environmental and women's movements), there is sufficient evidence to justify optimism. Change is possible when the time is right and the ideas involved are compelling enough to win wide support. This does not mean that all problems can be solved. Many will only be resolved when their deeper dimensions are more fully understood and more widely appreciated. Yet even now there are numerous ways ahead.

Re-negotiating meanings

The notion that words simply mean what they say and that texts embody a coherent experience or account of the world is a deeply held and comforting one. It is comforting because it preserves a simple view of language and meaning which naturalises a commonsense, taken-for-granted, view of the world. Yet, like the boundaries they enshrine, the comforts of realism are illusory. They obscure the ideological character and uses of language and leave individuals open to mystification and exploitation. There is insufficient latitude here to permit the full flowering of human communicative ability and expressiveness. In order even to notice ideological and linguistic traps (let alone to penetrate the fog of misdirection and escape them) it is essential to yield some degree of comfort and certainty. Yet in so doing, what is lost in narrowness and naivety can be gained in breadth and freedom to 'speak one's own word'.

Traditional literary criticism concentrated on understanding 'what the author meant' and classifying his/her stylistic attributes according to a pre-defined system of taken-for-granted criteria. Today the writer occupies a less privileged position and texts have been said to provide an open framework for the construction of meanings. While this view may readily be overstated, the reader has become much less a passive observer and more an active participant in the communication process. The reader is fully capable of calling forth meaning, purpose and intentionality from a range of sources, including texts. While in practice some texts may be susceptible to only a limited range of interpretations it is, of course, always possible for the reader to reject textual assumptions and claims, indeed to leap beyond them to quite new areas of concern. This is a key point: knowledge is never 'finished' and therefore meanings are always fluid and negotiable. The ramifications of this view are of great significance for people facing up to the decline of a worldview.

This is so because, in presuming a more equal status between author and reader, a principle can be established which applies equally to other contexts: advertisements, editorials, newscasts, political speeches and images/projects of the future. The concept of 'text' can be utilised as a metaphor and applied to cultures and traditions.

Contrary to received wisdom (if that is the right term), our present transition from industrial ways of life is not centrally a matter of economic and technical change. These features are 'noticed' and exaggerated by viewpoints founded upon or conditioned by, instrumental reason. Opposed to this perspective (which stresses externalities) it seems to me that by understanding the present cultural transition not so much in terms of the external regulation or control of techniques and technologies, than as a transformative process involving breakdowns and renewals of meaning, we penetrate to the core of all our major concerns.

In a critical futures view those concerns are perennial. They relate to the essentially human process of constituting meaning, significance, purpose and value. It follows that if individuals are free to reinterpret texts they are also free to reinterpret inherited traditions and normative views of 'desirable' futures. (In fact, we should doubt if they can do otherwise since meanings are never simply copied, duplicated, taken over intact.) If there can be no final or authoritative reading of history or futures, it follows that in principle each person has the same potential right of access to the crucial councils and commitments of the day. Those who so choose can, therefore, without regard for social status or academic qualifications, participate in cultural reconstruction and renewal at a very fundamental level.

Encouraging social learning and social innovations

Social learning is always necessary when a society must adapt to changing conditions. Yet there is always a time-lag between perception, decision-making and response. In the present century we have seen some highly effective group learning and innovation in areas like medicine, computing and space exploration. Yet in public policy fields such as transport, economics and the environment, we have witnessed a string of long-term failures. These are multi-dimensional failures of understanding, imagination, vision and response. Today our societies, environments and children are more at risk from a variety of significant threats than ever before, not less. Something is clearly very wrong with the social learning processes now in place. They are slow, ineffective and non-systemic.

Social learning can take place at a number of levels and in a number of ways (Figure 9.1). Surface learning refers to changes which can take place regardless of underlying structures. Organisational learning refers to changes in patterns of human activity within organisations and groups. Deep learning refers to changes in cultural programming at the level of epistemologies, fundamental values and ways of knowing. Social learning can occur informally, through planned incrementalism or via what has been termed 'crisis learning'. A further option is that of deliberate systemic change, but it goes without saying that this is extremely difficult under present circumstances. Perhaps it is something that a wise culture might attempt.

Figure 9.1 Social innovations

SURFACE LEARNING	Bike helmets Speed bumps Credit Cards	Play groups No-fault divorce Safe sex
ORGANISATIONAL LEARNING	Health insurance Ethical investing Futures workshops	Strategic planning Neighbourhood watch schemes Publicly-funded foresight institutions
DEEP LEARNING	Universal suffrage Deep ecology Intergenerational ethics	Intrinsic value Post-materialist economies Critical and epistemological futures study

The modern crisis of social learning is at least five-fold.

1. The world is too complex to be understood easily. This makes it very hard to achieve consensus.
2. The cultural programming now in use is defective in certain major respects (manifested, for example, in short-termism and lack of foresight capability). This means that major social formations (politics, economics, commerce, education, entertainment) tend to incorporate redundant principles.
3. Social and political leaders seldom have access to the necessary tools, understandings or policy options. They are hamstrung by questionable pre-judgements, self-interest and industrial-era imperatives.
4. There are too few forums where social learning can be facilitated. The 'official' organs of the state which could facilitate social learning (the

judiciary, the parliament, the church, etc.) are, by and large, still playing old games by old rules. They do not appreciate that the game itself has changed.

5. Diversionary 'surrogate worlds' intervene between individuals and the reality of the social/economic/ecological context in which they live. These surrogate worlds have come to play a powerful role in shaping perceptions of the real world. But they occupy the human nervous system in an often closed and unproductive loop, exerting tranquilising and mystificatory effects which obscure major systemic problems.

Clearly there are no simple solutions to this mismatch between a deteriorating world picture and inadequate human responses. Yet social learning can be facilitated in many ways. Some possible responses include the following.

- Expose the theoretical and applied defects of the industrial world view.
- Pay careful attention to the critiques presented by marginal groups.
- Seek social support for necessary innovations.
- Highlight the critical role of social innovation and the role individuals can play in supporting it.
- Seek to rewrite rules, principles, procedures which are now unhelpful.
- Develop foresight capacity in many locations and link with long-term, sustainable visions.
- Reconceptualise present dilemmas as opportunities for human and social inventiveness.

Such a list should not be taken to suggest that social learning can be planned, manipulated or imposed from above. There are no blueprints. The process is much more subtle and diffuse. It is also important to note that social innovations are not limited to grand plans and schemes. The Institute for Social Inventions has fostered and collected many more modest examples. Yet the collective impact of many small innovative changes could be significant in the long term.

Social learning will, in all likelihood, take place through each of the means noted here. Some will be directed, purposeful change, some will be incrementally achieved from the margins, and some will be crisis learning which is driven by the social experience of disaster. The latter cannot be avoided. But there is much that ordinary people can do to understand the shifts they are living through, find appropriate means of responding to them and therefore participate in the task of cultural innovation and renewal.

Balancing instrumental rationality with participating consciousness

As noted in Chapter 1, instrumental reason (IR) is goal-oriented reason. It draws upon those parts of the human mind that follow clearly laid-down rules in order to carry out certain kinds of tasks. Reason is one of the greatest human and cultural achievements. It allows us to learn from experience and to perform a very wide range of mental and physical operations upon each other and the world. Using reason we transform the chaos and contradictions of sensory experience into rules, procedures, laws and devices of great technical sophistication and practical power.

The entire edifice of science and technology has been built with the power of IR. It is the cognitive force behind the industrial era. The scientific experiment is the heart, the powerhouse, of IR. The wealth of instrumental knowledge that supports our civilisation has poured forth from its steadily reproducible rhythm.

Our difficulties with IR stem from the fact that it has certain features which must be kept in check and not generalised into other domains. One key problem is that while IR provides us with very powerful tools (means), it can say little or nothing about the purposes (ends) those tools can serve. Another is the constant danger of reductionism: of saying that something is only this or that, when in fact it is much more. Reductionism rears its head when something cannot be measured, and that something is assumed not to be important, or worse, not to exist.

The sheer practical power of IR, and the range of enabling devices it has helped to create, have made other aspects of human life and culture seem less important. Indeed, IR has been 'read upon' domains (such as spirituality and myth) where it has very little explanatory power at all. The end result of this long process of cultural imperialism has been that we are rich in means, but poor in ends. An industrialised culture is one which has exaggerated the role of IR and thereby created for itself a one-sided view of the world. Without other countervailing principles, IR expands to take over the whole world, thereby providing fertile ground for the now-familiar technocratic nightmares.

On the other hand, participating consciousness (PC) is not instrumental or goal-oriented. It draws on our capacity for empathy and awareness. It is not precise and cannot be measured. It breaches the boundary of I and other. But this is not done by pretending that differences are illusory. Rather, boundaries are seen as provisional and permeable. Self and not-self do not exhaust all available categories. Some categories (and their boundaries) overlap. This means that a range of modes of awareness are possible. These modes are not in the making and doing field at all, but in the common process of knowing and being.

PC identifies elements of self in its environment. It perceives an unending flow of interactions between an extended self and its broad, long-term environment. These interactions occur in various ways: through physical structures, body functions, energies, symbolic exchanges and so on. What emerges from all this is a sense of a larger self; a self which merges into the environment and also extends into past and future. It is an involved self which contrasts plainly with the model of the uninvolved scientist 'objectively' operating upon nature.

A strong experience of PC has many powerful consequences. Among them are that it permits the direct experience of intrinsic value in nature (see below). This perception is pivotal. For it means that nature is no longer of value only for use or for exchange. It is seen in a non-instrumental way. If this perception of intrinsic value were to displace existing use- or exchange-oriented notions and become embedded in the foundations of our culture, the whole edifice would change. The qualities of participation support a responsible ethical stance toward the rest of the world. Empathy merges into responsibility, and this into a notion of service and pursuit of the higher good. PC therefore stands as a contrast to IR, and to some extent, a countervailing force. However, the two modes should not be seen in simple opposition.

The way forward is not simply to reject instrumental rationality, empiricism or technology in any simple-minded way but, rather, to situate each of them in their wider context. This sounds reasonable enough but the suggestion therein is radical. It is that rather than approaching knowledge in the usual narrow ways – through subjects, disciplines and specialities – we look for ways of beginning from this wider, broader context in space and time. There is, perhaps, no better way to start than with the search for new worldview commitments. Fortunately, there are many available options.

New, or renewed worldview commitments

Developing a Global, Systemic View

The present lack of systems consciousness is one of the greatest dangers to the future of this planet. Without it we cannot comprehend the consequences of our actions, nor anticipate their effects. Global thinking is the smallest frame within which to view human affairs. Anything less lacks the capacity to deal with the interconnectedness and systemicity that characterise the global system.

Such a view would not have been possible a few short years ago. But with the development of ecological, systemic and holistic perspectives it has rapidly become practicable. Furthermore, at the (admittedly low) level of data (as distinct from knowledge or wisdom) such a view is technically supportable. As suggested in Chapter 5, every classroom and home could have access to remote sensing via satellite on a real-time basis. That this has not yet happened is a consequence of the way that the agendas for info-tech (IT) have been subverted by vested interests and obsolete frameworks of understanding. As in so many other areas, a highly sophisticated technical capacity exists but the consciousness directing it remains preoccupied with power and control.

It is not merely that the nation state in its monolithic form is obsolete. As argued in Chapter 2, many of the institutions and power structures which took shape in the industrial era are reaching the end of their useful lives. Yet they persist in enforcing and sustaining radically limited interests rather than universal ones. The systematic application of merchandising recommends the misleading strategy of self-absorption to millions, and millions have believed it. The dynamic and imperative so created owe nothing to a fragile, interconnected world and everything to the abstracted nullities of money, profit and power. This is a system which feeds upon itself, devours its own children and is parasitic upon the shared foundations of life. Yet, properly understood, it also offers a powerful stimulus for rising above the compulsive escapism of cultures in crisis.

Many technical fixes have been put forward for dealing with social and ecological breakdown. But the lack of global systems consciousness cannot be rectified merely by installing computers and fine-tuning the economy. The answer to television is not media education but a recovery of human identity and purpose. The most significant step toward global consciousness would be a qualitative shift in human thinking beyond the present limitations of mental/egoic life to more universal concerns which are both global and long-term. A full flowering of global systems consciousness would require a combination of technical skill and highly advanced human motives.

Taking a broader view of time

I have written above about the drawbacks of Western linear time: its unidirectionality, narrowness and fractured, unlivable present. The whole edifice of this notion of time reflects an obsession with measurement, the empiricist's particular conceit. If empiricism and measurement were merely to occupy their legitimate place in the overall scheme (at the level of rationality and technical operations) there would not be a problem. But since they have become universalised, their correspondingly underdimensioned epistemology has been read upon the whole world, not least of all through time.

But Western linear time cannot represent, model or sustain for us the rootedness of our origins in the past, our very broad cultural present or our deep participation in many of the structural continuities of the future. It overlooks the fact that a globally-distributed culture equipped with powerful technologies already occupies a very broad span of space/ time. The dislocation between existing structures and processes and their conventional representations places severe limits upon the coherence of the Western worldview. It serves to sanction and obscure the unabated assault upon the planet's ecology and resource base. That is partly why we are now receiving such uncompromisingly powerful messages from the global environment.

In the heady years of post-war expansion it suited the powerful to sponsor an ideology which harked back to the past for its inspiration and rationale. But in present conditions it is very clear that we require credible models, coherent visions of a wide variety of futures in order to guide our choices in the present. There is a very large gap between the frequently mentioned 'speed of change' and the imaginative capacity to articulate credible future alternatives. However, the more careful use of time-frames would do much to overcome this limitation.

Time-frames are distinct periods of time, some of which can be associated with certain human activities. However, periods measured in, say nanoseconds, fall below perceptual thresholds, and geological millennia exceed our usual requirements by orders of magnitude. For most human purposes time-frames range between seconds and years. For each human activity there is an appropriate time-frame. Driving a car or typing each require a very short one (seconds or less). Listening to music typically requires a longer one (minutes to hours). Taking a course may extend over a year. Raising children obviously takes many years.

At a cultural level time-frames vary. However, for planning purposes, they seem to range between one year and perhaps five years. Typically, in politics a year is regarded as a very long time, and the ultimate time-frame is the next election. Yet human activities have implications which extend over millennia. Two test cases are the extinction of species through human action, and the creation, use and storage of fissile materials such as plutonium (which has a 'half-life' of 250,000 years). Such examples suggest that some time-frames have a 'default' status which may be mismatched with the activity in question. This is certainly the case with most major institutions which tend to regard the past as authoritative and discount the future.

It is tempting here to suggest that time-frames should just be extended. But that is too simple. The point is, can particular time-frames be matched with certain activities? For the purposes of social policy, economics and education, for example, there is a case for establishing a more extended time-frame (but not one which is unmanageable). The two-hundred year present may represent a more adequate 'default' standard for broad cultural purposes than the one-to-five-year plans now in evidence (see Figure 9.2). If the areas just mentioned were to reflect both halves of this period then the frame of reference would shift accordingly. This would be a major achievement.

However, the underlying point is more subtle. While, in general, some activities need to be matched with longer time-frames (so as to cover impacts, implications, responsibilities, etc.) the more important shift is toward the conscious use of time-frames. The study of human cultures in time lags far behind their study in space. Yet the interaction of temporal process with culture is a fascinating field of study with important implications for the organisation and pacing of human affairs.

By opening up the futures dimension beyond the technical/instrumental imperatives of forecasting and planning, humans can move out of the isolation and alienation of the minimal present and create 'a space in time' to re-negotiate futures worth living in. Within a wider, extended present there arise many possibilities that invite criticism, selection, reconceptualisation and choice. In this way the perceptual field may be extended such that we do not need to experience catastrophe before we act to prevent it. Once again, this corresponds to a shift in consciousness toward higher, more inclusive levels.

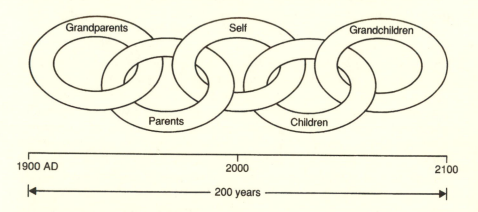

Figure 9.2 The 200-year Present

Recovering a sense of the future

Many cultures have, and have had, a clearly-articulated relationship to the future. Yet the cultural editing of most contemporary Western cultures has had two contradictory effects. As noted, it has mis-represented the futures dimension as a kind of empty space, an abstraction, which is not worthy of serious attention. (That is one reason why school curricula embody so many references to the past, but so few to the future.) In addition, two very different types of futures images have become current in late industrial cultures. One is the optimistic, high-tech, machine-dominated version which is found on popular TV and in young people's books. The other is the dark vision of dystopia, of decline, decay and eventual destruction.

Now while it may be true that both represent real alternatives, with roots in aspects of the present, neither begin to do justice to the much wider range of options and possibilities that lie ahead. Activating a developed sense of the latter has therefore become very important. How may this be done? Futures concepts and ideas are of enormous import-ance here. As suggested in Chapter 6, speculative fiction also has a major role to play. Many novels and short stories serve to elaborate futures potentials – that is, to illuminate futures and aspects of futures that tend to be inaccessible to reason in general or 'hard-headed' (i.e. empirical/ analytical) futures research in particular. A working familiarity with this literature demonstrates, as perhaps no other source can, that the idea of the future as 'empty space' is not valid. On the contrary, many futures-related stories actually demonstrate the wider range of options, dangers and possibilities that lie ahead. Instead of remaining an abstraction, the imaginative and intellectual space of the future begins to coalesce around a variety of themes, scenarios and lines of development.

Why Futures Perspectives Are Essential

A rationale is outlined below for reintegrating futures perspectives into daily life and culture.

- Decisions have long-term consequences
- Future alternatives imply present choices
- Forward thinking is preferable to crisis management
- Further transformations are certain to occur

Repairing the damage, reducing risk

Given the enormous costs which the industrial system has exacted upon the world, repairing the damage has become a major imperative. There are very many areas and ecosystems which have been completely destroyed. Others have been severely compromised; entire species of plants and animals have been lost. This dynamic of destruction must be replaced with a new dynamic of restoration. Hence there is scope for a series of new professions to develop from the confluence of ecological science and environmental activism.

Beyond this there is a dawning possibility that humans may, in some sense, be able to 'reinvent nature'. Of course, this instantly recalls the notion of hubris, or unjustified pride. But in a different cultural context, i.e., one which had re-established a sense of the sacred and developed a strong stewardship ethic, it is conceivable that one part of nature (humans) could act with other parts (animals, plants, ecosystems) to create new patterns of life. If habitats can be recovered and restored there may be no reason why future humans should not reanimate extinct species, adapt existing species (as is now being done with many crops and transgenic transfers) and invent new ones. When guided by a higher ethic humans might actually improve upon what nature has achieved blindly.

However, for any of this to happen, and to be viable, the present serious risk factors would need to be reduced or eliminated: stocks of nuclear weapons, military action, overpopulation, further deterioration of ecosystems and genetic pools. Resolving these is a *sine qua non* of a viable future. Systematic foresight will be needed to establish the dimensions of opportunity and risk involved.

Creating sustainable economies

This will not be easy, but in a sense it could be inevitable because a non-sustainable economy is just that. However, there are many contradictions to resolve. Advertising, consumerism, materialism, competitive individualism and the pursuit of old-style growth all make it difficult to embark on the transition.

Growth will need to be redefined. Resources will need to be revalued and seen in their wider context. The environment will need to be brought fully into all economic calculations instead of being dismissed as a mere 'externality.' Energy will need to be conserved and used much more efficiently. At a deeper level, the ideologies and power systems which drive the technocratic machine will have to be challenged and replaced. Similarly, the time-frames which are applied to human economic life will need to be re-assessed. Most importantly, it will be necessary to reverse the chronic short-term thinking now common in business, government, industry and education.

It is important that such developments are seen together: a critique of industrial era economics, the rise of a different time sense and the implementation of a range of conserving measures and practices all reinforce each other in the longer term.

Finding new purposes and meanings

The purposes and meanings which powered the social system over some two hundred years have created a world of contradictions. The process of selecting new ones will not be easy since powerful groups always have interests bound up in the way things were. Yet the de-legitimisation of redundant social principles and practices is overdue. This is a major focus of critical futures work. As shown above, it begins with the critique of what is wrong, redundant, no long helpful in contemporary cultures. It proceeds to develop alternative ways of knowing and being. These alternatives thrive upon new purposes and meanings, examples of which have been given above. I want here to touch on three more: stewardship, selfless love, and obligations to future generations.

A stewardship ethic could well be a motivating force in the establishment of new intentional communities which will spring up in formerly ravaged areas. Such communities are likely to differ from the communes of the 1960s. For example, they will be much more sophisticated, both technically and culturally, and they will exist to repair landscapes and reinvigorate ecosystems. They may be regarded as part of a common shift toward long-term responsibility for the well-being of the earth.

Selfless love may be part of a shift away from the me-ness and materialism of the 20th century. It reflects an established trend from outer-directedness to inner-directness, or, from having to being. This is an important distinction. The having mode is insecure, needing constant reassurance and material inputs. On the contrary, the being mode is self-sufficient. It is centred in 'that which is' and sees the material realm as only one among others.

Obligations to future generations are likely to emerge as a new (or renewed) social/cultural concern. Humans will no longer see themselves as cut off from past and future, but as participating in a cosmic process with no discernible beginning or end. In that process the generations are partners in time, each contributing to the overall journey.

Such developments will be supported by changes in worldviews which reveal the interwoven, interconnected, layering of reality. The latter will no longer be seen to reside primarily in material objects and physical powers, but will embrace other domains: emotional, mental and spiritual.

The recovery of intrinsic value

It seems clear that present-day negative views of futures are driven by fairly primitive human instincts which are magnified and augmented by powerful technologies (particularly tools of communication and the mass media). The interaction of an industrial worldview with the political and commercial opportunism of the 20th century has permitted a crass, short-sighted marketing culture to become dominant. Yet it is entirely possible to 'breach the bounds' of present social reality and to imagine a very different world structured according to different values and assumptions. This could be the role of a 'wise culture'. It may not be achieved tomorrow, next year or even next century. What it does do is much more immediate and practical. It creates a contrast which, like the best speculative fiction, de-familiarises the present, makes it seem strange (i.e. historically contingent). A compelling vision therefore appears which transcends the catastrophic futures endemic to technocratic scenarios.

How can one define a wise culture? This is discussed in Chapter 10. The actual details are less important than the quality of consciousness which they evoke, for it is this which is arguably the pivot, rather than the technical or other means by which it is expressed. Nor need this quality be wholly displaced into future time. The startling thing is that people have always been capable of it. Today one such person may be **Thomas Berry**. His *The Dream of the Earth* seems to presage exactly the kind of shifts outlined here. He points towards a 'new sense of reality and value' which, perhaps, is one of the keys to a new historical dynamic. The new sense turns not on the intellectualisation of experience, and still less upon the reductionist interrogation of nature by naturalistic science; but rather upon the direct experience of intrinsic value. This stands in stark contrast to use-value and exchange-value which still remain core assumptions of the late industrial era. Imaging workshops which can bring participants to this point in living experience are clearly promoting social change at a very profound level.

Intrinsic value gives back to the earth, its wildlife and ecology the right to independent existence, regardless of the needs or uses of human kind. In this way, nature can be reconstituted at the heart of the social order.

Towards a new world view

As noted above, the way we see the world dictates the way we use it. So the commitments embedded in the foundations of industrial culture can be examined and, where necessary, transformed or discarded. A renewed worldview will retain much that is good and useful from earlier times. It will retain notions of justice, equity and so on. But it will also include other elements such as sustainability, stewardship and a global, long-term view. Such developments are not immediately obvious because they are not tangible and visible. It takes time to understand them and to feel empowered to address them. However they are powerful tools in the re-shaping of the epistemological, and hence the cultural, order.

The foregoing supports a view of the world in which we recognise our embeddedness in a series of contexts. We begin to see only too clearly that our understanding of reality is dependent upon the quality of the models used and the quality of consciousness using the models. Problem solving is no longer about making small, isolated changes. It is about participation and intervention in mutually-interacting webs and processes. In this sense, solutions tend not to be 'right', but elegant. As ever, the threads which create the world lead back to us.

The final Chapter suggests that such a culture can arise in part from the inner dynamic of higher-order human capacities, founded on wisdom. But we must also bear in mind the limitations noted above. The fact is, no one knows in detail how we might move from one culture to another. What follows on from industrialism cannot be specified fully in advance. But that is by no means the end of the story.

What is certain is that if the human race is to survive in a world worth living in, a world rich in other life forms, rich in resources, rich in human and non-human options, then it will be with a culture based on assumptions very different than those now operating. So, finally, we turn to the outlines of the new. What would a wise culture be like?

CHAPTER 10

Towards a Wise Culture

The idea of a wise culture is not a simple one. From within the confines of late industrialism it may seem impossibly distant. Yet stepping stones to this future certainly exist. Three are discussed below. First, the transpersonal perspective offers us a distinctive way of looking at human development and human futures. Second, 'Homo Gestalt' provides a model of a more advanced human. Third, a revised map of knowledge may open out quite new, or at least hitherto untried, options. Finally, the question of how wisdom may be developed and nurtured is addressed.

There are several grounds for using the notion of a wise culture in a futures context. First, it supplies a rationale and, to some extent, a method for transcending (literally 'going beyond') the conflicts of late industrial culture and establishing a different dynamic for cultural development. Second, it represents a humanly-compelling goal to aim at. The goal is quintessentially one of human and social development. As such it may begin to correct the present imbalance between these and our presently one-sided preoccupation with technical change. The loss of balance between the human world and the technical one represents a continuing threat to all cultures. Third, the exploration of human possibilities at the peak of knowledge and experience reveals options for the future which are impossible to reach from within an industrial worldview. Finally, if a compelling view of a wise culture can be developed, it may become a guiding image which positively encourages moves in that direction.

There is a regrettable tendency to label eras with instrumental titles like 'the industrial age' or 'the information age' – as if these technical terms identified the essence of a period. But this is not necessarily the case. Why should technology or economics dominate an entire era? Why not use some desirable human quality instead? What might a culture be like which aspired towards a real, substantive and applied wisdom? The question can be approached through Figure 10.1.

In this account, DATA is raw information. It could be any statistic or fact, but these are meaningless without a context. INFORMATION includes data and indicates what category the data refers to. However, note that MISINFORMATION can occur when information is filed in the wrong category or when individuals or groups deliberately use information to mislead. KNOWLEDGE is created from information and data. It draws on values and traditions to create humanly significant meaning from patterns, relationships and accumulated judgements. Finally,

WISDOM is the process and the product of searching for higher-order meaning and purpose. Wisdom goes beyond the instrumental questions of 'how?' to consider 'why?' Hence, data, information and knowledge can be seen, not as ends in themselves, but as stages on the path towards wisdom.

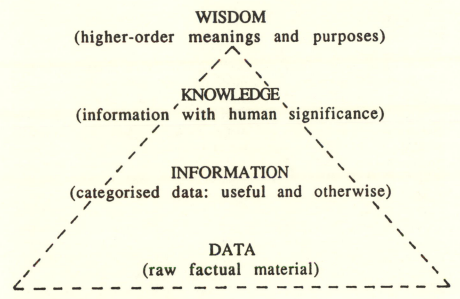

Figure 10.1 A hierarchy of knowledge

So what might a wise culture be like? Figure 10.2 gives one possible overview. Note that if one assumes the highest motives possible (instead of the basest) then many existing problems and dilemmas seem to vanish. This clearly suggests that the consequences of a vertical shift of consciousness can be intensely practical. However, it is a long-term process. The reality of a wise culture could well take many centuries to achieve. But, in the meantime it has enormous present-day value as a goal, a direction and a powerfully suggestive contrast to cultures which have become over-committed to rationality and technology.

Figure 10.2 Aspects of a wise culture

- Vivid understanding of common humanity
- Move beyond roles based on race, gender, etc.
- Local differences set in context of universals
- All people and religions seen as one in spirit
- Balanced use of rationality and intuition

- Higher motivations reshape economic life
- Methods and institutions to foster growth of consciousness
- Education as a discipline in transcendence
- Technology as aid to transcendence, not substitute
- Governance depends upon mastery of the system at each level: body/mind/soul/spirit

Source: K. Wilber, *Up From Eden: A Transpersonal View of Human Evolution* (London, UK, RKP, 1983).

To reproduce such a list risks trivialising the underlying perspective. But nothing could be further from the truth. Take the first four items. A view of the world which assumes a common humanity, discards many ascribed roles, sees differences united in a higher-order unity and regards all peoples and religions as essentially one in spirit – such a view has wide cultural implications. For example, there would be a huge reduction in endemic violence and aggression. The time, energy and resources which are needed to create and sustain modern armed forces would be greatly reduced. The balanced use of rationality and intuition would provide a more capable, flexible outlook that facilitated a fluid and easy movement across different ways and levels of knowing.

The idea that higher motivations could affect economic life is a proposition that still lies outside conventional political and economic discourse. Yet stewardship, loving kindness and what has been called an ethic of 'enoughness' provide some of the most potent solutions to the problems of material growth and a real stimulus to sustainability. Similarly, the notion that societies might deliberately create specific places where consciousness itself was the substantive focus of concern may seem radical or outlandish. Yet what better antidote can there be to anxiety and fear? Current strategies of distraction via the entertainment industry clearly do not work. They are only a holding operation. To see education not merely in terms of cognitive development, but also as a discipline in transcendence, opens up the prospect of reintegrating the arts of contemplation into educational theory and practice. These are not trivial options.

In this perspective technology is not seen as a major determinant of the present or the future. When used at all it is bent to some higher purpose. Similarly the arts of governance are seen in a quite different light – that is, in terms of the mastery of the human system at each major level. Even to put this as a theoretical proposal affects the nature of the political debate and implicitly critiques the usual criteria for selection of politicians. Yet, as discussed in Chapter 5, a new generation of politicians is needed. Whatever else they may offer, it begins to seem as if a strong ethical commitment is a minimum qualification.

It may be that a wise culture, or something very like it, represents the only long-term solution to the cultural dilemmas discussed throughout this book. For it will take the higher-order imperatives of true wisdom to repair the earth, reconceptualise the relations between people, and create a new balance between people and nature. It will take such wisdom to look beyond the instrumental imperatives of faster . . . further away . . . bigger . . . more.

A culture inspired by the 'Perennial Tradition' (i.e., the universal spiritual heritage of humankind) would neither be flat nor boring. It would be resonant with a vibrant new outlook fully capable of articulating new meanings and purposes. This, perhaps, is the nearest we can approach to 'solving' the human predicament. But such a view does have major consequences. For example, it means that our pre-occupation with tools and technologies may be diverting our attention from more vital possibilities. It also suggests that the present preoccupation with information industries and systems may well be more of a passing phase than a lasting solution. Without being guided by higher-order ethical norms, information societies will remain crippled by some of the defective programming they have inherited from the industrial era.

The transpersonal perspective, 'homo gestalt' and a new map of knowledge

One of the most persistent themes in the futures literature is the struggle between human intentions and the abstract imperatives which arise from technical systems. Yet as I suggested in Chapter 2, the issue is badly fudged in education and the mass media (particularly in young people's media dealing with futures). Similarly, Chapter 1 argued that Western culture adopted an instrumental, use-oriented view of the world which bestowed a special status upon the products of science and technology. It marginalised religion and permitted technical systems to impose their own dynamic upon human cultures and the natural environment. Over 200 years the world was transformed. People (in the West) became healthier and lived longer. But their underlying make-up changed little. So it became easy to see the historical imperative drifting away from people and steadily becoming invested in the products of human ability and intelligence.

From this point on it is but a small step to seeing people as relatively powerless servants (or even victims) of an infinitely more powerful social/technical system. This creates a genuinely depressing outlook. As we have seen, the futures which then arise are wholly dystopian in character. However, the fact remains that a future dominated by technical systems is not a future for humans. So there is a very great need to locate a counter-dynamic to compulsive technical innovation and development. The transpersonal perspective may provide this or, at least, point us in the right direction.

The transpersonal perspective

Belief in the isolation and separateness of individual human selves is a very persistent Western myth. In this view personal identity ends at the surface of the skin which encapsulates a single, unitary being. Yet skin-as-boundary sanctions a wide range of self-centred, exploitive values and behaviours which have plagued the history of the species. A more productive view suggests that the surface of the skin is simply a line, and not a boundary at all. Discussions of what may be termed 'the biodance' reveals some of the interactions between individuals and the wider environment: flows of food, energy, oxygen and relationship in many dimensions. Close regard for these connections reveals our immersion in a diverse web of being.

The record of sages and mystics from many cultures shows that this underlying 'oneness' need not be merely deduced. It can be directly experienced. The path to transcendent awareness is not particularly easy to achieve but it is a true and direct one. The recognition that there is a path and a means of liberation from technocracy lends the notion a compelling edge.

Humanistic psychology represented an advance over behaviourism and psychoanalysis. Its major concern is less with repression and control than with the whole and healthful personality. But towards the end of his life, Abraham Maslow looked beyond humanistic concerns to a small minority of individuals who had passed beyond self-realisation to self-transcendence. That is, they had passed beyond personal and egoistic concerns to universal and transpersonal ones. They tended to: 'think in terms of planetary humankind ... transcend the dichotomy between selfishness and unselfishness ... be innovators, discovers of the new ... shun luxury, possessions, honour and privilege'.

The study of transpersonal phenomena is of major interest because it opens out human options for development and change that cannot be readily articulated within the confines of a technocratic world view. It provides a basis for renegotiating accepted views of the cultural past and also for making the imaginative leap toward wholly 'other' futures. **Ken Wilber** is an exponent of this approach and his works provide essential background. In *Up From Eden* he takes the view that history may be understood as 'a slow and tortuous path to transcendence'.

Wilber traces the historical emergence of the ego from the undifferentiated 'ground unconscious' of nature up to the present mental/egoic stage. At each level he distinguishes typical preoccupations which are seen in the cultural record of the period. The scheme is elegant and suggestive. For in venturing beyond the mental/egoic it sketches in a framework for human (as opposed to technical) development and aspiration. While the earlier stages operated according to subhuman, subcon-

Figure 10.3 The great chain of being

Unity Consciousness

Spirit	Ultimate Causal	Super- consciousness (transpersonal)
Soul	Subtle Psychic	Self-consciousness (personal)
Advanced mind	(rational, mental- egoic, reflexive)	
Early mind	(verbal, mythic, social)	
Body	(higher bodily forms, magical)	Subconsciousness (pre-personal)
Nature	(physical nature and lower life)	

Source: K. Wilber, *Up From Eden: A Transpersonal View of Human Evolution* (London, UK, RKP, 1983).

scious and prepersonal impulses, the higher stages may be characterised by spiritual and transpersonal concerns. The evidence here comes both from the self-transcending individuals studied by Maslow and others and from the traditions that were summarised in **Aldous Huxley**'s now-classic work, *The Perennial Philosophy*. This evidence is interpreted to represent the 'growing tip' of human ability and awareness.

It is important to note that this does not usher in the millennium. Wilber cautions against 'New Age enthusiasm' and points out that since it took 'a terrible 15 billion years' to reach the present stage, the millennium is unlikely to occur tomorrow or next year. Levels of consciousness beyond the mental/egoic can certainly be achieved now but may not be widely attained for decades or even centuries. However, understood as contributing to a view of humanly compelling futures, they are of immediate interest and value.

Wilber's characterisation of 'The Great Chain of Being' provides a general framework of wide practical utility (Figure 10.3). In this view, the whole thrust of human development is up and out of undifferentiated oneness with nature toward states of clarity and integration fore-shadowed by great spiritual leaders. Just to begin to think of the future in terms of subtle awareness, causal insight and ultimate identity (with the Source, Atman, That Which Is) is to radically alter the terms of the debate. Again, the stage of 'psychic intuition' is characterised as 'the beginning of transcendent openness and clarity, the awakening of a sense of awareness that is somehow more than simple mind and body'.

Openness . . . clarity . . . awareness. Such terms indicate qualities and powers which have hardly figured in present-day debates about futures. To begin to place them at the very centre of our future vision is to shift the focus of concern away from technocratic narrowness to the

Figure 10.4 Aspects of *homo gestalt*

- More advanced mode of consciousness: wisdom, sagacity, awareness, wakefulness, playfulness
- Non stimulus-bound, prolonged maturation, abstract in view, flexible and reflexive
- Global abstract thought, freedom from fixed, limited view and fixed ego
- Routine experience of void consciousness
- Restructuring of own system to operate in new sensory modes
- Transcendence of ego identity and thus also of destructive activity associated with fear of death
- Attainment of full systems consciousness
- Rapid and easy alternation between incoming information and projections
- Full and easy access to intuitive knowledge (Gnosis)
- A more refined set of feelings
- An ever-widening and spiralling of consciousness
- Movement beyond gender identity toward androgyny
- Dissolution of partitions in the being and the growth of love

Source: Laughlin, C. and Richardson, S., 'The Future of Human Consciousness', *Futures* 17, 3, 1986, 401-409.

constitution of significance in a wider and essentially human world. This places within imaginative grasp the means to reverse the ancient reversal. That is, to de-centre the machine and the technocrat, thereby returning to individuals and groups options that had seemed to be lost forever.

Homo Gestalt

This term was coined by two researchers who wanted to create a model of a possible future human along these lines. Charles Laughlin and Sheila Richardson provide a fascinating view of possible future developments. It is a vision not merely of what we can have, but what we may be. Figure 10.4 lists some of the possible attributes of 'Homo Gestalt'.

What Laughlin and Richardson have envisaged is a being in full control of perceptual and cognitive processes; one that is able to tap into and use quite new functional modes of operation. For example, the routine experience of void consciousness would illuminate intrinsic value not as an esoteric theory, but as a living reality. Similarly, full systems consciousness would eliminate learning lags and ensure that local phenomena would be experienced as dynamically 'nested' in the global context. Such capacities would not only permit individuals to engage more fully in the present, but to profoundly empathise with past and future alike. The seeds of alternative futures would be as real and substantial as the roots of the past. Such a being would clearly have left behind low level motives such as fear and anger, would transcend gender and would place much less emphasis on technology and external manipulation of the world.

Indeed, what we call 'inner' and 'outer' would fuse into a rich and fascinating tapestry of unfolding meaning.

Such visions are perhaps a little daunting, in part because of the implicit challenge they offer to our own ego-based identities. Yet they are also of immense value in offering an alternative to the more usual preoccupation with technical evolution and development. They represent a significant departure from the stale conventionalism of much cultural thinking and can begin to inform necessary shifts in theory and practice in many fields: shifts from past to future, from quantitative growth to qualitative growth, from technology to human evolution. From this perspective, western cultures are in a state of continuing crisis not primarily because of commercial greed, not because they are ungovernable, and not merely because of technologies or patterns of social organisation, important as these may be. Explanations of this kind only supply part of the answer. The crisis arises most profoundly from inadequate ways of knowing and the consequent confusions between different integrative levels of existence; that is from reductionist epistemologies and category errors. That is essentially why we have reached the era of 'irreversible effects' in which social learning takes place in a context of severe ecological and climatic change. Here is the most profound source, or origin, of the global problematique and the source of every durable solution.

Many are becoming aware of the fractured and incoherent character of the Western worldview. Fewer are aware that the mere extension of present trends leads on to futures few would wish to live in. But what the transpersonal perspective in general, and Homo Gestalt in particular suggest, is that where the simplifications of the industrial outlook end, exactly there, a whole new world of significance begins. This alters the whole aspect (or prospect) of the future. It means that instead of being dark and depressing, there is something to look forward to. Metaphorically-speaking, there is 'light at the end of the tunnel'. Moreover, there are maps to help us reach it.

A broader map of knowledge

Implicit in the above is the view that our ways of constructing the world are deeply implicated in our misuse of it and hence underlie all the threats to our common futures. So this section considers a model which holds out more optimistic alternatives.

As suggested above, Ken Wilber has probably done as much as anyone to re-establish the grounds for a comprehensive paradigm of knowing and being, and in doing so he has covered an enormous amount of ground by way of developmental psychology, anthropology, consciousness and religion. In each of these areas he found evidence of hierarchical structures and distinct levels or ways of knowing. His simplest account has three main levels.

Figure 10.5 A map of knowledge: three ways of knowing

	Realm	Method	Goal
Senses (Body)	Nature	Number	Empirical fact (science)
Reason (Mind)	History	Theory	Philos. & psych. insight
Contemplation (Spirit)	Transcendence	Direct perception	Spiritual wisdom

Source: K. Wilber, *Eye to Eye: The Quest for the New Paradigm* (Anchor, USA, 1989 & 1990).

Wilber takes his lead from St. Bonaventure who distinguished between an eye of flesh ('by which we perceive the external world of space, time, and objects'), an eye of reason ('by which we attain a knowledge of philosophy, logic and the mind itself') and an eye of contemplation ('by which we rise to a knowledge of transcendent realities'). Though the wording of this account is Christian, similar ideas can be found in other schools of psychology, philosophy and religion.

The eye of flesh corresponds to the gross world experienced through the senses. It is an empirical way of knowing of which number is the paradigmatic method and empirical science the product. It operates upon the realm of nature. The eye of reason is more subtle and it corresponds to the inner world of ideas, images, meanings and concepts. This is a way of knowing whose method is theory, whose subject is history and whose goal is philosophical and psychological insight. The eye of contemplation is more subtle still. Its method is direct perception of suchness; its goal is spiritual wisdom and its realm is transcendence. Figure 10.5 illustrates some of these relationships.

Wilber amplifies his schema into three modes of knowing. He calls the data dealt with in the three modes sensibilia, intelligibilia, and transcendelia. It is worth considering them in more detail. Sensibilia is that familiar zone in which science has traditionally operated. This domain deals with sensory experience. Its raw material is empirical data, observed and analysed by means of the scientific method. The knowledge derived from this domain we recognise as the 'hard sciences'. The mode of inquiry in this domain is a monologue. It requires only the detached observer, collecting data alone and subjecting them to rigorous, rational analysis. Verification is essentially instrumental; if the theory 'works', then it is valid.

Intelligibilia is of a different order from sensibilia. In this domain, the relevant phenomena are thoughts as they display themselves to the inward mental eye. The raw materials are therefore reported, for they cannot be physically observed by someone else as is the case with sensibilia. Thus the mode of inquiry is mental and phenomenological (an experience which is related and described). The domain deals with the analysis of one's thought processes, with symbols (things or experiences which carry deeper meanings), with language and linguistics. Intelligibilia therefore give rise to the disciplines of philosophy, psychology, and history. Knowledge processing within this domain is clinical (rather than empirical). Importantly too, the mode of inquiry requires dialogue (where sensibilia rest upon monologue). In order to come to terms with the data, the one experiencing them has to discuss them with another person; there is no other way to make the data accessible. Thus the mode requires communication and interaction (where sensibilia required only detached observation, documenting what one 'sees'). The verification is intuitive, a coherence born of congruent interpretation.

Transcendelia occupy a domain which has been acknowledged by countless generations of human beings who testify to deeper perceptions and experiences which cannot be encompassed either by the senses or by reason. In this domain the mode of inquiry is meditative or contemplative. Data are derived from 'transcendental perception' which 'cannot be perceived with the mental or the sensory eyes'. Included in this domain are experiences described as religious, spiritual, or mythological, the perceptions which come from 'altered states of consciousness'. This area, then, is open only to those who have learned to comprehend the data. Interestingly, however, the data are verifiable, for they are communal, shared, repeatable. The saints of all ages and all cultures tend to speak a similar language, attesting to a commonality of experience. While recognising the inadequacy of language to describe the sublime, they fall back on the same imagery, the same symbols, the same archetypes, which Wilber, Campbell and others believe constitute 'a sound and valid transcendental methodology'.

Wilber's analysis here is very useful, for he clarifies the problem of 'category errors'. In other words, there is consistency and logic in each domain; each has its own mode of operation and inquiry; each has aspects that are appropriate to that domain and to it alone. A major problem arises when we try to extract inappropriate data from the wrong domain, or when we apply the methods of inquiry and analysis from one domain to another domain. Several points stand out here. The first is that contemplation cannot be reduced to reason, nor reason to the senses. Each is ontologically distinct. To take the lower for the higher is to commit a category error. To put it differently, the truth of ideas cannot be seen by the senses, the reality of direct perception cannot be 'seen' by reason – or as Wilber puts it, 'sensation, reason and contemplation disclose their own truths in their own realms and any time one eye tries to see for another eye, blurred vision results'.

There could not be a more concise critique of industrialised culture than this, for such a culture, based on the simplifications of the Newtonian synthesis, validates number and theory and discounts direct perception. It commits a double category error and obscures the most crucial area for future development. This goes a long way toward explaining why the culture has lost its coherence and why many attempted solutions to problems do not work. As noted above, there are very often no effective solutions at the level at which they are experienced. It is often only by understanding the broader structure and the creative potential within the problem or conflict that a conscious decision can be made to transcend the level upon which the problem first manifests.

Taken together, writers in this tradition establish a strong case for re-establishing the qualitative dimension of human experience. Here, then, are the makings of a different outlook. It is one which:

- provides an explicit basis for superseding reductionism;
- provides a constructive framework from which to address the underlying sources of global problems;
- suggests a way to examine the taken-for-granted and to move to a more fluid, open and inclusive awareness;
- explains why many phenomena appear mysterious in their original terms (since higher integrative levels tend to appear mysterious or paradoxical in the language and view of the lower) and therefore are not addressed;
- helps us recognise the positive potential within conflict and crisis; and
- reveals how the future options for western societies can be inspired by shifts toward higher levels of integration and consciousness.

This outline does not negate empiricism, rationality or measurement. What it does show is that it is unnecessary to be limited to these ways of knowing. Beyond this, it provides access to a much wider range of human knowledge and experience.

Much conflict and confusion has been created in Western culture by our failing to distinguish between different levels of existence. Numerous false solutions have thrived on the resulting contradictions. For example, if I am ill at ease, it is pointless to engage in an outer, sense-based, activity such as buying something, eating something or diverting myself by passively watching TV. Instead, what I may need to do is to attend to the inner life and discover how to manage the system from the highest level I can reach. Similarly, if I feel threatened by someone, I am missing the point if I respond by designing and building weapons systems to create a counter threat. Such responses developed during pre-history and they continue to threaten our present and future. They need to be understood, worked through and discarded, along with the insane weapons they have spawned.

This map of knowledge can certainly be elaborated. But even in this simple form it helps to explain why, at first sight, there are often no apparent solutions to problems. A problem at the level of the senses may be genuinely irresolvable. However, a shift to reason or to contemplation may reveal answers via informed insight or spiritual wisdom. Similarly, a problem at the level of reason and argument may seem to have no clear answer. Yet the exercise of a higher motive (such as selflessness or compassion) may provide the grounds for a genuine resolution. In other words, problems that cannot be solved may, in some cases, be transcended in a higher-order unity. Such are among the practical consequences of higher-order human capacities.

The ability to grasp the particular uses of number, theory and direct perception brings clarity to some vexed issues. For example, it allows us to maintain some critical distinctions between machines and people. At present the former may be said to 'belong' to that part of the universe accessible through number and instrumental reason. So long as this remains true, there are strong ontological grounds for seeing machines as inferior and derivative entities (however 'intelligent' they may appear). Again, the academic world is replete with theories and intellectual activity. Yet much of this may be barren, unhelpful or beside the point if not illuminated by truths available through contemplation. Many university professors would shudder at the thought. But this may be an indication of how far the universities are lagging behind the reality of a differentiated, re-enchanted world.

The consequence of this brief discussion is basically straightforward: Western culture is caught up in the confusions and dilemmas of inadequate ways of knowing, of false maps and false solutions. In order to make real progress, the last thing we need is a continuation of compulsive technical dynamism, linked to low-level human impulses (profit, power, aggression, etc.). This only leads to absurd nightmares such as the aptly-titled 'Star Wars' scenario. The most important kind of progress we could make at the present time would be to move out of the sterility and irresolvable conflicts generated by inappropriate, reductionist ways of knowing. That is why the three foci examined here are so helpful.

In summary, the transpersonal perspective provides us with a framework for seeking solutions through human, as opposed to technical, development. The notion of 'Homo Gestalt' is only one of many possible models, but it puts some fascinating detail on what this might involve. Finally, the idea that our inherited maps of knowledge are partly responsible for the present global predicament returns our attention to the nature of the epistemological frame within this culture has developed and thrived. It suggests that we have a great deal of work to do in reconstructing these invisible – but immensely powerful – foundations.

From ideas to practice: developing and nurturing wisdom

Grand theories and schemes of the future are all very well. But how can we move from words on paper to implementing some of the real-world changes that would encourage a wise culture? There is obviously no simple answer to this question. However, the beginnings of answers may be found by considering responses at three levels: individual, institutional and social.

The individual level

Individuals often feel overwhelmed by the scale and complexity of the problems facing them. Yet a careful look at the work of social movements, social innovators, critics of technology, futurists, spiritual leaders and 'leading-edge' thinkers, suggests a different response. It suggests that informed and determined people who are driven by higher-order motives can become very powerful indeed. It seems that the adoption of motives such as stewardship, foresight and service to humanity permits people to transcend many of the earlier limitations of their lives (including ego) and to thereby acquire great cultural and symbolic power. This is the power to de-legitimise (or undermine) aspects of the past that are no longer useful and to articulate or envision aspects of futures that may be pursued in the present.

The most culturally powerful leaders, such as Gandhi, Martin Luther King and the present Dalai Lama, clearly draw immense strength from contemplative knowledge. That is, from direct, inner knowing on a spiritual level. Clearly this requires discipline, application, practice. They use the authority so gained to intervene in processes of meaning-making such as were outlined in Chapter 9. They re-negotiate aspects of social reality and embody this in new social practices, i.e. through social innovations. While few people would aspire to the status of such great leaders, the principles underlying their greatness – and their practical success – can be developed and applied by anyone. So, while no-one should pretend that the route to a wise and far-sighted culture is simple or direct, there are clearly ways forward.

At their simplest, social innovations can be broken down into the stages given above.

1. Get informed about a social problem or need.
2. Research the topic over a period of time.
3. Discuss the early conclusions with a number of advisers.
4. Evolve and present a project or a proposal in an appropriate way.
5. Expect opposition, but if the project/proposal is important, don't give up.

Of course various elaborations can be considered, depending on the context or purpose of the work. For example, in schools, a local example of a successful social innovation can best be illustrated by those who made it happen. The research component can be elaborated in many ways, not least of which is through the futures literature and associated networks. The checking phase is important for young people and should be taken seriously by teachers. Much discussion may be needed to discover just what a proposal should look like, whom to present it to and in what form. Finally, dealing with opposition, learning to move from open conflict to a position of negotiation, clearly involves a whole range of skills. Thus, a grounding in social innovations is a fine way to develop practical and applied wisdom.

Personal wisdom is difficult to define. In part it implies a broad grasp of human affairs past, present and future; profound insight into contemporary life; a familiarity with different forms of knowledge, their uses and limitations; access to motives that transcend ego-based existence and an open, questing spirit that is ever ready to listen and to learn. In the most ethically advanced humans wisdom is softened by humour, modesty and a genuine love for all living beings. Clearly, the sources of such wisdom are many and varied. The study of history, patterns of causation, the role of human actors and the rise and fall of institutions over time provide a sense of the context of human life. Within this context the role of myth, religion and spiritual practice play an important part. It seems that the pursuit of true wisdom invariably involves subjecting oneself to the discipline of an higher-order authority. Hence many wise people tend to have spent some time as an apprentice to one or more great teachers. Others have withdrawn to the wilderness, or to lives of great simplicity in order to pursue the arts of contemplation. In modern times this may not be practical for most people who, nevertheless, can still access the insights of great leaders and teachers through books and other media.

Books have been described as 'the royal road to wisdom' (though clearly book-learning is not enough on its own). Yet they not only give access to the wisdom of the past. They also provide seekers after knowledge with in-depth critiques of technicised cultures. As Chapter 1 suggested, these help to provide a diagnosis of what has gone wrong in the world. Foresight shows very clearly what the implications of 'business-as-usual' are likely to be. So a wise response is to look carefully at the nature of the industrial worldview, to understand its weaknesses and blind spots and then begin the search for a renewed worldview. This is not simply an intellectual matter. It is a spiritual, rational and practical one.

The results are several. First, industrial outlooks, beliefs, forms of knowledge and so on, can be reinterpreted. Second, higher-order purposes and meanings for people, organisations and cultures can be developed. Typically these look beyond personal, material and short-term ends to collective and long-term ones. Third, more advanced models of human and social life can be articulated. Hence, in this view, personal wisdom may emerge from a long-term engagement with these concerns at each of the levels indicated.

The institutional level

Perhaps the key institutions in this book are those directly involved in learning, and the key issues are all related to the nature of the maps of knowledge adopted by a culture. So three institutions are centrally involved in nurturing or inhibiting wisdom: schools, universities and institutions of foresight.

It follows from the above that a map of knowledge is not simply a matter of knowledge content but of the role of different forms of knowing on different levels. At present, schooling addresses the realm of the senses and of the mind. It ignores transcendent knowing, and therefore misses what many have considered to be the most potent sources of insight and inspiration. So a major task for schools seeking to pave the way towards a wise culture would be to broaden the map with regard to forms of knowledge. That is, to look more closely at how different traditions – both East and West – have pursued direct perception. This leads on to the practice and the uses of the arts of contemplation.

But the point is not simply to teach children how to meditate. It is rather to draw insight from such sources to strengthen individuals and prepare them for the work of managing a culture in transition. Thus all the usual rational/intellectual skills are needed, as well as a wide range of practical competencies. All can contribute to the task of envisioning alternative futures and that of creating appropriate, timely social innovations. The primary goal for schooling therefore is to shift the focus from past to future and then to explore a broader map of knowledge in the light of the best available foresight.

Universities could play a substantial part in the transition process. In some ways they could be considered institutions of foresight in their own right. Indeed, some do attempt to do this. However, most are caught up in the narrower business of territorial defence, short-term thinking and economic survival. This is not good enough. University entrance requirements determine secondary curricula and thus exert a strong impact upon what is considered central to the whole educational process. Generally speaking, they are caught up in the process of reproducing an obsolete past. Though the 21st century is only a few years away, there are still very few departments or schools of prospective studies around the world. H. G. Wells complained of this in the 1930s in a radio broadcast entitled 'Wanted: Professors of Foresight'. Yet not much has changed. So how could universities help to support some of the changes discussed here?

In the first place, they could pay a lot more attention to studying the nature of the global transition out of industrialism. Up-to-date knowledge about the state of the global system is needed by everyone, particularly those with responsibility for policy, research and governance. Secondly, they could begin to create departments or schools of prospective studies and give the futures profession some long-overdue support. It should not be merely the servant of business and (occasionally) government. It should be developed and applied in the broad public interest. Third, new ways of representing and communicating complex knowledge should be explored. In part this will involve developments in software, graphics and communications media. Ways are needed of presenting up-to-date insights (not merely information) on a real-time basis to anyone who needs them. Finally, and in general terms, the universities should show a willingness to re-draw the boundaries of knowledge that they have inherited from the industrial era. While there have been many horizontal extensions of existing fields, and indeed, many new sub-fields, the old cultural editing is still very strong. For example, phenomena that are distant, contemplative or related to the future are generally disregarded. These epistemological oversights need to be addressed.

Finally, institutions of foresight were discussed in Chapter 7. The point of them in regard to wisdom is not simply to set up a whole new generation of think-tanks intended to deliver strategic advantage to a few limited constituencies. It is rather to respond to the wider needs of societies in stress and in transition. As I have argued above, particularly in Chapter 7, this requires that attention is drawn to the cultural commitments, values and assumptions – the social 'software' – that serve to drive cultures in particular directions. These directions need to be re-set away from industrial imperatives to ones that tally more closely with the real limits of the Earth and the real needs of its people and other life-forms. This is demanding work. So it will require many more scholars, writers, teachers, media people and so on than are at present employed in these ways.

In many ways institutions of foresight can be 'midwives', helpers at the birth of a new era. Some, such as the Worldwatch Institute and the Network for Future Generations, are already active. But they are not numerous enough and not yet strong enough to carry out a decisive cultural role. These institutions can help to clarify the picture of the near-term future, explain what is at stake and provide access to some of the many options that are presently obscured. By its very nature, foresight contributes to wisdom. Indeed, the two are mutually reinforcing. They draw attention to the wider, long-term world overlooked by empiricism and industrial profiteering. They suggest that we learn to 'steer' our civilisation with far greater insight and skill; indeed, that we re-animate

Figure 10.6 Alternative operating assumptions

	INDUSTRIAL CULTURE	WISDOM CULTURE
Growth	Rapid, and quantitative	Problematic or qualitative
Limits	Non recognised	Re-conceptualised and chosen
Nature	Seen as resources	A community, re-sacralised
Person/Person Person/Nature Relations	Exploitative, exclusive	Reverent, participatory
Present	Fleeting	Extended
Future	Linear, expansionist	Open, varied
Technology	Violent, dominant Destructive	Appropriate, secondary Peaceful

the care and the concern of those earlier cultures that provided a voice for the unborn in all their important councils.

The social level

If a wise culture is to emerge, it will need to do more than simply pass new laws or seek a new view of limits. In time it will need to consider, and then implement, a range of different operating assumptions. Some examples are given below.

Each of the seven areas illustrated in Figure 10.6 represent a challenge and an opportunity to deploy greater wisdom in our collective affairs. The struggle to transform growth-addicted societies into sustainable ones will not be easy. Yet the means are available to reconceptualise growth and rebuild economics on a different basis. Similarly, the nature of global limits will test human ingenuity in countless ways. It is not simply a matter of redesigning the infrastructure but of revising our relationship with the whole natural world. The adoption of a stewardship ethic could play a major role here.

Western notions of time, and particularly our notions of 'the present' are badly in need of revision. If this happens the future will no longer be seen as a simple linear extension, still less as an empty space. Rather it may come to be seen as a vital part of the here-and-now. In such a context we will require much wisdom to tame the threats posed by technology and to harness it to higher ends.

As discussed above, the empowerment principle suggests that the single most important insight is that the keys to the future are not found in the focus, or causes, of fears and concerns but in the human and institutional responses to them. This is consistent with the view that human beings are, or can choose to be, agents of history. From such a viewpoint the 21st century looks less like a continuing disaster and more like an historic challenge.

The promise of that century lies precisely in the kinds of work outlined here; work that places in people's hands a powerful set of tools and methods for re-humanising the future, for matching technological virtuosity with advanced ethics and a profoundly altered worldview.

Conclusion: The Promise of the 21st Century

The end of one millennium and the prospect of another to follow is not merely symbolic; it provides us with an opportunity to take stock and consider our position. Why are such turning points important? They reflect two powerful aspects of our reality. One is the capacity (even the need) of the human mind to range at will over time past, present and future. The other is the fact of our interconnectedness with all things past and future.

During the course of everyday life we become entrained in short-term, ego-bound, thinking, in the limited demands of the present. But the transition into a new century reminds us (as few other events can) of the wider macro-historical process. Looking back over the last hundred years we contemplate our roots in the lives and cultures of our parents and their parents. Over the next hundred years we look forward with our children and theirs to the world which is growing organically, day by day, from our present reality. This 'two-hundred year present' is our space in time. And when we reach the changeover, as dictated by the calendar and our numbering system, for a brief moment we seem to stand on a pivot of history.

The perspective catches our imagination. It is, perhaps, the temporal equivalent of the view from a high mountain. The details which had absorbed us stand revealed in a breathtaking panorama. Yet that is where the analogy ends. For we are keenly aware that the 20th century has been harrowing for us, for the Earth and certainly for our children. It is highly significant that at the end of the 19th century people looked ahead with optimism and hope. As we have seen, they believed that the rational application of scientific knowledge and technical skill would re-make the world and usher in an era of peace and prosperity. Nowadays it takes a profound act of imagination to reconstruct that sense of boundless possibility. For we carry the experience of the souring of that dream, of wars, catastrophes and the steady deterioration of our prospects and our images of the future.

Approaching the new millennium we know at a deep, incontrovertible level that everything is at stake. Of course there have been countless other crises, other cultures, systems, empires in decline. This leads some to suggest that there is nothing new about this particular time. But that is a grave error which overlooks the concrete facts of the age: our numbers, the kinds of tools and technologies we deploy, the change of scale in human activity and the increasingly compromised status of planetary life-support systems. Such facts suggest that something profound has indeed changed. It is now clear that, with few exceptions, previous generations always assumed that other generations would follow. However, in the mid 1990s, many have lost the age-old certainty that the species will even have a future, and have therefore withdrawn to denial and diversion in a minimal present, the here-and-now. At some level, this loss is felt by everyone. So it is no surprise that Macy calls it 'the pivotal psychological reality of our time'.

It seems clear that there is no transcendent principle which dictates that the experiment of life on planet Earth must succeed. Our very success as a species, coupled with the extraordinary assumptions and habits of the industrial era have brought us to a real 'hinge in history', not an imaginary one nor merely a calendar change. So it is not surprising that people have come to fear the future. To the extent that substances such as plutonium will be around for up to 250,000 years, or that the viability of forests and other ecosystems is threatened, such a response could be entirely appropriate. However, it is also possible that a keen awareness of both halves of this two-hundred year period may, in fact, stimulate changes, shifts of perception, processes and actions which could lead in an entirely different direction. That is the view developed in this book.

Part One was concerned with establishing the context. It began by looking back at the origins of the Western worldview in the patterns of thinking which gave rise to the so-called 'enlightenment' (as if there were only one in a single cultural context) the industrial revolution and, much later, to what I have termed 'the metaproblem'. The latter has been overlooked by many futurists. Yet it helps to account for 'world problems' in the foundations of culture: in paradigms, worldview assumptions and ways of knowing. Chapter 2 showed how a number of key institutions remain caught up in this overall pattern and are seriously malfunctioning, or at least being much less productive and useful than they might be. Chapter 3 raised the question of how we may 'know' anything about the future. It suggested that, while future events may be unpredictable, a careful reading of continuity and change can provide a surprisingly elaborate 'decision context' or account of the near-term future. This highlights options and choices, giving rise to a new kind of 'steering capacity'. Chapter 3 also introduced the 'futures field', considered some global trends and reviewed a number of critical issues to provide the beginnings of a broad overview of the next twenty years. It suggested several reasons why things may get harder before they get easier. In all, Part One established the context of this period at the end of the industrial era. The look back, the look around and the look forward encapsulate the basic movement of all futures study.

Part Two sought to extend the notion of foresight. Chapter 4 began with a review of the ways that foresight is already understood and applied in everyday life. It showed that, crucially, we don't have to invent a new principle, merely extend an historically-sanctioned and socially-validated one. This is encouraging, since the former would clearly be a quite different proposition and take much longer to achieve – if, indeed, it were possible at all. Chapter 5 looked at how changing ideas and worldview assumptions affect the way we conceptualise the global outlook, thereby deepening our understanding of what is at stake. This led on to a consideration of how foresight could be used to improve the institutions critiqued in Chapter 2. Chapter 6 looked at extensions of foresight through a range of analytic, imaginative and creative options. Besides considering a 'divergence map' for exploring alternative futures, it also considered the QUEST technique and ways of dealing with the imaging dilemma (the view of the future as necessarily dark and gloomy) in part through workshops. Chapter 7 considered some examples of institutions of foresight and asked 'what do they actually deliver'? It provided some pointers for future work and discussed costs and benefits. Finally it outlined the view that foresight has become an historical imperative, albeit that depends more on a shift of perception than upon the simple availability of resources.

Part Three linked foresight with the theme of cultural recovery. Chapter 8 considered the plight of young people as they come to grips with a challenging and dangerous world. A number of empowering strategies were set out. Chapter 9 looked at some of the ways that the Western worldview might be reinvented, in part through understanding cultural editing and creating social innovations. Finally, Chapter 10 used the transpersonal perspective, the notion of 'Homo Gestalt' and a new map of knowledge to explore some possible aspects of a wise culture. These, it was suggested, could be used to help create a new 'guiding image' or vision, to light the way beyond the decline of industrialism.

In all the above there is, of course, a danger here of wishful thinking, of 'finding good in everything', a silver lining in every cloud. But that is not what this book has suggested. Instead it has taken the view that the species as a whole is in very great peril (a fact which is already fully appreciated by the collective unconscious; otherwise, why would images of disaster, decay and decline dominate our popular and visual media?). However, properly handled, that fact may jolt us into a new awareness of where we are and what we need to do. It is most emphatically not a case of thinking good thoughts and being good, positive people. The point is that we face a challenge of unprecedented proportions. We have known it for some time. But late industrial culture has provided us with so many diversions and avoidance strategies that most of us are simply not paying attention.

The approach of a new century provides a genuine chance to take stock. It raises three simple, but very critical questions. Where have we come from? Where are we going? How can we get there? In other words, for a short time, 'the future' stops being an abstraction, an empty box. Suddenly it crashes through the defences and insists on our attention. If we are at all responsive, we will look back at the horrors of the century: at Auschwitz, Hiroshima, Bhopal, Chernobyl and the rest. In so doing, we will also look right into the abyss of equally disastrous futures in which the old industrial game was the only game in town and the foresight principle was never seriously applied. However, that is not the only choice. For beyond the abyss lie all the many processes of recovery and renewal which point in quite different directions. This is not an illusion. There is plenty of evidence that within the vast span of human cultures and responses there can be found all the resources necessary to re-conceptualise our predicament and steer in a different direction. It is from this viewpoint that we can discuss, indeed more than discuss, create, the promise of the 21st Century, for promise there is.

The single greatest impediment is a partially defective worldview that lurks out of sight beneath the surface of social and cultural life. It is invisible, yet it arguably affects everything that we do and think. So it is therefore necessary to account for the kind of cultural editing which has occurred within Western cultures. Of central concern is the way that this long historical process has either ignored or misrepresented the higher levels of a qualitatively differentiated world, made them appear mysterious or esoteric, the realm of gurus, mystics or charlatans. In fact they are simply part of a wider pattern. Just as a clock is more than the sum of its parts and a living organ is more than the sum of its cells, so the more highly evolved manifestations of human consciousness reach transcendent levels. Accounts of these processes suggest very strongly that higher levels of awareness tend to be inclusive rather than exclusive. They reach out to broader spans of space and time and have therefore become essential in healing the planet, creating peace and moving toward new stages of civilised life.

Transcendent knowledge is taught in very few schools, colleges or universities in the West. Yet in the view developed here, it occupies the highest level of a re-drawn 'map'. This is not because it is 'better' but because it is more highly differentiated. It does not involve a rejection of empiricism or rationality but rather an understanding of where their appropriateness lies, of where they fit. In losing this scheme of vertical differentiation, our culture has cut itself off from some of the most potent sources of value and meaning. One result is that problems (of power, ownership, conflicting interests and viable futures) genuinely appear irresolvable. They are irresolvable in these terms. Yet lasting solutions can rapidly appear in a vertical movement which transcends and resolves lower-level contradictions.

If one accepts the the view that human consciousness is emergent from the pre-personal ground of undifferentiated oneness with nature, then the present level of advanced mind is an enormous achievement. But the promise of the next century, indeed of all centuries, is that the whole thrust of human development goes beyond this toward states of clarity and integration which have been foreshadowed by great spiritual leaders. The work of transpersonal psychologists, as well as the accumulated wisdom sometimes known as the 'Perennial Philosophy', confirm that new worlds of significance lie beyond the mundane. In the context of a re-enchanted world, the radical loss of meaning and significance in the old world picture is decisively reversed.

Schumacher pointed out the necessity of there being within the knower something which was adequate to that which is to be known. He called this 'adequateo'. It has become a collective necessity if we are to move beyond the industrial era. It was also Schumacher who observed that, at the level of human beings, no upper limit to capacity can be found. We know that this is the case because we have evidence from many cultures and traditions that higher states of knowing and being have been achieved by outstanding individuals for many centuries. So, in contrast to the usual machine-led view of the future, a more humanly-compelling option can be envisaged. Essentially it is one in which human development accelerates to the point where it can exert dominance over technical development. Even a cursory look at the evidence shows that within each culture there exist all the potentials needed to empower other lines of development. They are accessible through clarity of insight, through deepened perception, creativity and certain forms of spiritual practice. All reveal new possibilities precisely because they progressively refine the instrument of knowing itself. As the latter changes, so does the wider world of which it is the most highly developed part. This is a pivotal insight of enormous power.

Though it has been widely overlooked there remains a persistent thread throughout most cultures and spiritual traditions which suggests that we are all and always immersed in a stream of knowing in a world brimming with immanent meaning. Since language cannot fully encompass those realms, the descriptions may appear paradoxical. From within the desert of scientific empiricism that is the end of the story. But the account given above suggests that in any particular context the higher may not be noticed from within the lower and certainly cannot be explained by it. Thus, far from sustaining an adequate worldview, the tired rationalism now solidly embodied in social, political, educational, cultural and economic discourse around the world, itself represents a radically limited frame to read upon an interconnected world rich in hierarchical truths.

Higher awareness is not an illusion, but a constant inspiration and challenge. It is refined, peaceful, compassionate. It is not under threat. It does not need to consume the world, still less destroy it. It recognises, with Siddhartha, that 'meaning and reality (are) not hidden somewhere behind things, they (are) in them, in all of them'. The widespread recognition of such insights will not be quickly achieved. It is a distant goal. Yet the lines of development which are implied can energise very many changes in the here-and-now. The innovations and insights discussed above are steps on a long journey. It is a journey which leads up and out of the abyss toward new stages of personal and cultural development.

Possible futures for humankind are many and varied. The inert, radio-active desert is still a possibility, though less likely than it once was. More likely at present is a planet whose life-support systems are devastated beyond all hope of repair. In that scenario the four horsemen would ride at will across the densely-populated landscapes, wreaking their age-old havoc through famine, war, disease and pestilence. In some areas they are already doing so, and the foresight principle comes too late. By contrast, there are some who place their hope on 'the high frontier', i.e. the promise of space, orbiting colonies, mining the asteroids and so on. Others are unlocking the DNA code, pursuing nanotechnology and other such wonders. However, the fatal flaw in so many enterprises is that they leave the question of human motives unaddressed.

As noted above, when primitive human instincts or motives such as fear, greed, hostility, etc. become associated with powerful technologies, the result is, indeed, a long-running disaster. This is the subtext of much 20th Century speculative writing (which as Brian Aldiss wittily put it, demonstrates how 'hubris is clobbered by nemesis'). We have seen both many times in recent history. But when higher motives such as selfless love, stewardship and what Buddhists call 'loving kindness' come into play the grounds of many otherwise serious problems seem to disappear! Ethical concerns such as 'enoughness', a deep identification with the natural world and a developed interest in future generations come to the fore. In other words, when a right relationship is re-established between people, culture and technology a whole new world of options emerges. This is the key which unlocks the future, takes us beyond the collapse of industrialism, moves us decisively away from the abyss, proves that there can indeed be 'light at the end of the tunnel'.

There is little prospect of going back to some pre-industrial condition of innocence, for in many ways we have as a species 'needed' the 20th century to make available to us certain kinds of experience, along with the experience of their costs and limitations. We have learned that the industrial assumptions about materialism, growth, the world as a machine or a resource and so on, are untenable. Consequently, we are challenged to create a new synthesis, and that has been the culmination of this work. Since we have no 'book of rules' and no blueprint will suffice, the creation of this synthesis is a huge challenge. It calls for modesty and humility on one hand and a kind of adventurous risk-taking on the other. Insofar as it is guided by human values, perceptions and concerns, it is a direct process. Yet it is also unpredictable and collective. It will emerge from the actions and insights of very many people from different cultures.

It follows that the promise of the 21st century cannot be found solely in the products or processes of rational intelligence, in displays of technical virtuosity or in new tools or techniques. Therein lies the industrial trap and the roots of unlivable, dystopian futures. Rather, this book has argued that it lies primarily in human and cultural development, in our ability to learn from this and other centuries and to collectively strike out in new (or renewed) directions. In part this means taking up the foresight principle and applying it in many different contexts. In so doing, human cultures can become responsive to a much wider variety of futures concerns, including that of their own long-term viability. As noted, acknowledging the different layers of meaning in an expanded map of knowledge and celebrating a re-enchanted world leads toward a sence of informed optimism and greatly enhanced options for the future. Finally, we are collectively challenged to release the disastrous conceits of the past and to embark on a journey to explore the heights of human ability and potential. From that viewpoint the future not only looks less daunting, but positively compelling.

The central myth of the 20th century is that the path to human destiny is by way of science, machines and rationality. This book has argued that these have been over-valued and that a more productive path will also require foresight and the pursuit of wisdom.

Annotated Bibliography

Brian Aldiss and David Wingrove: *Trillion Year Spree: The True History of Science Fiction* (1986, Gollancz, London)

An encyclopedic and authoritative survey of the development of speculative writing over some 150 years from Mary Shelley's 'Frankenstein' (1818) to the late 1980s. Successor to Aldiss' earlier Billion Year Spree (1973) and highly recommended for its breadth, balance and sympathetic analysis both of a wide range of works and the genre subculture associated with them. Essential reading for its portrayal of the development and evolution of popular images and concerns about technology, progress and futures.

J. G. Ballard: *Vermilion Sands* (1973, Cape, London)

Linked set of evocative short stories set in an ambiguous desert-like beach environment. A rich fantasy environment of the future with distinct resemblances to the late 20th century present. Highly recommended.

Gregory Bateson: *Steps to an Ecology of Mind* (1978, Paladin/Granada, London)

First published in 1972, this work remains a standard text on systems thinking. Bateson develops a unified body of theory that illuminates many diverse fields and provides support for a non-reductionist account of order, organisation and ecology. Demanding but highly recommended.

Gregory Bateson: *Mind and Nature* (1979, Wildwood House, London)

A more unified and concise statement of the author's perspective. Draws parallels between genetic and cultural evolution. Further develops his approach to applied systems thinking.

Hedley Beare and Richard Slaughter: *Education for the 21st Century* (1993, Routledge, London)

An attempt to show how education can be transformed by an understanding of the shift from industrialism and by the adoption of an explicit futures perspective. Looks at: dimensions of change, consequences of industrialism, global consciousness, the view beyond scientific materialism, the future of schools, the shift from past to future and a number of bridging strategies. Suggests that, while the view ahead is exceptionally challenging, there are substantial grounds for informed optimism through a renewed worldview and an active engagement with the future.

Catherine Belsey: *Critical Practice* (1980, Methuen, London)

A fine, concise introduction to the principles and applications of critical practice. Makes clear why this method is so productive when applied to futures and cultural change. An essential part of the critical futurist's tool kit.

Morris Berman: *The Re-enchantment of the World* (1981, Cornell University Press; 1988, Bantam, New York)

One of the most penetrating and useful books listed. Berman traces the birth of scientific consciousness and its subsequent evolution into an obsessive system which permitted humans to develop a powerful, but one-sided and destructive culture. Drawing on Bateson (q.v.) and others, he explores the grounds for recovering participating consciousness and a more viable set of cultural assumptions and practices. This is an important book.

Thomas Berry: *The Dream of the Earth* (1988, Sierra Club, San Francisco)

If there is a single text which demonstrates the viability of a post-materialist worldview, this is it. Berry is one of those rare writers who clearly sees where the resolutions to our current cultural predicament lie. He writes from a quality of consciousness which itself models those resolutions. The book therefore has depth as well as breadth. Yet it does not preach or over-intellectualise. It sets out the grounds of cultural recovery more clearly than any other book I have read. A fine companion to Berman (above) and Wilber (below). Most highly recommended.

Charles Birch: *Confronting the Future* (1976, 1983, Penguin, Australia).
New edition 1993

An under-valued book which attempts to argue for fundamental changes
in Western economics and culture away from material growth and
toward sustainability. The analysis is applied to Australia; it is suggested
that the country has natural advantages which make such a shift possible
and desirable. The book anticipates many later issues and was, perhaps,
ahead of its time. It is of continuing interest as an early statement (in
this context) of arguments for sustainability, arguments which become
more pressing as time passes.

David Bohm: *Wholeness and the Implicate Order* (1980, Routledge
London; 1983, Ark, London)

A demanding, yet influential, work in which the author argues against
the pervasive fragmentation of Western culture and consciousness. Bohm
draws on concepts from quantum physics to outline an implicate order
within which usual notions of time, space and causality break down.
Ultimately he believes that 'the entire universe . . . has to be understood
as a single undivided whole, in which analysis into separately and inde-
pendently existent parts has no fundamental status.' Problematic in some
respects but essential reading towards a new worldview.

Elise Boulding: *Building a Global Civic Culture: Education for an Inter-
dependent World* (1988, Teachers College Press, Columbia University,
New York)

Elise Boulding has spent a lifetime working for peace, justice and the
future. This book ranges widely over her many interests. It considers a
number of important conceptual, organisational and human innovations.
It also considers problems of knowledge in high-tech cultures and how
to recover a broader range of ways of knowing. A thoughtful and productive book.

Stewart Brand: *The Media Lab* (1987, Viking Press, New York)

An outstanding book providing an overview of research and developments in electronic media in the USA. Of particular interest because it is
written by a truly independent-minded author with no great faith in
technology *per se*. The result is a witty, penetrating and thoroughly enjoy-

able work which opens out this fascinating area for wider consideration. Notable also for its insight that 'information wants to be free'.

Lester Brown (and others): *State of the World* (Series) (1989-Worldwatch Institute/Allen and Unwin, London & New York)

Series of annual reports. They have steadily gained recognition internationally and have become essential background reading for anyone wishing to be informed about the contemporary facts about human/ environmental/climatic change at the global level. Each contains several topical essays with much useful analysis and information. Worth buying for courses on development, futures, the global problematique and so on. Highly recommended.

Lester Brown (and others): *Vital Signs 1992: The Trends that Are Shaping Our Future* (1992, Norton, New York)

Valuable insight into the state of the planet through the analysis of thirty-six vital signs covering many key areas. This is an invaluable reference work for the 1990s. Recommended.

Gro Harlem Brundtland (and others): *Our Common Future* (1987, Oxford University Press)

A much-heralded contribution to the debate initiated by *Limits to Growth* (q.v. 1972). Notable for its stress on interdependence and global development, but lacking in other areas. It fudges the central growth issue and retains an instrumental and anthropomorphic attitude toward nature (as merely constituting a set of resources for human manipulation and use). The book is therefore useful to those with vested interests in the status quo and it appeals to superficial environmentalists, futurists etc. However, it provides an inadequate basis for social or economic reform. An extra chapter (on sustainable development) added to the 1990 Australian edition is worth attention for its attempt to bend conventional economics to progressive ends. But its suggestions are modest and it too misses the deeper, more productive options.

John Brunner: *The Sheep Look Up* (1972, Harper & Row, New York)

The most successful of Brunner's dystopias. Deals primarily with the possible effects of unrestrained pollution. Creates a very dark vision of a future to avoid.

Brian Burrows, Alan Mayne and Paul Newbury: *Into the 21st Century: A Handbook for a Sustainable Future* (1991, London, Adamantine Press)

A very useful, detailed and readable book. Divided into three sections: approaches to current problems, new paradigms and future scenarios. These open out to chapters on detailed topics. I particularly liked part two for its accessible focus on ideas, worldviews and paradigms. The book is richly annotated and provides useful access to other literature. It will therefore be useful to many people, including students. Recommended.

Salvino Busuttil (and others): *Our Responsibilities to Future Generations* (1990, Foundation for International Studies/UNESCO, Malta)

Anthology of high-quality papers on inter-generational equity and associated ethical and legal concerns. A useful primer on the dimensions of this important debate.

Leonie Caldicott and Stephanie Leland (editors): *Reclaim the Earth: Women Speak Out for Life on Earth* (1983, Women's Press, London)

A stimulating collection of essays by women on a range of contemporary issues. Contains Hazel Henderson's fine essay: 'The Warp and the Weft; The Coming Synthesis of Eco-Philosophy and Eco-Feminism'. Highly recommended for the way it integrates environmental and feminist concerns.

Joseph Campbell: *The Hero's Journey* (1990, Harper, San Francisco)

Fascinating insight into the author of The Hero With a Thousand Faces. Campbell's influence after his death has been enormous – partly due to taped conversations with Bill Moyers. Essentially, he shows how myth and ritual have served countless cultures in their search for meaning, and how the West has ignored the mythic dimension to its very great cost.

Fritjof Capra: *The Tao of Physics: An Exploration of the Parallels between Modern Physics and Eastern Mysticism* (1975, Wildwood House; 1976, Fontana, London)

Early standard work on this subject. Provides a fascinating insight into the cosmic dance perceived by ancient and more recent disciplines. Serves to underpin some aspects of a post-materialist world view and manages to be readable without being popular or over-intellectual.

Fritjof Capra: *The Turning Point: Science, Society and the Rising Culture* (1982, Wildwood House, London; 1984, Ark)

Clear account of the cultural impasse encountered by obsolescent views of the world. Contrasts the latter with emerging visions of reality and social life. Highly recommended as an introduction to this crucial area and some of the issues and debates therein.

Ian Clarke: *The Pattern of Expectation 1644–2001* (1979, Cape, London)

An exhaustive study of changes in society, technology and culture in relation to successive views of the future. Draws on Professor Clarke's wide knowledge of popular and scientific writing over the period indicated. Demonstrates some of the many interactions between knowledge, social context and futuristic images. Usefully illuminates the crucial role of the latter.

Joseph Coates and Jennifer Jarratt: *What Futurists Believe* (1989, Lomond/World Future Society, Washington DC)

An in-depth analysis of the philosophies, approaches and methods of seventeen male American futurists. Notable for providing clear summaries of each, but unintentionally demonstrating the serious limitations of the American futures tradition. Contrast with Marien and Jennings: *What I have Learned . . .* (q.v.).

Joseph Coates (and others): *Issues Management* (1986, Lomond, Washington DC)

A clear, concise and authoritative exposition of the concepts, principles and practices of issues management. Stresses the concept of foresight as a process rather than a technique.

Peter Cock: *Alternative Australia: Communities for the Future* (1979, Quartet, Melbourne)

A sympathetic account of the social alternatives movement in Australia from the 1960s to the late 1970s. Surveys over fifty communities and comments on their experience and wider significance. Documents this movement which attempted to establish a separate and more sustainable mode of life. Notable now for the way much early idealism has been lost. However, the questions raised by these initiatives, and the implicit critique of mainstream culture, both remain highly relevant (q.v. Smith and Crossley, 1975).

Edward Cornish: *The Study of the Future: An introduction to the Art and Science of Understanding and Shaping Tomorrow's World* (1977, World Future Society, Washington DC)

A very accessible, if somewhat pedestrian introduction to the field of futures study by a prominent American futurist. Theoretically shallow, but a useful introductory source for younger students.

Kjell Dahle: *On Alternative Ways of Studying the Future* (1991, Alternative Future Project, Oslo, Norway)

Useful review of the Norwegian project, futures studies institutions around the world and annotated bibliography. Mainly of value for extensive bibliographic details of various rare and little-known sources. Dated in some respects, but a worthy effort from an informed European perspective.

David Darling: *Deep Time* (1990, Bantam, New York)

A stunning account of the story of the universe from the big bang to the distant future. Written with an elegance that is rare in this genre. A truly mind- and vision-expanding book. Also one that tackles the role of the individual in this vast space/time context and comes up with a fascinating view of the necessity of the observer. Highly recommended.

James Dator: *Surfing The Tsunamis of Change* (1993, Proceedings of Construction Beyond 2000, Espoo, Finland)

Iconoclastic and penetrating critical survey of five broad global processes: population, economics, environment, technology and globalisation. Stresses reality of the future and the role of human responsibility for it.

Paul Davies: *The Mind of God* (1992, Penguin, London)

Davies is one of the key interpreters of the new science and explorer of the interface between science and religion. In this book he argues that there is a deep and significant link between the human mind and the structure of the universe. He concludes that the universe is not an accident, but structured in a way that provides a meaningful place for individual thinking beings. The perfect companion to Darling, above.

Bill Devall and George Sessons: *Deep Ecology* (1985, Gibbs Smith, Salt Lake City)

Clear and systematic treatment of this vital area. A lucidly written introduction to the subject and a wide range of associated references.

Phillip K. Dick: *The Man in the High Castle* (1965, Penguin, London)

Accomplished portrait of an alternative world in which the USA lost World War II and is divided between Japan to the West and Germany to the East. Widely regarded as a masterpiece. The book dramatises the sheer contingency of what we take to be the present.

Larry Dossey: *Space, Time and Medicine* (1982, Shambhala, Boulder, Colorado)

Wide-ranging attempt to develop a new paradigm for health in relation to emerging world views. Slightly over-optimistic in places, excellent in others. Dosseys account of the bio-dance is exemplary in the way it evokes the wider context of space and time in which we are immersed.

Terry Dowling: *Rynosseros* and *Blue Tyson* (1990 and 1992, Aphelion Press, Adelaide, Australia)

Compelling tales of a far-future Australia very different from the present. In this scenario, Western civilisation has withered and the aboriginals have re-claimed their land. Moreover, they are now equipped with a range of powerful technologies. Dowling's prose is sometimes obscure, but he succeeds in portraying a plausible and fascinating future populated by nearly-real people and almost magical artefacts.

Eric Drexler: *Engines of Creation* (1986, Anchor/Doubleday, New York)

A provocative and stimulating book which explores the implications of nanotechnology – a new suite of developments which may emerge from the confluence of information technology, micro-engineering and biotechnology. While Drexler is overcommitted to promoting this technology, he nevertheless provides a coherent account of it and explores many of the social implications, both positive and negative. The book is therefore more substantial than naively technophilic works. This is the test case for the necessity of implementing foresight at the social level. It depicts a frightening future which promises hugely augmented technical power – but at the cost of radically undermining human society and cultures. As such the book should be taken seriously.

Freeman Dyson: *Infinite in All Directions* (1988, Harper & Row, New York)

A book derived from the authors' series of Gifford Lectures and ranging widely over science, ethics, politics and futures. Dyson is noted for his almost visionary descriptions of vast futuristic engineering projects in space. But this book shows a broader concern with human life and ecological diversity.

Paul Ehrlich, Carl Sagan (and others): *The Cold and the Dark: The World After Nuclear War* (1984, Sidgwick & Jackson, London)

Scientific picture of the likely effects of even a small nuclear exchange. Draws on several major research projects to explore the atmospheric, climatic and biological consequences. Not a depressing book if its detailed analyses are understood and broadly accepted. Provides a clear view of a future to be avoided at all costs.

Riane Eisler: *The Chalice and the Blade* (2nd edition, 1990, Unwin, London and New York)

A theory of cultural evolution based on two models: the dominator model, symbolised by the blade, and the partnership model, symbolised by the life-giving chalice. Eisler argues that long before the global shift to patriarchy became established, there was a long period of peace and contentment based on holism and a goddess culture. This account of human history and pre-history can usefully be contrasted with that of Wilber in *Up From Eden* (q.v.).

Duane Elgin: *Voluntary Simplicity* (1981, Morrow, New York)

An exploration of the rich personal and social consequences of adopting a way of life which is 'outwardly simple and inwardly rich.' Sees this kind of shift as prefiguring a renewed global culture. Complements Berman (q.v.) though at a less penetrating level.

Jaques Ellul: *The Technological Bluff* (1990, W. B. Eerdmans, Grand Rapids, Michigan)

Trenchant critique of technology by the author of The Technological Society, now more certain than ever that the costs may outweigh the benefits. Provides a broad critical discourse on many aspects of technology/culture relations. A bit dense and idiosyncratic in places, but about the nearest thing we have to a comprehensive theory about the negative impacts of technology upon culture.

Frank Feather (editor): *Through the 80s; Thinking Globally, Acting Locally* (1980, World Future Society, Washington DC)

A wide-ranging collection of papers of varying quality produced for the First Global Conference on the Future, Toronto 1980. Contains sections on Change, Global perspectives, Resources, The International Context, Economics, Values, Communications, Education, Health Futurism and Methods. Now dated in some respects. But useful as an indication of how various debates in the USA have since moved on.

Frank Feather (editor): *Optimistic Outlooks* (1982, Global Futures Network, Toronto)

Generally anodyne collection of short papers mostly by big names. However, a useful summary of (largely American) upbeat views of futures. As with the previous volume, the book suffers from a lack of critical and comparative perspectives.

Marilyn Ferguson: *The Aquarian Conspiracy: Personal and Social Transformation in the 1980s* (1980, Tarcher, Los Angeles)

A very influential, sometimes overstated, exposition of the good news about the prospects for, and process of, change. Ferguson captures the sense of potential inherent in several related areas of the futures movement but fails to convince that this potential is more than marginally realised. (Compare with Wilber, below.)

Robert Fitch and Cordell Svengalis: *Futures Unlimited: Teaching About Worlds to Come* (1979, National council for the Social Studies, Washington DC)

Concise and readable introduction to the theory and practice of teaching futures as it has developed in North America. Covers: the futures field, curriculum approaches, methods, values, images of the future, evaluation and resources. Easily the most accessible and useful American publication on this subject. Highly recommended.

Tom Forester (editor): *The Microelectronics Revolution* (1980, Blackwell, Oxford)

A valuable reference work containing source materials on a range of micro-related issues. Major sections deal with the revolution itself, social and economic implications, speculations about the microelectronic age.

E. M. Forster: 'The Machine Stops' in *The Eternal Moment and Other Stories* (1929, Harcourt, Brace, Jovanovich, New York)

Salutary tale of over-reliance upon the machine and the inevitable result when it breaks down. One of the most significant and insightful works of fiction in the 20th century. Identifies one of the key drawbacks of technological dependency. Still directly relevant many decades later.

Viktor Frankl: *Man's Search for Meaning* (4th edition, 1985, Washington Square Press)

Provides important support for the view that the major dynamic in human behaviour is not, as has been popularly supposed, the will to power, but the will to meaning. This important distinction is sustained by the authors experiences in Nazi concentration camps. He is thus eminently qualified to speak with deep insight on questions of pain, suffering and purpose. This, and his insistence that 'logos is deeper than logic' helps to provide part of the grounding for a post-materialist worldview. Highly recommended.

Marie von Franz: *Time: Rhythm and Repose* (1978, Thames & Hudson, London)

A concise, cross-cultural, account of the significance of time, its measurement and rhythms. Fruitfully influenced by eastern concepts and a strong intuitive feel for the subject. Many interesting illustrations provide starting points for students and others.

Julius Fraser: *Time as Conflict: A Scientific and Humanistic Study* (1978, Birkhauser Verlag, Basel and Stuttgart)

J. T. Fraser is an unusual writer who appears to have devoted the post-war years to the study of time. He has edited and written several volumes on the subject and this book clearly draws on that impressive foundation. His account of distinct *Umwelts*, each with its own characteristic mode of temporality, makes a very brave and substantial bid to unravel the microstructure of time and its human and cultural significance. This is a major work and one that amply rewards the diligent reader. Very highly recommended.

Julius Fraser: *Time the Familiar Stranger* (1987, Microsoft, Washington)

A rich and satisfying exploration of the thesis set out in Time as Conflict (q.v.). Fraser deploys an impressive range of material in his journey through the different levels and aspects of time. He throws new light on each and provides many deep insights into the rich character of temporality as mediated through culture and experience. Essential reading.

Christopher Freeman and Marie Jahoda (editors): *World Futures: The Great Debate* (1978, Martin Robertson/S.P.R.U., London/Brighton)

One of the earlier and more substantial books produced within the futures field. Some particularly useful chapters on the global futures debate, worldviews and scenarios, images of the future and war. Clear, considered and – in the best sense – critical. Stands in sharp contrast with the woolly speculations produced elsewhere. Highly recommended even though dated now.

Erich Fromm: *To Have or to Be?* (1978, Cape, London)

There are not many books which attempt to engage with the human (as opposed to technical) significance of alternative futures. This volume productively explores the having/being dichotomy, drawing on a wide range of historical material to discuss the implications of each. While the best use of dichotomies is often to transcend them for higher-order wholes, Fromm argues that a tendency to one or other pole of the present one has pervasive effects. Not a particularly easy book, but a useful one.

Buckminster Fuller: *Critical Path* (1983, Hutchinson, London)

Fuller is the archetypal technological optimist. In his view most pressing problems have appropriate technical solutions. As inventor of the geodesic dome, the dymaxion world map and much else besides, he writes with some authority. Yet to this reviewer the book is both stimulating and irritating. The former because few have explored technical possibilities and alternatives with more thoroughness and dedication. The latter because Fuller's breadth in some areas cannot hide his narrowness and idiosyncrasy in others. He also has an annoying habit of coining odd neologisms. Nevertheless, the book is of interest in demonstrating the uses and limitations of a technicist view.

Denis Gabor: *Inventing the Future* (1963, Secker & Warburg, London)

Dedicated to Aldous Huxley, this work is mainly of interest for the way it provides perspective on more recent insights. It is one of a number of books produced in the post-war years which attempted to come to grips with fundamental threats and dangers facing humankind. It is included here because its calm reasonableness and earnest rationality are certainly commendable, though they no longer ring true in a more sophisticated, more embattled age. Works of this kind remain useful insofar as they indicate how far the futures field has moved on from its earlier attempts to map out and understand the area.

Martha Garrett (and others): *Studies for the 21st Century* (1991, UNESCO, Paris)

Valuable overview of numerous 21st century studies from around the world, with a critical commentary on lessons learned. Shows how far the Institute for 21st Century Studies has come over the last decade. An important publication, foreshadowing a developing 'global prospective outlook' of major significance for policy, planning, education and so on.

Susan George (and others): *The Debt Boomerang* (1992, Pluto Press, London)

A hard-hitting critique of the global economic system and the World Bank. Shows how old-style development re-bounds not merely upon the recipients but also upon the rich West through: environmental damage, the drug trade, bank rorts, lost jobs and markets, immigration problems, conflict and war. This is one of the clearest expositions of the centrality of the foresight principle in coming to grips with global concerns. Highly recommended.

Jonathan Gershuny: *After Industrial Society: The Emerging Self-service Economy* (1978, Macmillan/S.P.R.U., London/Brighton)

A penetrating analysis of the shift from industrial social and economic patterns. Shows that, far from a simple transition to a service economy, we are witnessing a shift toward a self-service economy. The latter is fuelled by the purchase and use of consumer durables in place of certain services and by a shift towards new developments in the non-formal economy.

William Gibson and Bruce Sterling: *The Difference Engine* (1990, Gollancz, London)

Alternate world novel in which Babbage's mechanical computer succeeded and helped to transform Victorian England. A bit too focussed on the atmosphere of the time, rather than on the social implications, to be a great novel; but an intriguing one.

Herbert Girardet (editor): *Land for the People* (1978, Crescent Books, London)

Underlying many views of the desirability of a return to more rural and self-sufficient ways of life are major issues of land redistribution and land reform. This interesting volume touches on many of the relevant questions and provides suggestions for further reading.

Michel Godet: *Scenarios and Strategic Management* (1987, Butterworth, London)

A demanding but refreshingly original work describing the approach and methodology of 'la prospective'. Based on extensive experience with governments and corporations in France, the author has a shrewd and detailed grasp of futures research techniques and of their underlying problematics. Provides a valuable contrast to American writing on the same subject.

Michel Godet: *From Anticipation to Action: A Handbook of Strategic Prospective* (1993, UNESCO, Paris)

Detailed and valuable account of the methodology and approach of 'la prospective'. This is probably the 'state of the art' book on the subject. Highly recommended.

Edward Goldsmith (and others): *A Blueprint for Survival* (1972, The Ecologist, Camelford, Cornwall, UK)

A catastrophist view of social, economic and environmental trends. Advocates massive de-industrialisation and a wholesale return to sustainable ways of life, particularly in relation to agriculture. Always controversial, Goldsmith's theories have never appealed to more than a lunatic fringe of the ecology movement – and for good reason. The changes demanded are repressive, authoritarian and wholly unworkable as they stand.

Albert Gore: *Earth in the Balance: Ecology and the Human Spirit* (1992, Houghton Mifflin, New York)

Examines the origins of the environmental crisis and suggests ways of dealing with it. Concludes that restoring the environment should become the central organising principle of civilisation. Clearly sees a major role for foresight. Connects the external picture with the inner world and concludes that some kind of spiritual awakening is required.

Steven Jay Gould: *Time's Arrow, Time's Cycle* (1987, Harvard, Boston, 1987, and 1989, Penguin, London)

This is one of the most literate and penetrating books ever written on time and metaphor. It is particularly resonant when describing the Victorian discovery of deep time – the millions of years of geological history. But it also uses the history of geology itself to show how these two central metaphors guided and conditioned discourse on time and change over several centuries. From this emerges a clear and insightful picture of the nature of scientific controversy and thought. Highly recommended.

Lindsay Grant: *Foresight and National Decisions: the Horseman and the Bureaucrat* (1988, University Press of America, Maryland)

Grant surveys the US government's record on foresight and, predictably enough, finds it wanting. He calls for better foresight through the application of systematic and interdisciplinary techniques to complex issues. Among the proposals put forward are: establishment of a foresight ombudsman, a foresight working group and a similar policy group. He also suggests a separate and private foresight foundation. The book is a useful review of past practice and future possibility in this crucial area. However, it misses some of the strongest grounds for establishing foresight and portrays the latter largely in organisational terms.

John Gribbin: *Future Worlds*, also *Time Warps* (1979, Abacus, Sphere, London)

Two competent and readable summaries of their respective subjects. Though dated by now, **Future Worlds** is one of the best popular introductions to futures study. **Time Warps** considers some of the conundrums raised by discoveries in astrophysics and relativity. Both are recommended as good introductory material. Unfortunately they are also out of print – but may often be found in second-hand bookshops.

Ursula le Guin: *Always Coming Home* (1986, Gollancz, London)

Not so much a novel as a tapestry of culture. The culture in question is in a far-future California. It differs from our own in many ways, particularly the relative prominence given to technology versus ritual and participation in nature. The book works so well partly because le Guin's parents were well-known anthropologists. Much of this material emerges in the book. But it is the author's particular gift to make this alternative future a powerfully evocative and contrasting statement. It therefore stands as a challenge and a rebuke to machine-based societies such as our own. Most highly recommended.

Jurgen Habermas: *Towards a Rational Society* (1971, Heinemann, London)

This is not an easy read. However chapters 4–6 (and particularly chapter 4: 'Technical Progress and the Social Life-world') are essential reading for anyone attempting to understand the role of science, technology and instrumental rationality in creating the central problematic of our time. Habermas not only penetrates the dark corners of technocracy, he also specifically argues for an 'interdisciplinary, future-oriented research' capable of looking beyond the status quo. Hard work in places, but well worth the effort.

Peter Hall (editor): *Europe 2000* (1977, Duckworth, London)

This work considers future options in the broad context of European life and a changing world order. Few books retain the coherence that this one does in such a field. Furthermore, the author penetrates to what he calls 'the heart of the matter'; that is, the implicit mode of rationality which underlies social and economic change. This emphasis gives the book a depth which few others of its type have achieved and the thesis remains fully pertinent many years later.

Willis Harman: *Global Mind Change* (1988, Knowledge Systems Inc., Indianapolis)

If there is one readable book which penetrates to the heart of the global predicament – and then beyond it to a transformed world, this is it. Harman manages to cover a lot of ground clearly, simply and accessibly. His treatment of three metaphysical perspectives is exemplary in its understated economy. The analysis is sound, the approach is right and hence the book opens out the prospect of cultural recovery on a global scale – no mean feat. Recommended most highly.

Willis Harman and Howard Rheingold: *Higher Creativity* (1984, Tarcher, Los Angeles)

Useful addition to the literature on human potentials and the evolution of consciousness. Argues that higher forms of creativity are available to everyone and that these permit us to address the 'fundamental crisis of meaning' in modern societies. Strikes a careful balance between inner and outer work. Recommended.

Peter Hawken, James Ogilvy and Peter Schwartz: *Seven Tomorrows* (1982, Bantam, New York)

Many futures books speak of alternatives, but few illustrate them with such clarity. The authors utilise assumptions about energy, climate, food, the (American) economy and values to construct seven distinct scenarios. Each is outlined clearly and the main choices are described. Some of the material is inevitably dated but the soundness of the approach makes the book a useful model to be emulated.

Hazel Henderson: *Creating Alternative Futures* (1978, Berkeley, New York)

Essential reading for the serious student of futures. Henderson's essays on the decline of classical economics represent a damning indictment of much conventional thinking. But the criticism is balanced by her shrewd grasp of the significance of innovative socio-cultural developments. Highly recommended, as are all works by this writer.

Hazel Henderson: *The Politics of the Solar Age: Alternatives to Economics* (1981, Doubleday: 1988, Knowledge Systems, Indianapolis)

The second major collection. Comments as above.

Hazel Henderson: *Paradigms in Progress* (1991, Knowledge Systems, Indianapolis)

Reflects a marvellous breadth of insight into the institutions, players, ideas and theories of economics. A world-spanning catalogue of structures in transition, with details about how many organisations are attempting to adapt to, and create, the new conditions. Falls short of providing a new theory of economics, but provides a stunning critique and a large number of insights, examples and pointers for further work.

Hermann Hesse: *Siddhartha* (1951, New Directions, New York)

To this reviewer, too much of the futures literature is preoccupied with externals, so it is useful to have books like this which re-affirm the primacy of human beings as actors and agents in culture. While *Siddhartha* is set in the distant past, it speaks powerfully to our present and future by depicting contrasting modes of consciousness and their different consequences. This is a perennial concern which should be located at the heart of futures work (q.v. Huxley 1946).

Stephen Hill: *The Tragedy of Technology* (1988, Pluto Press, London)

The tragedy Hill speaks of refers to the apparent inevitability of technical systems. The author examines them from the point of view of technology as a cultural text. While this text may appear to be constituted autonomously and distantly, there are numerous opportunities in everyday life to reconstruct meanings and to direct tools and technologies. This is a thoughtful book which repays close attention. Also see Winner, *Autonomous Technology* (q.v.).

Mark Hilligas: *The Future as Nightmare: H. G. Wells and the Anti-Utopians* (1967, Oxford University Press)

Useful review of the crucial transition from Utopian visions in literature to the rise, and continuing elaboration, of dystopia. Traces the development of the new tradition within Wells' own work and in reactions to it by other writers. Recommended.

Fred Hirsch: *Social Limits to Growth* (1977, Routledge, London)

Most discussions of future limits centre upon economic, resource and environmental factors. Hirsch argues that there are inherent social limits. With increasing affluence new types of scarcity come into being so that 'getting what one wants is increasingly divorced from doing as one likes.' A provocative and well-argued thesis which has received less attention that it deserves.

Donald Horne: *The Great Museum: The Re-presentation of History of History* (1984, Pluto Press, London)

The key is in the term re-presentation. Here the author explores the ways that European countries reconstruct their past to serve present social interests. It is a useful reminder of the gulf which separates what we take to be the past and the realities of life as known and experienced at other times. Both past and future require imaginative construction, but the task is a perilous one when the great museum of Europe turns its monuments and hallowed buildings to new, socially convenient uses. Recommended.

Barbara Hubbard: *The Evolutionary Journey: A Personal Guide to a Positive Future* (1983, Turnstone, Wellingborough, Northants)

Frothy and self-indulgent attempt by a prominent American futurist to till well-turned soil. The author is painfully 'inspirational' and the book lacks any concession to rigour or to critical thought. Included here mainly as a contrast, e.g. to Wilber, below.

Nicholas Humphrey and Robert Lifton (editors): *In a Dark Time* (1984, Faber, London)

The title is from a poem by Roethke that 'in a dark time, the eye begins to see'. A very effective anthology of writing from a wide variety of sources forming a kind of tapestry of responses to the dilemmas of the late 20th century. Truly a selection for the nuclear age.

Aldous Huxley: *The Perennial Philosophy* (1946, Chatto & Windus, London)

Now-classic synthesis from the world's spiritual traditions of the ways that people have ventured beyond conventional knowledge and experience to the clarity and tranquillity of higher states of being. Included here because the perspective outlined (and later elaborated by Wilber, below, and others) provides perhaps the basis for articulating futures wherein people do not yield up their autonomy to machines but, in some sense, aspire to states of consciousness and being which transcend the banalities of technocracy. Highly recommended.

Ivan Illich: *Tools for Conviviality* (1973, Calder Boyars, London)

Incisive critique of repressive norms in an industrialised, technicised, society. Like most of Illich's work this one is brilliant, iconoclastic and hopeful but some will find sections of the work impenetrable or obscure.

Chris Jenkins and Barrie Sherman: *The Leisure Shock* (1981, Methuen, London)

Sequel to *The Collapse of Work* which seeks to explore alternatives to mass unemployment but despairs of the requisite changes in official attitudes occurring in time to prevent chaos. Still relevant more than ten years later.

Barry Jones: *Sleepers Wake!* (2nd edition, 1990, Oxford University Press, London)

A penetrating analysis of work and leisure in the context of the new information technologies. Written by a leading Australian politician, this lucid and provocative work is essential reading for anyone involved in this area. Recommended.

Ralph Jones (editor): *Readings From Futures* (1981, Butterworth, Guildford, UK)

Rare and stimulating collection of papers from the journal *Futures*. Highly recommended, especially for libraries and research students.

Bertrand de Jouvenal: *The Art of Conjecture* (1967, Weidenfeld & Nicholson, London)

Despite its age this work remains one of the standard texts of the field. A fine, literate, introduction to rationales and methods of futures study. Still very well worth reading.

Robert Jungk: *The Everyman Project: Resources for a Humane Future* (1976, Thames & Hudson, London)

A compendium of constructive responses to the deepening dilemmas of the West as seen by a distinguished European writer. Much useful material though some of it now seems dated and over-optimistic.

Robert Jungk and Norbert Mullert: *Futures Workshops* (1987, Institute for Social Inventions, London)

Practical introduction to workshop techniques which permit communities and groups to define their aspirations and work toward them. The approach has been successfully applied in several European countries.

Herman Kahn, William Brown and Leo Martel: *The Next 200 Years* (1977, Associated Business Programmes, London)

Ambitious attempt by Hudson Institute analysts to assert a pattern for global development which, in their view, could lead to near-universal affluence. It pours scorn on most limits arguments and fails to grasp the significance of environmental politics and other cultural developments. Nevertheless, of considerable interest for its exploration of key issues in a perspective favoured by big business and multinationals. This represents one pole of a much more diverse debate and should therefore be taken seriously despite the clear ideological bias.

Mary Kaldor: *The Baroque Arsenal* (1982, Deutsch, London; 1983, Abacus, Tunbridge Wells, Kent)

For once the cover blurb is accurate: 'a baroque arsenal is one that is complex, expensive and impractical... By establishing a direct link between high arms expenditure and economic stagnation, Mary Kaldor shows how the funds which could be used to develop new jobs and industries are being squandered on obsolete weapons.' A fine example of critical, futures-related work. Highly recommended.

Draper Kauffman: *Teaching the Future* (1976, ETC Pubs., Palm Springs, California)

An early practical introduction to teaching futures based on American experience. Still holds up as an introductory text, though it obviously cannot include reference to later developments.

Paul Kennedy: *Preparing for the 21st Century* (1993, Harper Collins, London)

This book is well-written and comprehensively researched. It covers a range of general trends and their regional impacts in considerable detail. As a snapshot of the present (or, rather, the recent past) it provides a reasonable overview. Unfortunately, however, it provides only a stereotypical description of the problem and falls well short of the claim in its title. There are two major omissions. First, there is little or no recognition of the futures literature *per se*. Second, the analysis is empiricist and external. The author is neither aware of the ways futures people have approached the coming millennium, nor of the deeper analysis within the present which provides grounds for inspiration and hope.

Joel Kovel: *Against the State of Nuclear Terror* (1983, Pan/Channel Four, London)

One of the most impressive and incisive books on the present list. Kovel probes into the roots of technocratic culture and its psychology to account for the rise of what he calls 'official nuclear terrorism'. Not everyone will agree with this book but I believe it to be an important one, not least because of the way it faces the unthinkable and distinguishes specific ways forward through an 'anti-nuclear politics' which is rather more than rhetoric and flag-waving. Highly recommended.

Krishan Kumar: 'Prophecy and Progress' in *The Sociology of Industrial and Post-Industrial Society* (1978, Allen Lane, London)

Kumar's thesis is that most theories of post-industrialism fail because they misconstrue the nature and history of industrial society. He therefore sets out to correct the record and discusses options for the future that he believes go well beyond usual notions of the post-industrial society.

Richard Leakey: *The Making of Mankind* (1981, Michael Joseph, London)

A useful and informed historical perspective over many thousands of years of human development. Lends credibility to the idea that human aggression is not innate and therefore casts new light on our future aspirations. Leakey's views on the role of tools and technologies may usefully be compared with Mumford's, below. It becomes clear that the earliest humans shaped tools and built structures with a clear sense of future purpose, thus proving that futures thinking may well be innate.

Sara Lefanu: *In the Chinks of the World Machine* (1988, Women's Press, London)

A refreshingly original analysis of SF from an intelligent feminist viewpoint. Part one casts a critical eye over a number of genre themes. Part two looks in detail at four women SF writers (including Le Guin and 'James Tiptree'). An outstanding work of SF criticism.

William Leiss: *The Limits to Satisfaction* (1976, University of Toronto Press)

The author explores an under-regarded, but very important idea. Namely that: 'in our society individuals are encouraged to misinterpret the character of their needs and desires, and as a result the character of their attempts to assuage them becomes more and more ambiguous.' This is both a powerful condemnation of market-oriented values and an important contribution to the articulation of alternatives – one of which is here described as 'the conserver society'. Recommended. (Also see Elgin, above.)

Harold Linstone and Clive Simmonds (editors): *Futures Research: New Directions* (1977, Addison-Wesley, Reading, Mass.)

An outstandingly high quality collection of papers on various aspects of futures research. For those who are sceptical about whether futures study is a discipline, and those who question if futures can be studied at all, this is essential reading. Highly recommended for doubters and serious students of the field.

John Livingstone: *The Fallacy of Wildlife Conservation* (1981, McClelland & Stewart, Toronto)

Systematically considers the various major arguments for wildlife conservation and their respective limitations. Contains a fine section on the 'Root Problems' which locates these difficulties firmly in the nature of embedded cultural assumptions. Concludes finally that conservation is not dependent upon reason and logic, but upon a 'state of being.' Hence it sketches in the grounds for 'deep ecology.' (q.v. Seed *et al*, below.)

James Lovelock: *Gaia: A New Look at Life on Earth* (1979, Oxford University Press)

A provocative thesis presented in a cool and sympathetic way. The author suggests that the Earth can, in some sense, be regarded as a self-regulating system which somehow intentionally maintains its environment in precisely the way suitable for life. He dubs this greater entity Gaia, the ancient Greek term for the earth goddess. Qualifies as an increasingly resonant modern myth.

Amory Lovins: *Soft Energy Paths: Toward a Durable Peace* (1977, Pelican, London)

A now-classic work on the desirability and practicability of non-nuclear energy options. In retrospect the book seems somewhat optimistic, but the issues raised remain pertinent. Since it was published the nuclear industry has run into major problems. But the soft alternatives, implying quite different social and economic patterns, look increasingly attractive as time goes by.

Eleonora Macini (editor): *Visions of Desirable Societies* (1983, Pergamon, Oxford)

Outstanding collection of essays emerging from a two-year UN university project. Essential reading for visions of futures and cultural change themes. One of the most useful books to have emerged from the World Futures Studies Federation. Highly recommended.

Eleonora Macini (and other editors): *The Futures of Development* (1991, UNESCO, Paris)

Proceedings of the 1988 WFSF Beijing conference of the same title. Wide-ranging selection of papers, most of good quality and above.

Joanna Macy: *Despair and Personal Power in the Nuclear Age* (1983, New Society Publications, Philadelphia)

An in-depth approach to transforming despair into empowerment via workshop techniques. Based on the authors extensive experience of this work over many years. Highly recommended.

Joanna Macy: *World as Lover, World as Self* (1991, Parallax Press, Berkeley, California)

A fascinating journey through despair and empowerment work, back to the source of Macy's inspiration in Buddhist texts and traditions, and on to the flowering of insight and activism which this permits. A luminously intelligent book which plumbs perennial wisdom in ways that make it accessible to late 20th century dilemmas and needs.

Jerry Mander: *In the Absence of the Sacred* (1991, Sierra Club, San Francisco)

One of the key books on this list. Mander decisively calls the bluff of technological neutrality and science-and-technology-led views of progress and the future. His critique is sound and first-rate. He complements it by showing with enormous sympathy and skill how native peoples have been abused by the West, yet have also struggled to maintain the integrity of aspects of their pre-modern worldview and cultures. A fascinating, challenging and important book. It should be read by all those who are concerned about the directions, costs and viability of Western-style development. Highly recommended.

Herbert Marcuse: *One Dimensional Man* (1972, Abacus, Tunbridge Wells, Kent)

Standard work on the domination thesis, i.e. that what passes for freedom in the West is a repressive and confining state in which institutions serve vested interests. Over-stated in some respects, but a useful, penetrating, analysis for those who can stay the course.

Michael Marien and Lane Jennings (editors): *What I Have Learned* (1987, World Future Society, Washington DC)

Fascinating and varied collection of essays by futurists who look back over their experiences and attempt to draw out principles and conclusions. Very useful introduction to futures thinking in spite of the by-now stereotypical emphasis on the USA.

Michael Marien (editor): *Future Survey Annual* (1979, series WFS, Bethesda, Maryland)

Annual compendium of abstracts from *Future Survey*, organised under various headings, with highlights, summaries and index. While suffering a bit from being mainly US-oriented, *Future Survey* and the annual provide the most useful bibliographic overview of futures- and futures-related material yet available. A tool for research and scholarship, with the nearest to a substantive critical perspective yet produced in the US. Recommended.

Bill Mc Kibben: *The End of Nature* (1990, Penguin, London)

During the 20th century there have occurred a number of fundamental changes in the human condition and the environment in which human life exists. This volume captures the profound significance of the shift from nature as a given, a vast and unknowable realm within which societies are framed, to nature as part of society. The latter does not refer to the indissoluble quality of participation indicated by Berry (q.v.) and Berman (q.v.) for example, but the fundamental compromising of nature's integrity by increasingly powerful waves of human activity. The book is written in the tradition of Muir and Thoreau, but it does not descend into sentimentalism or preservationism. It conveys a powerful sense of loss but also faces up constructively to some of the human and cultural implications.

John McHale: *The Future of the Future* (1969, Braziller, New York; 1971, Ballantine)

A better than average introduction to the futures field and some of its early concerns. Useful concepts and conceptualisations of futures issues and concerns. Another book to provide perspective on later development.

John McHale: *The Changing Information Environment* (1976, Elek, London)

A well-documented account of the impacts and implications of successive revolutions in the development of communications technology. Now dated, but still useful.

Corinne McLaughlin and Gordon Davidson: *Builders of the Dawn* (1985, Stillpoint, New Hampshire, USA)

Fascinating review of a wide variety of alternative communities throughout the world. Suggests that they represent an important medium of social learning and cultural innovation. (Also see Cock, 1979 q.v.; and Smith and Crossley; 1975 q.v.)

Barry McWaters: *Conscious Evolution: Personal and Planetary Transformation* (1983, Turnstone Press, Wellingborough, Northants)

Above average work on now fashionable theme. Better than Hubbard (above), nowhere near Wilber (below). From the blurb: 'the aim of Conscious Evolution is two-fold: to encourage deeper personal meaning through conscious participation in a larger reality; and to seed the idea of the planet as a living, intelligent, organism in the evolutionary process.' Intellectually suspect, perhaps, but of possible inspirational value.

Dennis Meadows (and others): *The Limits to Growth* (1972, Universe Books, New York)

A book which stimulated a major and continuing debate. It argued that a combination of population growth, agricultural production, resource depletion, industrial output and pollution would lead to the collapse of civilisation unless limits to growth were observed before they became compelling. The use of simple computer modelling techniques gave this thesis great superficial credibility though later studies showed that underlying assumptions and methodologies were suspect (see *Futures* vol. 5, no. 1, Feb 1973: 'The Limits to Growth Controversy'). Nevertheless, in general terms, the discussion remains an important one (q.v. Freeman and Jahoda, 1978 above).

Donella Meadows, Dennis Meadows and Jorgen Randers: *Beyond the Limits* (1992, Earthscan, London)

A worthy successor to *Limits to Growth*. Begins with a lucid account of exponential growth, continues with a review of the nature of limits and considers the dynamics of growth in a finite world. Demonstrates beyond all doubt that foresight has become a structural necessity since 'a system with inherent physical momentum needs to be looking decades ahead'. Concludes by outlining necessary shifts in culture, human behaviour and governance. Essential reading for anyone interested in the future. Most highly recommended.

Donald Michael: *On Learning to Plan and Planning to Learn* (1973, Jossey-Bass, San Francisco)

Ground-breaking work on the social psychology of long range social planning and a learning society. Looks in detail at many of the social/perceptual problems involved, skills and metaskills, the personal and organisational burdens of change. Recommended.

Lester Milbrath: *Envisioning a Sustainable Society* (1989, SUNY Press, New York)

Impressive account by a noted political scientist of the need for such a society and the ways it may be brought about. Begins with an enquiry into why modern society is not sustainable. Elaborates a vision of the transition process (with an important chapter on an appropriate structure of governance) and finishes with possible scenarios. A fine, wide-ranging book of great practical significance. Highly recommended.

Ian Miles: *The Poverty of Prediction* (1975, Saxon House, Farnborough, UK)

Critical analysis of futures research and social forecasting. Exposes the dominance of technocratic images of the future and argues for greater public participation in decision making. Now dated, but the main argument remains important. (q.v. Kovel 1983, above).

Edward Mishan: *The Economic Growth Debate: An Assessment* (1977, Allen & Unwin, London)

A perceptive and still relevant critique of the assumptions and implications of standard economic doctrines concerning growth. Sketches out an alternative view of steady-state economics with discussions of social and human issues involved. A handbook for Green politics (see Porrit 1984, below) and for those suspicious of western-style progress.

Ian Mitroff and Warren Bennis: *The Unreality Industry* (1989, Carol Publishing Group, New York)

Within the limitations of the chosen metaphor (with its simple reality/ unreality dichotomy) the authors skilfully explore the implications of 'the deliberate manufacturing of falsehood and what it is doing to our lives.' Like other critics of unrestrained technical and social innovation, they deplore the penetration of media hype and unreality into every aspect of our lives. They see two great features of the present century (complexity and trivialisation) standing in opposition, greatly to our detriment. However, in lacking a critical futures methodology the book lacks penetration and cannot resolve the dilemmas it outlines so clearly. (Also see Postman q.v.)

Peter Moll: *From Scarcity to Sustainability. Futures Studies and the Environment: the Role of the Club of Rome* (1991, Peter Lang, Frankfurt)

Valuable account of the history of the Club of Rome and its connection with the development of modern futures studies. Takes a critical view of both and provides important indicators for future development. Some by typos and grammatical errors, but, nevertheless, a rare and outstanding work of scholarship in the futures area.

Sir Thomas Moore: *Utopia* (1516)

The original work which attempted to describe a different and ideal society based on rational, enlightened government and religious freedom. A template for much of the varied literature that followed.

Ward Moore: *Bring the Jubilee* (1953, Morrow, New York)

A time traveller goes back to the battle of Gettysburg and changes the outcome of the American Civil War. In so doing the narrator becomes stranded in the past, and his manuscript is discovered in 1953. An outstanding combination of time-paradox and alternative world themes.

Anthony Moncrieff: *Messages to the Future: The story of the BBC Time Capsule* (1984, Futura, London)

A fascinating little book detailing the time capsule project and contents thereof. Of interest here because it makes explicit what is often implicit; namely, that we have important, shared, interests in the future. To send it messages is to begin to uncover the nature of those interests. Provides a good basis for school projects on this subject. Recommended.

Sheila Moorcroft (editor): *Visions for the 21st Century* (1992, Adamantine Press, London)

Fascinating anthology of over twenty short essays from a very wide variety of authors. Given this diversity, the book succeeds because it illuminates the area in so many different ways. From the sum of these accounts there emerges a convincing overview of the whole field. Most are clear and well-written. Hence this is an easy-to-read and lively introduction which will appeal to a broad audience. Recommended.

Lewis Mumford: *The Myth of the Machine, vol 1: Technics and Human Development, vol 2: The Pentagon of Power* (1967, & 1970, Harvest/HBJ, New York)

In many ways two of the most important works on this list. Mumford's panoramic view of the development of technics within successive civilisations lends his analysis an authority few others possess. His description of the archaic 'Megamachine' in Pyramid-Age Egypt prefigures very many contemporary concerns about technology and technocratic values. Similarly, the discussions of kingship, money, the introduction of clocks and the increasing mechanisation of life, illuminate the foundations of our present culture, its aspirations and many blind spots. Both volumes deserve and fruitfully reward, extensive study. Highly recommended.

Norman Myers: *The Sinking Ark: A New Look at the Problem of Disappearing Species* (1979, Pergamon, UK)

Review of the impact of human activity upon habitats and wildlife. Looks at rationales for conservation, the roles of various agencies and sets out a comprehensive strategy for reducing the growing damage worldwide. A clear exposition of the standard view. Contrast with Livingstone (q.v.).

Norman Myers (editor): *The Gaia Atlas of Planet Management* (1985, Pan, London)

An impressive, large format, copiously illustrated volume on key global issues. There are major sections on land, ocean, elements, evolution, humankind, civilisation and management. The book is a mine of information and is attractively presented. It deserves a place in all school libraries and all concerned homes.

John Naisbitt: *Megatrends: Ten New Directions Transforming Our Lives* (1982, Warner, New York)

A controversial book which claims to sort out the confusion of the present and distinguish ten clear trends in American society that are shaping its (and hence our) future. There is no doubt that Naisbitt is a professional who has mastered the technique of content analysis of newspapers to the point where digests can be widely marketed. He serves up a fine collection of detailed observations and reports. But it is doubtful if the trends he distinguishes are as important as he suggests, nor are they the only ones. Interesting only if taken with a large dose of scepticism. Dangerous if taken without.

John Naisbitt and Patricia Aburdene: *Megatrends 2000* (1990, Morrow, New York)

Predictable re-run of the above. Lists the key trends as: the global economic boom of the 1990s; renaissance of the arts; emergence of free market socialism; global lifestyles and cultural nationalism; privatisation of the welfare state; rise of the Pacific rim; 1990s as the decade of women in leadership; age of biology; religious revival of the third millenium and the triumph of the individual. These easy-to-digest themes are skilfully distilled for maximum impact but are poor guides to the future because they are over-optimistic and overlook more fundamental shifts of meaning and purpose. To be used with caution, if at all.

Burt Nanus: *Visionary Leadership* (1992, Jossey Bass, San Francisco)

Useful introduction to the art of visionary leadership in organisations, as seen by one of America's leading practitioners. Highly practicable, but not profound.

OECD Interfutures: *Facing the Future: Mastering the Probable and Managing the Unpredictable* (1979, OECD Paris)

A demanding and detailed work on global economic and development issues. Valuable for its insistence that 'mankind is involved in an irreversible process of progressive and fundamental transformation' and that 'the complex relationships between values, growth and structures now make any linear view of development untenable.' Flawed by size, very dull presentation and lack of index. For reference only.

James Ogilvy: *Futures Studies and the Human Sciences* (1992, Futures Research Quarterly vol. 8, no. 2, World Future Society, Washington DC)

A masterly account of key developments in the humanities which help to support a more sophisticated and helpful view of futures studies. An important paper.

Keniche Ohmae: *The Borderless World* (1990, Collins, London)

An important book which explores a range of management and corporate implications of the globalisation process. Useful for an inside view of this approach, but also exhibits paradigm blindness in that it overlooks other approaches to the subject.

Gerard O'Neill: 2081: *A Hopeful View of the Human Future* (1981, Simon & Schuster, New York)

There is a major divide in the futures field between those who adopt an earth-centred perspective and believe that human survival is dependent upon what happens here, and those who adopt a space-centred perspective. Drawing upon the author's earlier work on the high frontier (i.e. space colonies) O'Neill suggests a number of ways in which the journey into space could enhance human prospects.

Seymour Papert: *Mindstorms: Children, Computers and Powerful Ideas* (1982, Harvester, Brighton)

The inventor of the computer language logo argues that it can lead to new educational and cultural developments. Clearly overstated in retrospect, but some useful points about the role of computing in education.

Faith Popcorn: *The Popcorn Report* (1991, Random House, Sydney)

An interesting application of the trend analysis technique as developed in a US consultancy. The author shows how trends affecting middle America can be used as guidelines for business strategy and product development. The method obviously works. Yet the book is also of interest for what it leaves out – which is most of the rest of the world. This is pop-futurism at its best and empiricism at its worst.

Jonathan Porrit: *Seeing Green: The Politics of Ecology Explained* (1984, Blackwell, Oxford)

The writer's long association with the Ecology Party and the Friends of the Earth provide an informed basis for a work of this kind. But the author is a more accomplished activist than he is theorist and some parts of the book are banal and superficial. Nevertheless, he half succeeds at what is certainly a very difficult task and many will find ample food for thought herein.

Neil Postman: *Amusing Ourselves to Death* (1986, Heinemann, London; 1987, Methuen, London)

Trenchant critique of the ways that television is transforming American culture into a showbiz arena in which public affairs are being turned into forms of entertainment. Argues that TV has achieved the status of a meta-medium, i.e., one that 'directs not only our knowledge of the world, but our knowledge of ways of knowing.' A polemical and penetrating analysis. Highly recommended. (Also see Mitroff and Bennis, q.v.)

Ira Prigogine and Isobel Stengers: *Order out of Chaos: Man's New Dialogue with Nature* (1985, Fontana, London)

A demanding, yet fascinating, book which traces some of the major controversies arising from scientific developments over the last three centuries. Attempts a new synthesis which seeks to reconcile long-standing disputes and dualities. Not a light book, but a fruitful one.

Frederick Rawlence (editor): *About Time* (1985, Cape, London)

Fascinating and visually attractive work on temporality as explored in a TV series of the same title. By concentrating on many people's experience of time the book (and series) shows that many commonplace notions of it are inadequate. Here is conveyed something of the richness of temporality, some of the meanings, interpretations and cultural forms entwined within it. Overall, a rich tapestry of individual and collective experience. Highly recommended, especially in combination with Fraser (q.v.).

Darryl Reanney: *The Death of Forever, a New Future for Human Consciousness* (1991, Longman Cheshire, Melbourne)

A rare book which probes the human condition with enormous skill and deep insight. Shows up many of the illusions of a vapid, commodity-oriented culture. Reminds us of some of the irreducible facts of existence, and attempts to portray the grounds from which ways to resolve the irresolvable may be attempted. A challenging and valuable book. Recommended.

Keith Roberts: *Pavane* (1968, Gollancz, London)

Short stories set in an alternative England in which Queen Elizabeth I was assassinated, the Reformation did not happen and, by the 20th century, the country is still in the so-called Dark Ages. One of the finest of this genre.

James Robertson: *The Sane Alternative* (2nd edition, 1983, Robertson, UK)

For anyone overwhelmed by the prospect of futures study this is a good place to begin. Robertson has produced an accessible little book which covers a lot of ground fairly painlessly. He outlines five scenarios for future social and economic development, argues for a 'new economic direction', a 'shift of paradigms' and a 'process of transformation'. While dated in some respects, it is still worth recommending as a starting point.

James Robertson: *Future Wealth: A New Economics for the 21st Century* (1989, Cassell, London)

An important book which goes a long way toward reconceptualising the work/leisure conundrum. It is readable, original and relevant.

Kim Robinson: *Pacific Edge* (1990, Unwin, London)

A fine modern novel in the utopian tradition. Portrays a future in which present-day alternatives have become mainstream. The politics of water play an important part. A very successful book which succeeds where many have failed.

Stephen Rosen: *Future Facts* (1976, Heinemann, London; 1978, Corgi, London)

Futures study usually proposes that there are no future facts. Yet here is a writer who claims to have assembled a volume of them! In fact it is a speculative and popular survey of possible 'things to come in technology, science, medicine and life'. More comprehensive and better illustrated than other examples and similarly useful as source material. But amongst all this extrapolation there is little real vision, little of true human significance.

Andrew Ross: *Strange Weather* (1991, Verso, London)

As a doyen of the new field of cultural studies, Ross has a rare ability to creatively ignore boundaries and to cross-fertilise ideas and sources. In this book he looks at new age science, computer hacking sub-cultures, the origins of SF, the cyberpunk scene, corporate futurism and the weather. From these disparate sources he weaves a fine web of comment, criticism and informed insight. A fascinating and useful book. (My only quibble being that he obviously does not know about the several counter-traditions of futures work that are not oriented to the corporate sector.)

Theodore Roszak: *Where the Wasteland Ends: Politics and Transcendence in Post Industrial Society* (1972, 1989, Doubleday, New York)

Masterly exploration of the limits of Newtonian thought and of the basis for a wider world of meaning and significance. A brilliant commentary on instrumental world views and traditions which, being written before more recent syntheses (e.g. Prigogine, above) is mildly dated in some respects. However, the underlying critique of instrumental reason is excellent. Highly recommended.

Theodore Roszak: *The Cult of Information* (1986, Pantheon, New York)

Useful and highly critical counter to the usual upbeat views of computers and the information society. Roszak problematises the debate and points out some important defects and limitations. Compare with Stonier, below.

Peter Russell: *The Awakening Earth* (1982, Routledge, London)

Another rendering of the Gaia hypothesis (see Lovelock 1979, above) about which I remain frankly ambivalent. I agree with the writer that 'the real problem lies not in the physical constraints imposed by the external world, but in the constraints of our own minds', and am sympathetic to his vision of a high synergy society. But some aspects of the argument are barely credible and, while there is much of genuine interest here, some essential components are missing.

Jonathan Schell: *The Fate of the Earth* (1982, Picador, London)

This powerful work considers the biological and cultural implications of nuclear war. After describing the 'republic of insects and grass' which would result, the writer uses Hannah Arendt's concept of the common world to argue that megadeath amounts to something quite different from the passing of individuals. He is also right that 'formerly the future was given to us, now it must be achieved.' If the significance of this notion were more widely appreciated, we could look forward with greater confidence.

Fritz Schumacher: *Small is Beautiful: Economics as if People Mattered* (1974, Abacus, London)

Now-classic critique of western economic and political structures and priorities. Among many other things, it suggests that education could be our greatest resource and makes the case for intermediate technology. The book's title passed into the language and some of its proposals have been embodied in real life projects. Recommended.

Fritz Schumacher: *A Guide for the Perplexed* (1977, Cape, London)

Schumacher's final work. Provides an accessible introduction to his philosophy. Covers the concept of adequateo and levels of being. Leads up to a discussion of two kinds of problem. Highly recommended.

Fritz Schumacher: *Good Work* (1979, Cape, London)

An attempt to formulate a theory of work in the light of the author's Buddhist economics. It explores a number of alternatives based on this and shows that new, or renewed, options are possible and desirable.

Barrie Sherman and Phillip Judkins: *Glimpses of Heaven, Visions of Hell: Virtual Reality and its Implications* (1992, Hodder & Stoughton, London)

Competent review of VR realities and possibilities. Essential background reading for the debate we should be having. Considers impacts and implications in many areas. But lacks a sound critical perspective, so probably underestimates the subversive potential of VR.

Richard Slaughter: *Recovering the Future* (1988, Graduate School of Environmental Science, Monash University, Melbourne)

Explores how a critical futures approach can facilitate a reconceptualisation of the global predicament and therefore a movement beyond crisis and despair. The four sections are (1) Futures Now – Exploring the Extended Present (2) Taking Issue With the Way Things Are (3) Futures in Education – A Quiet Revolution? and (4) The Answer is a Journey. Core text for tertiary level courses.

Richard Slaughter (editor): *Studying the Future* (1989, Bicentennial Futures Education Project, Commission for the Future, Melbourne)

This anthology is one of the main products of the Australian Bicentennial Futures Education Project. It provides a concise introduction to those aspects of futures which are relevant to secondary education. Part 1, Perspectives, considers anticipations, overviews, visions, principles and practice. Part 2 includes reports from participating schools and the project director. Part 3 outlines some of the resources available: books, journals and organisations.

Richard Slaughter: *Futures Concepts and Powerful Ideas* (1990, Futures Study Centre, Melbourne)

A distillation of core material from critical futures studies. Presented in thirty short sections, with graphics and OHP blanks. Suitable for secondary, tertiary and a range of creative and professional uses.

Margaret Smith and David Crossley (editors): *The Way Out: Radical Alternatives for Australia* (1975, Lansdowne Press, Melbourne)

A time capsule anthology of readings which captures the breadth and depth of radical idealism in the 1960s and 1970s. Some excellent contributions, and a fine overview of the social alternatives movement. Raises the question of the extent to which this is, or was, indeed the way out.

Brian Stableford and David Langford: *The Third Millenium: A History of the World AD 2000–3000* (1985, Sidgwick & Jackson, London; 1988, Paladin)

A partly tongue-in-cheek, but also highly informed and fascinating look at possibilities for the next thousand years. The original edition is profusely illustrated and well worth reading. The two authors are both noted SF writers. They have a rare grasp of their subject. Hence the book is an unusually rich imaginative romp through unknown territory. A fine contrast to the earnest endeavours of some professional futurists.

Olaf Stapledon: *First and Last Men,* and *Star Maker* (1930 and 1937, Methuen, London)

Two of the most visionary, long-term novels ever written. Both of vast and cosmic scope. Mined ever after by generations of writers and others. These are in a class of their own.

Bart Steenbergen (and other editors): *Advancing Democracy and Participation: Challenges for the Future* (1992, Catalonian Centre for Futures Studies, Barcelona)

Proceedings of the 1991 WFSF conference in Barcelona. A carefully edited collection of twenty-four high-quality papers on issues relating to democracy and participation. A selective and useful resource for those working in this area. Recommended.

Tom Stonier: *The Wealth of Information: A Profile of the Post-Industrial Economy* (1983, Thames/Methuen, London)

The writer argues that wealth is created when new knowledge transforms a non-resource into a resource. Knowledge and the means to produce it (i.e. education) are therefore of central importance to a post-industrial economy. However the book has been criticised for omitting political factors and ignoring well-known counter arguments. A provocative and interesting thesis, but not perhaps a fully convincing one.

David Suzuki: *Inventing the Future* (1990, Allen & Unwin, New York)

Edited collection of the author's Canadian newspaper columns. Some pieces are excellent. But the chatty, provocative style becomes irritating in places and the book certainly lacks depth. Hence, the promise of the borrowed title (q.v. Gabor 1963) is unrealised. While media personalities like Suzuki may play a useful consciousness-raising role, the lack of substantive analysis makes this an unsatisfying collection. For introductory use only.

Alvin Toffler: *The Third Wave* (1980, Collins, London)

Like its predecessor (Future Shock, 1970) this book is ambitious and over-hyped. The author specialises in simplistic theses which are then built up by selective examples and often painful neologisms. After agriculture and industrialisation (the first two waves) he proposes that a new cultural synthesis is taking place, mediated by information technologies. This is a book in which the good ideas, the real insights, are almost submerged by the dross. It is better understood as part of the Toffler industry than as a serious contribution to debates on futures which, for this reader at least, this volume tends to obscure.

Allen Tough: *Crucial Questions About the Future* (1991, University Press of America, New York)

Very readable introduction to some simple to ask, but difficult to answer questions about the future (e.g. What is most important of all? and Why do we act in ways that hurt our future?). Tough is a thorough-going humanist who cares deeply about the future and tries in this short book to lead us to think about it in a more sustained and caring way. Recommended.

Francis Tugwell (editor): *Search for Alternatives: Public Policy and the Study of the Future* (1975, Winthrop, Mass.)

Useful, high-quality, collection of papers by American authors of the early 1970s. Good for reference. Some of the contributions hold up very well indeed – particularly Elise Boulding's summary of Polak's thesis on images of the future.

John Tydeman: *Futures Methodology Handbook* (1987, Commission for the Future, Melbourne)

Useful review of standard futures methods and research techniques. Brief sections on these, but only limited guidance on how to apply them in detail. Has a clear corporate bias, and lacks a broad view of other paradigms and approaches. But, within these limitations provides a useable overview.

Jaques Vallee: *The Network Revolution* (1984, Prism/Penguin, London)

Stimulating and accessible commentary on implications of developments in computer-mediated networks. Stresses the human dimension more than most. Recommended.

Kimon Valaskakis (and others): *The Conserver Society: A Workable Alternative for the Future* (1979, Harper & Row, New York)

Summary of a Canadian think-tank report exploring future options in pursuit of a sustainable society. Considers several basic scenarios and ways they could be implemented. Avoids the faults of Blueprint for Survival (Goldsmith 1972, above); q.v. Birch 1976.

Francis Vaughan: *The Inward Arc* (1985, Shambhala, Boulder, Colorado)

A fine and clear exposition on the nature of the inner journey towards wholeness and well-being. The book takes the framework developed by Wilber (q.v.) and applies it to human development. Highly recommended and relevant in a futures context.

Geoffrey Vickers: *Freedom in A Rocking Boat: Changing Values in an Unstable Society* (1970, London, Allen Lane; 1972, Penguin)

Classic work on social and cultural change. Vickers was less concerned with the usual litany of problem issues than with the cultural and institutional milieu in which values and attitudes are actively shaped. Remains of continuing interest and value.

Warren Wagar: *The Next Three Futures* (1992, Adamantine, London)

Wagar is a US professor of history, with an interest in H. G. Wells and a long-standing teaching record in futures. His book suffers a bit from its US bias, but is literate and well-written. His view of three coming cultural eras (technoliberal, radical and countercultural) provides a useful framework for intelligent speculation. The epilogue is brilliant, though frustratingly brief. In short, a flawed, but useful addition to the literature.

Barbara Ward: *Progress for a Small Planet* (1979, Temple Smith/Pelican London)

Like the previous volume *Only One Earth* (co-authored with Rene Dubos in 1972), this book takes a panoramic, yet detailed, look at the global predicament. Part One considers new directions for the industrial order (the rich north). Part Two outlines a strategy for Third World development. Part Three argues that the inequities of the world economic order can be reduced to mutual benefit. A comprehensive and well argued work which stands up well against later work.

Marilyn Waring: *Counting for Nothing: What Men Value and What Women are Worth* (1988, Allen & Unwin)

A challenging and important book on the ways in which domestic work has been excluded and under-valued in systems of national accounting. Marilyn Waring is a rare combination of activist and theoretician. Here she provides both a well-grounded critique of existing practice and a key component of an alternative economics. The approach and the book are fine examples of action-oriented critical enquiry. To be read with Henderson's (q.v.) forays into similar territory.

Anthony Watts: *Education, Unemployment and the Future of Work* (1983, Open University Press, UK)

A balanced, clear and well-written analysis of educational and political choices pertaining to work. Examines four scenarios (unemployment, leisure, employment and work). Concludes that work can be seen in much broader terms than the usual employment/unemployment dichotomy, that political education is important and that schools badly need to develop credible views of the future. Highly recommended.

Christopher Weeramantry: *The Slumbering Sentinels: Law and Human Rights in the Wake of Technology* (1983, Penguin, Australia)

A useful review of technical developments from the points of view of law and of human rights. The author argues convincingly that legislators have 'slept on the job' by allowing important principles to be overridden by the march of technology. Concludes with an agenda for action. Compare with Jones, and with Hill (q.v.).

H. G. Wells: *A Modern Utopia* (1905)

Wells definitive attempt to show how a technologically developed society could be governed by inspired socialism. Also touched by intimations of war. Could be considered one of the last expressions of Victorian optimism.

Joseph Weizenbaum: *Computer Power and Human Reason: From Judgement to Calculation* (1976, Freeman & Co., USA; 1984, Penguin, London)

Weizenbaum is concerned to de-mystify the computer and to expose the wide gulf between computer programs and natural language, between calculation and judgement, between machines and people. Like Roszak (above) this is an important antidote to technocratic visions of a wired society. The final chapter 'Against the Imperialism of Instrumental Reason' is required reading, particularly for those who perceive no conflict between technical progress and human development.

Thomas Whiston (editor): *The Uses and Abuses of Forecasting* (1979, Macmillan/S.P.R.U., University of Sussex)

A varied collection of articles on forecasting issues and related case studies. It does concentrate upon analytic/cognitive approaches. However several excellent chapters hold up well. In particular, Ian Miles paper on the early development of forecasting deserves close attention.

Michael Wiener: *English Culture and the Decline of the Industrial Spirit 1850–1980* (1981, Press Syndicate of the University of Cambridge, USA; 1985, Penguin, London)

Important historical and cross-disciplinary analysis of the peculiarly ambivalent English attitude to industry over the past 130 years. Major contribution to this debate. Recommended.

Ken Wilber: *No Boundary: Eastern and Western Approaches to Personal Growth* (1979, Shambhala, Boulder, Colorado)

Major work integrating insights from a wide range of disciplines and approaches. A variety of psychologies and therapies are located upon a 'spectrum of consciousness.' Suggests an overall framework for human growth and development. Chapter 2, on opposites, is an exemplary treatment of dualist traps. A profound and important book – the antidote, perhaps, to Kahn, Heilbronner, Goldsmith, Naisbitt and Toffler, above.

Ken Wilber: *The Atman Project: A Transpersonal View of Human Development* (1980, The Theosophical Publishing House, Wheaton, Illinois)

Wide-ranging account in the tradition of *No Boundary* of the process of individual development from the primitive roots of awareness to higher states pioneered by mystics and sages.

Ken Wilber: *Up From Eden: A Transpersonal View of Human Evolution* (1983, Routledge, London)

Companion to the above. Panoramic view of human history as a 'slow and tortuous path to transcendence'. Outlines distinct stages in the development of consciousness from the most primitive to the present mental/egoic level. Outlines possible developments beyond the latter and thereby provides a human (as opposed to technical) basis for future vision. Essential reading. Contrast with Eisler (q.v.).

Ken Wilber: *Eye to Eye: the Quest for the New Paradigm* (2nd edition, 1990, Anchor/Doubleday, New York)

Possibly the most important of Wilber's books in that it sets out the ground for a more comprehensive map of knowledge which integrates different ways of knowing in a 'right relationship' one to the other. It therefore provides part of the basis for a post-materialist world view. Very highly recommended.

Raymond Williams: *Towards 2000* (1983, Chatto & Windus, London; 1985, Penguin, London)

A chastened look at 1980s Britain by an observer whose preferred future seemed to have vanished. Acute observation vies for dominance with a lack of imaginative insight. For such an accomplished writer there is a surprising dearth of future vision. A comment, perhaps, on the dominance of the past in British psychology.

Anthony Wilson: *War Gaming* (1970, Pelican, London)

This useful volume sheds light on a little-advertised sequence of development in the evolution of modern futures research. It shows how military uncertainties led to the strategic use of computer simulations and scenario forecasting – techniques which later diffused into business and other contexts. Suggests that were it not for the military uses of futures research the field would not have developed so fully or so fast. Mainly of specialist interest.

Langdon Winner: *Autonomous Technology: Technics-out-of-Control as a Theme in Political Thought* (1977, MIT Press, Cambridge, Mass.)

Winner argues that advanced technologies are often 'tools without handles' and cannot be controlled in the usual sense of the term. Rather, they tend to bring about the conditions needed for their own elaboration and growth. A major work in the tradition established by Marcuse and Mumford (above). Essential reading for those interested in the adaptations required by technologies and the grounds for recovering human agency and control.

Langdon Winner: *The Whale and the Reactor: A Search for Limits in an Age of High Technology* (1986, University of Chicago Press)

A more personal and reflective extension of the above thesis in which the author makes effective use of new material. The contrasts drawn between whale and reactor are memorable, as is the description of post-war change in a middle California town. A useful complement to the more academic work above.

Brian Wynne: *Rationality and Ritual: The Windscale Inquiry and Nuclear Decisions in Britain* (1982, British Society for the History of Science Monograph 3, Lancaster)

Detailed analysis of the Windscale enquiry into nuclear reprocessing and issues raised therein. The author questions the validity of 'judicial rationality' and concludes that 'democracy is gradually abandoned to those who, through fact-finding rituals, can pretend not to choose our future but to make it safe'. A rare insight into the nature of big technology decision-making. Highly recommended for detail, authenticity and relevance.

Michael Young (editor): *Forecasting and the Social Sciences* (1968, Heinemann/SSRC, London)

Unusual collection of papers commissioned by an unusual (and ephemeral) Social Science Research Council Committee on 'The Next Thirty Years'. The contributors are drawn from a range of disciplines and they discuss approaches, methods and specific problem areas. While now dated in some respects this volume is useful as a model of prospective, inter-disciplinary, enquiry: a model that has been infrequently emulated in the British context.

Index

About the Author

RICHARD A. SLAUGHTER is director of the Futures Study Centre in Melbourne, Australia. Until recently, he was Lecturer in Futures and Social Policy and convenor of the Foresight Research Unit at the Institute of Education, University of Melbourne, Australia. His previous works include *Futures Tools and Techniques* (1987) and *Recovering the Future* (1989). He is also the coauthor, with Hedley Beare, of *Education in the 21st Century* (1993).

ISBN 0-275-95292-4

90000>

9 780275 952921

HARDCOVER BAR CODE

EAN